Multimedia Learning

Second Edition

For hundreds of years verbal messages such as lectures and printed lessons have been the primary means of explaining ideas to learners. Although verbal learning offers a powerful tool, this book explores ways of going beyond the purely verbal. Recent advances in graphics technology have prompted new efforts to understand the potential of multimedia and multimedia learning as a means of promoting human understanding. In *Multimedia Learning, Second Edition*, Richard E. Mayer asks whether people learn more deeply when ideas are expressed in words and pictures rather than in words alone. He reviews twelve principles of instructional design that are based on experimental research studies and grounded in a theory of how people learn from words and pictures. The result is what Mayer calls the cognitive theory of multimedia learning, a theory introduced in the first edition of *Multimedia Learning* and further developed in *The Cambridge Handbook of Multimedia Learning*.

Richard E. Mayer is Professor of Psychology at the University of California, Santa Barbara, where he has served since 1975. He is the author of *Multimedia Learning* (Cambridge University Press, 2001) and editor of *The Cambridge Handbook of Multimedia Learning* (Cambridge University Press, 2005). In 2008 he received the American Psychological Association's Distinguished Contributions of Applications of Psychology to Education and Training Award.

Multimedia Learning

Second Edition

Richard E. Mayer

University of California,
Santa Barbara

CAMBRIDGE
UNIVERSITY PRESS

CAMBRIDGE UNIVERSITY PRESS
Cambridge, New York, Melbourne, Madrid, Cape Town, Singapore,
São Paulo, Delhi, Dubai, Tokyo

Cambridge University Press
32 Avenue of the Americas, New York, NY 10013-2473, USA

www.cambridge.org
Information on this title: www.cambridge.org/9780521735353

First edition published 2001
Second edition published 2009
Reprinted 2009 (twice), 2010

Printed in the United States of America

A catalog record for this publication is available from the British Library.

Library of Congress Cataloging in Publication Data
Mayer, Richard E., 1947–
    Multimedia learning / Richard E. Mayer. – 2nd ed.
        p.   cm.
    Includes bibliographical references and index.
    ISBN 978-0-521-51412-5 (hardback) – ISBN 978-0-521-73535-3 (pbk.)
    1. Computer-assisted instruction.   2. Interactive multimedia.   I. Title.
    LB1028.5.M36 2009
    371.33′467–dc22   2008021185

ISBN 978-0-521-51412-5 Hardback
ISBN 978-0-521-73535-3 Paperback

Dedicated to Beverly

Contents

Preface

Multimedia instruction refers to presentations involving words and pictures that are intended to foster learning. How can we design effective multimedia instruction? In this book I review twelve principles of instructional design that are based on experimental research studies carried out by my colleagues and me and that are grounded in a theory of how people learn from words and pictures, which I call the cognitive theory of multimedia learning. In short, the premise underlying this book is that the design of multimedia instruction should be based on research and grounded in theory. If you are interested in an evidenced-based and theory-grounded approach to multimedia design, then this book is for you.

For hundreds of years, verbal messages – such as lectures and printed lessons – have been the primary means of explaining ideas to learners. Although verbal learning offers a powerful tool for humans, this book explores ways of going beyond the purely verbal. An alternative to purely verbal presentations is to use multimedia presentations in which people learn from both words and pictures – a situation that I call *multimedia learning*. Recent advances in graphics technology have prompted new efforts to understand the potential of multimedia as a means of promoting human understanding – a potential that I call *the promise of multimedia learning*. In particular, my focus in this book is on whether people learn more deeply when ideas are expressed in words and pictures rather than in words alone.

Multimedia encyclopedias have become the latest addition to students' reference tools, and the Internet is full of messages that combine words and pictures. Educational games, interactive simulations, and online pedagogical agents are touted as the wave of the future in education and training. Do these multimedia forms of presentation help learners? How do people learn from words and pictures? What is the best way to design multimedia messages?

These are the kind of questions prompted by advances in information graphics technology. My premise in this book is that the answers to these questions require a program of careful, systematic research. To understand how to design multimedia messages, it is useful to understand how people learn from words and pictures.

During the past twenty years, my colleagues at Santa Barbara and I have been conducting research studies on multimedia learning. This book provides a systematic summary of what we have found. The outcome is a set of twelve principles for the design of multimedia messages and a cognitive theory of multimedia learning. In short, this book summarizes research aimed at realizing the promise of multimedia learning – that is, the potential of using words and pictures together to promote human understanding.

People learn better from words and pictures than from words alone. This is the thesis I investigate in the book you are holding. This straightforward statement is what got me started doing research on multimedia learning in the first place, and it has sustained my interest over two decades and nearly 100 experimental comparisons. In short, I began with curiosity about whether people learn more deeply from a verbal lesson when graphics are added. This curiosity prompted questions about whether value is added when we incorporate graphics into a verbal lesson, under what conditions graphics improve learning, and how graphics help people learn. If these questions also pique your interest – and you want some research-based answers – then this book is for you.

Multimedia Learning, Second Edition, is intended for anyone who is interested in the scientific underpinnings of multimedia learning. This book could be used in courses across the university, including courses in psychology, education, and computer science, as well as in specialties such as educational technology, instructional design, applied cognitive psychology, and human-computer interaction. I do not assume that the reader has any previous knowledge of psychology, education, or technology. I do assume that the reader is interested in the promise of multimedia learning – that is, in understanding how to tap the potential of multimedia messages for improving human understanding.

This book has both a theoretical and a practical orientation. On the one hand, it is aimed at those with interests in basic theory and research in the cognitive psychology of how people learn from words and pictures. On the other hand, it is aimed at those with practical interests in designing effective multimedia presentations. If you are interested in the theoretical or practical bases of multimedia learning (or a combination of the two), then this book is for you.

Writing this book has been my labor of love. I hope that you enjoy reading it as much as I have enjoyed writing it. If you have any comments or suggestions, I would like to hear from you at <mayer@psych.ucsb.edu>.

WHAT'S NEW IN THE SECOND EDITION?

The first edition of this book, published in 2001, appeared when the field of multimedia learning was still in its childhood. Since then, the research base and theoretical base of multimedia learning have continued to grow, as is indicated by numerous special issues of journals highlighting multimedia learning and numerous edited books on multimedia learning. In 2005, I had the privilege of editing *The Cambridge Handbook of Multimedia Learning*, which contains thirty-five chapters by leading multimedia researchers around the world who were charged with highlighting empirical research on multimedia design principles. Portions of this second edition of *Multimedia Learning* are based on corresponding chapters in the first edition of *Multimedia Learning* and on my four chapters (2005a, 2005b, 2005c, 2005d) in *The Cambridge Handbook of Multimedia Learning*.

There are four major changes in the second edition – concerning the growth of the research base, the growth in the number of principles, the theoretical reorganization of the principles, and the boundary conditions of the principles. First, our research base has more than doubled: In the first edition, I reported on forty-five experimental comparisons involving transfer test performance carried out by my colleagues and me, whereas in this edition that number has increased to ninety-three experimental comparisons. Second, the number of principles has increased from seven to twelve. Six original principles are retained in the second edition: coherence, redundancy, spatial contiguity, temporal contiguity, modality, and multimedia principles. Six new principles are added: signaling, segmenting, pre-training, personalization, voice, and image principles. One of the original principles – the individual differences principle – is recast as a boundary condition (i.e., the individual differences condition is the idea that design principles that are effective for beginners may not be effective for more experienced learners).

Third, the underlying theory has been expanded to incorporate the triarchic model of cognitive load, which consists of extraneous, essential, and generative cognitive processing. Correspondingly, the twelve principles of multimedia instructional design have been reorganized into three sections – reducing extraneous processing, managing essential processing, and fostering generative processing. Although the main focus of the first edition was on reducing extraneous processing, the second edition adds new foci on managing essential processing and fostering generative processing. Finally, an indication of the maturity of the field is that the second edition highlights *boundary conditions* for each principle – research-based constraints on when a principle is likely or unlikely to apply. The boundary conditions are interpreted in terms of the cognitive theory of multimedia learning, and help to both test and enrich theories of multimedia learning. A focus on boundary conditions is consistent with the idea that principles of multimedia design must be applied in light of an understanding of how people learn.

ACKNOWLEDGMENTS

Much of the work reported in this book was conducted in collaboration with colleagues and students at the University of California, Santa Barbara, as well as collaborators from around the world. I am pleased to acknowledge the substantial contributions of those with whom I have published research articles on multimedia learning: Richard B. Anderson, Robert Atkinson, Paul Ayres, Monica Bulger, Julie Campbell, Paul Chandler, Dorothy Chun, Ruth Clark, Heather Collins, Krista Deleeuw, Gayle Dow, Joan Gallini, Stefan Hagmann, Shannon Harp, Egbert Harskamp, Mary Hegarty, Julie Heiser, Terry Inglese, Cheryl Johnson, Lewis Johnson, James Lester, Detlev Leutner, Steve Lonn, Laura Massa, Patricia Mautone, Sarah Mayer, Roxana Moreno, Peter Nenninger, Jan Plass, Bill Prothero, Valerie Sims, Hiller Spires, Andy Stull, and Ning Wang. My most frequent research collaborator, Roxana Moreno, deserves special mention for her tireless efforts to conduct research on multimedia learning. I also wish to thank the forty-five authors and coauthors from around the world who contributed to *The Cambridge Handbook of Multimedia Learning*, which I edited in 2005, as their chapters have helped me better understand our field. Special thanks are also due to Ruth Clark, with whom I coauthored *e-Learning and the Science of Instruction* in 2003 and *e-Learning and the Science of Instruction, Second Edition*, in 2008, for reminding me of the importance of communicating with instructional-design practitioners. I also wish to acknowledge the contributions of my faculty colleagues and students at UCSB who have helped me better understand the nature of multimedia learning, and the many faculty and student visitors from around the world who have spent time with me in Santa Barbara. Although they cannot be held responsible for any failings of this book, they all deserve credit for maintaining my interest in multimedia learning.

I appreciate the excellent research environment in the Department of Psychology at the University of California, Santa Barbara, as well as the opportunity to interact with a talented group of students and professors. Throughout my thirty-three years at UCSB, I have always enjoyed the opportunity to pursue research issues that come my way. I fondly acknowledge the influence of my parents, James and Bernis Mayer, who instilled in me a love of learning and helped me appreciate the indispensable value of intellectual honesty, hard work, and boundless curiosity. Their memory is never far from my thoughts. I appreciate the interest of my children – Ken, Dave, and Sarah – who often asked, "How's the book doing?" They have brought much light into my life, as has our new grandson, Jacob. Finally, this book would not have been possible without the encouragement and support of my wife, Beverly. I am pleased to dedicate this book to her, with love.

Finally, I gratefully acknowledge the contributions of the staff at Cambridge University Press.

RICHARD E. MAYER
Santa Barbara, CA

Section I

Introduction to Multimedia Learning

People learn better from words and pictures than from words alone. This hypothesis is the basis for the promise of multimedia learning. Multimedia instruction consists of words and pictures rather than words alone. How can we design multimedia instruction that improves learner understanding of the presented material? This is the central question addressed in this book.

Chapter 1 explores the promise of multimedia learning by offering definitions of key terms and by examining fundamental distinctions that will help you understand research on multimedia learning. A key distinction is between two goals of multimedia research – to contribute to instructional practice (i.e., the science of instruction) and to contribute to learning theory (i.e., the science of learning). The multimedia design principles presented in this book are intended to address both goals and reflect an example of what Stokes (1997, p. 73) calls "use-inspired basic research."

Chapter 2 explores the science of instruction by summarizing the methods we used to test the instructional design principles described in this book. The chapter gives you examples of the multimedia lessons and tests we used, including computer-based narrated animation, paper-based annotated illustrations, and computer-based games and simulations. I also show you how we created experimental comparisons in which we compared the test performance of a group that learned from a multimedia lesson containing a to-be-tested feature versus a group that learned from the lesson without the feature. In short, this chapter helps you see how the instructional design principles described in this book are based on evidence.

Chapter 3 explores the science of learning by summarizing a research-based theory of how people learn from words and pictures, which I call the cognitive theory of multimedia learning. The theory is based on research in cognitive science, including the ideas of dual channels, limited capacity, and active processing. The cognitive theory of multimedia learning can help you understand how we generated to-be-tested design principles and how we explained when the principles do and do not apply. In short, this chapter helps you see how the instructional design principles described in this book are grounded in theory.

1

The Promise of Multimedia Learning

Multimedia learning refers to learning from words and pictures. Multimedia instruction refers to the presentation of material using both words and pictures, with the intention of promoting learning. The case for multimedia learning rests on the premise that learners can better understand an explanation when it is presented in words and pictures than when it is presented in words alone. Multimedia messages can be based on the delivery media (e.g., amplified speaker and computer screen), presentation mode (e.g., words and pictures), or sensory modalities (e.g., auditory and visual). The design of multimedia instructional messages can be based on a technology-centered approach that focuses on the capabilities of advanced technologies or on a learner-centered approach that focuses on the nature of the human cognitive system. Multimedia learning may be viewed as response strengthening (in which multimedia environments are used as drill-and-practice systems), information acquisition (in which multimedia messages serve as information delivery vehicles), or as knowledge construction (in which multimedia messages include aids to sense-making). Three possible learning outcomes are no learning (as indicated by poor retention and poor transfer performance), rote learning (as indicated by good retention and poor transfer performance), and meaningful learning (as indicated by good retention and good transfer performance). Meaningful learning outcomes depend on the cognitive activity of the learner during learning rather than on the learner's behavioral activity during learning. The goal of basic research is to contribute a theory of learning (i.e., science of learning), whereas the goal of applied research is to derive principles of instructional design (i.e., science of instruction); merging these goals results in basic research on applied situations where the goal is to derive principles of multimedia design that are both grounded in cognitive theory and supported by empirical evidence.

■ ■ **Chapter Outline**

WHAT IS MULTIMEDIA INSTRUCTION?

People learn better from words and pictures than from words alone. This straightforward statement summarizes the promise of multimedia learning and is the guiding thesis of this book. In short, I am intrigued by the idea that we can improve people's learning by incorporating effective graphics into verbal material. Does adding graphics to words help people learn better? What makes an effective graphic? How do people learn from words and pictures? These are the questions I address in this book – questions about what works with multimedia instruction and how people learn from multimedia instruction.

The term *multimedia instruction* means different things to different people. For some people, multimedia instruction means that a person sits at a terminal and receives a presentation consisting of on-screen text, on-screen graphics or animation, and sounds coming from the computer's speakers – as with an on-line multimedia encyclopedia. For some people, multimedia instruction means a "live" presentation in which a group of people seated in a room views images presented on one or more screens and hears music or other sounds presented via speakers. Watching a video on a TV screen can be called a multimedia experience because both images and sounds are presented. Another example of multimedia instruction is a PowerPoint presentation in which someone presents slides from a computer projected onto a screen and talks about each one. Even low-tech environments allow for multimedia instruction, such as a "chalk and talk" presentation in which an instructor writes or draws on a blackboard (or uses an overhead projector) while presenting a lecture. Finally, the most basic form of multimedia instruction is a textbook lesson consisting of printed text and illustrations.

I define multimedia instruction as the presentation of material using both words and pictures, with the intention of promoting learning. By words, I mean that the material is presented in *verbal form* – using printed or spoken text, for example. By pictures, I mean that the material is presented in *pictorial form*, including using static graphics such as illustrations, graphs, photos, or maps, or dynamic graphics such as animations or video. This definition is broad enough to cover each of the multimedia scenarios I just described – ranging from multimedia encyclopedia entries to textbook lessons. For example, in a multimedia encyclopedia the words can be presented as on-screen text or as narration, and the pictures can be presented as graphics or animation. In a textbook, the words can be presented as printed text and the pictures as illustrations (or other kinds of graphics).

For purposes of conducting research, I have focused the definition of multimedia instruction on just two presentation formats. I have opted to limit the definition to just two formats – verbal and pictorial – because the research base in cognitive science is most relevant to this distinction. Thus, what I call multimedia learning is more accurately called dual-mode, dual-format, dual-code, or dual-channel learning.

Is *multimedia* a noun or an adjective? When used as a noun, multimedia refers to a technology for presenting material in both visual and verbal forms. In this sense, multimedia means multimedia technology – devices used to present visual and verbal material. When used as an adjective, multimedia can be used in the following contexts:

multimedia learning – learning from words and pictures

multimedia message or *multimedia presentation* – presentations involving words and pictures

multimedia instruction (or *multimedia instructional message* or *multimedia instructional presentation*) – presentations involving words and pictures that are intended to foster learning

My focus in this book is on the design of multimedia instructional messages that promote multimedia learning.

In the remainder of this chapter, I present the case for multimedia learning, and then I examine three views of multimedia messages, two approaches to multimedia design, three metaphors of multimedia learning, three kinds of multimedia learning outcomes, two kinds of active learning, and two goals of multimedia research.

THE CASE FOR MULTIMEDIA LEARNING

An instructional message is a communication that is intended to foster learning. In presenting an instructional message to learners, instructional designers have two main formats available – words and pictures. Words include speech and printed text; pictures include static graphics (such as illustrations or photos) and dynamic graphics (such as animations or video). For hundreds of years, the major format for presenting instructional messages has been words – including lectures and books. In short, verbal modes of presentation have dominated the way we convey explanations to one another, and verbal learning has dominated education. Similarly, verbal learning has been a major focus of educational research.

The advent of computer technology has enabled an explosion in the availability of visual ways of presenting material, including large libraries of static images as well as compelling dynamic images in the form of animations and video. In light of the power of computer graphics, it may be useful to ask whether it is time to expand instructional messages beyond the purely verbal. What are the consequences of adding pictures to words? What happens when instructional messages involve both verbal and visual modes of learning? What affects the way people learn from words and pictures? In short, how can multimedia presentations foster meaningful learning? These are the kinds of questions addressed in this book.

The case for multimedia learning is based on the idea that instructional messages should be designed in light of how the human mind works. Let's assume that humans have two information processing systems – one for verbal material and one for visual material. Let's also acknowledge that the major format for presenting instructional material is verbal. The rationale for multimedia presentations – that is, presenting material in words and pictures – is that it takes advantage of the full capacity of humans for processing information. When we present material only in the verbal mode, we are ignoring the potential contribution of our capacity to process material in the visual mode as well.

Why might two channels be better than one? Two explanations are the quantitative rationale and the qualitative rationale. The quantitative rationale is that more material can be presented on two channels than on one channel – just as more traffic can travel in two lanes than in one lane. In the case of explaining how a car's braking system works, for example, the steps in the process can be presented in words or can be depicted in illustrations. Presenting both is like presenting the material twice – giving the learner twice as much exposure to the explanation. While the quantitative rationale makes sense as far as it goes, I reject it mainly because it is incomplete. In particular, I am concerned about the assumption that the verbal and visual channels are equivalent, that is, that words and pictures are simply two equivalent ways of presenting the same material.

By contrast, the qualitative rationale is that words and pictures, while qualitatively different, can complement one another and that human understanding occurs when learners are able to mentally integrate corresponding pictorial and verbal representations. As you can see, the qualitative rationale assumes that the two channels are not equivalent; words are more useful for presenting certain kinds of material – perhaps representations that are more formal and require more effort to translate – whereas pictures are more useful for presenting other kinds of material – perhaps more intuitive, more natural representations. In short, one picture is not necessarily equivalent to 1,000 words (or any number of words).

The most intriguing aspect of the qualitative rationale is that understanding occurs when learners are able to build meaningful connections between pictorial and verbal representations – such as being able to see how the words "the piston moves forward in the master cylinder" relate to the forward motion of a piston in the master cylinder in an animation of a car's braking system. In the process of trying to build connections between words and pictures, learners are able to create a deeper understanding than they could from words or pictures alone. This idea is at the heart of the cognitive theory of multimedia learning that is described in Chapter 3.

THREE VIEWS OF MULTIMEDIA MESSAGES

The term *multimedia* can be viewed in three ways – based on the devices used to deliver an instructional message (i.e., the delivery media), the representational formats used to present the instructional message (i.e., the presentation modes), or the sense modalities the learner uses to receive the instructional message (i.e., sensory modalities).

The Delivery-Media View

The most obvious view is that multimedia means the presentation of material using two or more delivery devices. The focus is on the physical system used to deliver the information – such as computer screens, amplified speakers, projectors, video recorders, blackboards, and human voice boxes. For example, in computer-based multimedia, material can be presented via the screen and via the speakers. These devices can be even further broken down by defining each window on a computer screen as a separate delivery device and each sound track coming from a speaker as a separate delivery device. In lecture-based multimedia, material can be presented via a projector onto a screen and via the lecturer's voice. In the strictest interpretation of the delivery-media view, a textbook does not constitute multimedia because the only presentation device is ink printed on paper.

What's wrong with this view of multimedia? Technically, it is the most accurate view because it focuses on the media used to present information, but psychologically, it does more to confuse the issue than to clarify it. The focus is on the devices used to present information rather than on how people learn – that is, the focus is on technology rather than on learners. Therefore, I do not take the delivery media view in this book.

The Presentation-Modes View

A second view is that multimedia means the presentation of material using two or more presentation modes. The focus is on the way that material is represented – such as through the use of words or pictures. For example, in computer-based multimedia, material can be presented verbally as on-screen text or narration and pictorially as static graphics or animation. In lecture-based multimedia, material can be presented verbally as speech and pictorially as projected graphics or video. In a textbook, material can be presented verbally as printed text and pictorially as static graphics.

This view is consistent with a learner-centered approach if we assume that learners are able to use various coding systems to represent knowledge – such as verbal and pictorial knowledge representations. Although conventional wisdom is that a picture can be converted into words and vice versa, research on mental representations suggests that verbal ways of representing knowledge may be qualitatively different from pictorial ways of representing knowledge. In short, the presentation-modes view of multimedia is consistent with a cognitive theory of learning that assumes humans have separate information-processing channels for verbal and pictorial knowledge. Paivio's (1986, 2006) dual-coding theory presents the most coherent theoretical and empirical evidence for this idea.

The Sensory-Modality View

The third view, while also consistent with a learner-centered approach, takes a somewhat different approach. According to the sensory-modalities view, multimedia means that two or more sensory systems in the learner are involved. Instead of focusing on codes used to represent knowledge in learners' information-processing systems, the sensory-modalities view focuses on the sensory receptors the learner uses to perceive the incoming material – such as the eyes and the ears. For example, in a computer-based environment an animation can be presented visually, and a narration can be presented auditorially. In a lecture scenario, the speaker's voice is processed in the auditory channel, and the slides from the projector are processed in the visual channel. In a textbook, illustrations and printed text are both processed visually, at least initially.

This view is learner-centered because it takes the learner's information-processing activity into account. Unlike the presentation-modes view, however, the sensory-modalities view is that multimedia involves presenting material that is processed visually and auditorially. This distinction is based on the idea that humans process visual images and sounds in qualitatively different ways. In short, the sensory-modalities view of multimedia is consistent with a cognitive theory of learning that assumes humans have separate information-processing channels for auditory and visual processing. Baddeley's (1999) model of working memory presents the most coherent theoretical and empirical evidence for this idea.

Table 1.1 summarizes the differences among these three views. In sum, I reject the delivery-media view because it emphasizes the technology over the learner. Both the presentation-modes view and the sensory-modalities view focus on the information-processing system of the learner and assume that humans process information in more than one channel – a proposal that I call the dual-channel assumption. However, they differ in the ways in which they conceptualize the nature of the two channels: the presentation-modes view distinguishes between separate systems for processing verbal and pictorial knowledge, whereas the sensory-modes view distinguishes between separate systems for auditory and visual processing (i.e., for processing

Table 1.1. Three Views of Multimedia

View	Definition	Example
Delivery media	Two or more delivery devices	Computer screen and amplified speakers; projector and lecturer's voice
Presentation mode	Verbal and pictorial representations	On-screen text and animation; printed text and illustrations
Sensory modality	Auditory and visual senses	Narration and animation; lecture and slides

sounds and visual images). Although my definition of multimedia learning is based on the presentation-modes view (i.e., multimedia learning involves learning from words and pictures), the sensory-modalities view (i.e., multimedia learning involves learning from auditory and visual material) is also a useful way of conceptualizing the nature of dual channels in the human information system. A goal of the research presented in this book is to examine the relative contributions of both views of multimedia. The theory of multimedia learning presented in Chapter 3 relies on the sensory-modalities view to describe early processing and the presentation-mode view to describe later processing in the learner's cognitive system.

TWO APPROACHES TO MULTIMEDIA DESIGN

Multimedia represents a potentially powerful learning technology – that is, a system for enhancing human learning. A practical goal of research on multimedia learning is to devise design principles for multimedia presentations. It is useful to distinguish between two approaches to multimedia design – a technology-centered approach and a learner-centered approach.

Technology-Centered Approaches

The most straightforward approach to multimedia design is technology-centered. Technology-centered approaches begin with the functional capabilities of multimedia and ask, "How can we use these capabilities in designing multimedia presentations?" The focus is generally on cutting-edge advances in multimedia technology, so technology-centered designers might focus on how to incorporate multimedia into emerging communications technologies such as wireless access to the Internet or the construction of interactive multimedia representations in virtual reality. The kinds of research issues often involve media research – that is, determining which technology is most effective in presenting information. For example, a media research issue is whether students learn as well from an on-line lecture – in which the student can see a lecturer in a window on the computer screen – as from a live lecture – in which the student is actually sitting in a classroom.

What's wrong with technology-centered approaches? A review of educational technologies of the twentieth century shows that the technology-centered approach generally fails to lead to lasting improvements in education (Cuban, 1986, 2001). For example, when the motion picture was invented in the early twentieth century hopes were high that this visual technology would improve education. In 1922, the famous inventor Thomas Edison predicted that "the motion picture is destined to revolutionize our educational system and that in a few years it will supplant largely, if not entirely, the use of textbooks" (cited in Cuban, 1986, p. 9). Like current claims for the power of visual media, Edison proclaimed that "it is possible to teach every branch of human knowledge with the motion picture" (cited in Cuban, 1986, p. 11). In spite of the grand predictions, a review of educational technology reveals that "most teachers used films infrequently in their classrooms" (Cuban, 1986, p. 17). From our vantage point beyond the close of the twentieth century, it is clear that the predicted educational revolution in which movies would replace books has failed to materialize.

Consider another disappointing example that may remind you of current claims for the educational potential of online learning. In 1932, Benjamin Darrow, founder of the Ohio School of the Air, proclaimed that radio could "bring the world to the classroom, to make universally available the services of the finest teachers, the inspiration of the greatest leaders . . ." (cited in Cuban, 1986, p. 19). His colleague William Levenson, the director of the Ohio School of the Air, predicted in 1945 that a "radio receiver will be as common in the classroom as the blackboard" and "radio instruction will be integrated into school life" (cited in Cuban, 1986, p. 19). As we rush to wire our schools for access to the educational content of the Internet, it is humbling to recognize what happened to a similarly motivated movement for radio: "Radio has not been accepted as a full-fledged member of the educational community" (Cuban, 1986, p. 24).

Third, consider the sad history of educational television – a technology that combined the visual power of the motion picture with the world-wide coverage of radio. By the 1950s, educational television was being touted as a way to create a "continental classroom" that would provide access to "richer education at less cost" (Cuban, 1986, p. 33). Yet a review shows that teachers used television infrequently if at all (Cuban, 1986).

Finally, consider the most widely acclaimed technological accomplishment of the twentieth century – computers. The technology that supports computers is different from that of film, radio, and television, but the grand promises to revolutionize education are the same. Like current claims for the mind-enhancing power of computer technology, during the 1960s it was predicted that computer tutoring machines would eventually replace teachers. The first large-scale implementation occurred under the banner of computer-assisted instruction (CAI), in which computers presented short frames, solicited a response from the learner, and provided feedback to the learner. In spite of a large financial investment to support CAI, sound evaluations showed that the two largest computer-based systems in the 1970s – PLATO and TICCIT – failed to produce better learning than traditional teacher-led instruction (Cognition and Technology Group at Vanderbilt, 1996).

What can we learn from the humbling history of the twentieth century's great educational technologies? Although different technologies underlie film, radio, television, and computer-assisted instruction, they all produced the same cycle. First, they began with grand promises about how the technology would revolutionize education. Second, there was an initial rush to implement the cutting-edge technology in schools. Third, from the perspective of a few decades later it became clear that the hopes and expectations were largely unmet.

What went wrong with these technologies that seemed poised to tap the potential of visual and worldwide learning? I attribute the disappointing results to the technology-centered approach taken by the promoters. Instead of adapting technology to fit the needs of human learners, humans were forced to adapt to the demands of cutting-edge technologies. The driving force behind the implementations was the power of the technology rather than an interest in promoting human cognition. The focus was on giving people access to the latest technology rather than on helping people to learn through the aid of technology.

Are we about to replicate the cycle of high expectations, large-scale implementation, and disappointing results in the realm of multimedia technology? In my opinion, the answer to that question depends on whether or not we continue to take a technology-centered approach.

When we ask, "What can we do with multimedia?" and when our goal is to "provide access to technology," we are taking a technology-centered approach with a 100-year history of failure.

Learner-Centered Approaches

Learner-centered approaches offer an important alternative to technology-centered approaches. Learner-centered approaches begin with an understanding of how the human mind works and ask, "How can we adapt multimedia to enhance human learning?" The focus is on using multimedia technology as an aid to human cognition. Research questions focus on the relation between design features and the human information-processing system – for example, comparing multimedia designs that place light or heavy loads on the learner's visual information-processing channel. The premise underlying the learner-centered approach is that multimedia designs that are consistent with the way the human mind works are more effective in fostering learning than those that are not. This premise is the central theme of Chapter 3, which lays out a cognitive theory of multimedia learning.

Norman (1993, p. xi) eloquently makes the case for a learner-centered approach to technology design, which he refers to as human-centered technology: "Today we serve technology. We need to reverse the machine-centered point of view and turn it into a person-centered point of view: Technology should serve us." Consistent with the learner-centered approach, Norman (1993, p. 3) shows how "technology can make us smart" – that is, technology can expand our cognitive capabilities. Norman (1993, p. 5) refers to tools that aid the mind as *cognitive artifacts*: "anything invented by humans for the purpose of improving thought or action counts as an artifact." Examples include mental tools such as language and arithmetic as well as physical tools such as paper and pencils; as the twentieth century's most important new cognitive artifact, computer technology represents a landmark invention that has the potential to assist human cognition in ways previously not possible.

Norman's (1993, p. 9) assessment is that "much of science and technology takes a machine-centered view of the design of machines" so that "the technology that is intended to aid human cognition . . . more often interferes and confuses." By contrast, Norman's (1993, p. 12) vision of a learner-centered approach to technology design is that "technology . . . should complement human abilities, aid those activities for which we are poorly suited, and enhance and help develop those for which we are ideally suited." The design of multimedia technology to promote human cognition represents one exemplary component in the larger task of creating what Norman (1993, p. xii) calls "things that make us smart."

In his review of computer technology, Landauer (1995, p. 3) proclaims that "the computer and information revolution is widely predicted to be as consequential as the industrial revolution of the previous two centuries." Further, he describes two major phases in the use of computer technology – *automation* and *augmentation*. In the automation phase, computers are used to replace humans on certain tasks ranging from robots in manufacturing to imaging devices (such as CAT scans and MRIs) in medicine to computer-based switching in telecommunications. However, Landauer (1995, p. 6) observes that the automation phase "is running out of steam" because almost all of the easy-to-automate tasks have been computerized.

The second phase of computer application – augmentation – involves the use of computers to enhance human performance on various cognitively complex tasks. Augmentation involves designing computer systems "to act as assistants, aids, and power tools" (Landauer, 1995, p. 7). However, Landauer (1995, p. 7) is disappointed with progress in the augmentation phase: "It is here...that we have failed." A major challenge in making the augmentation phase work involves the learner-centered design of computer-based technologies: "They are still too hard to use" (1995, p. 7). The design of multimedia learning environments that promote meaningful human learning is an example of using computers to augment or aid human cognition – and thus one element in Landauer's augmentation phase.

The differences between the technology-centered and learner-centered approaches to multimedia design are summarized in Table 1.2. I take a learner-centered approach in this book.

THREE METAPHORS OF MULTIMEDIA LEARNING

Design decisions about the use of multimedia depend on the designer's underlying conception of learning. In this section, I examine three views of multimedia learning – *multimedia learning as response strengthening, multimedia learning as information acquisition,* and *multimedia learning as knowledge construction.* If you view multimedia learning as response strengthening, then multimedia is a drill-and-practice system. If you view multimedia learning as information acquisition, then multimedia is an information delivery system. If you view multimedia learning as knowledge construction, then multimedia is a cognitive aid.

Table 1.2. Two Approaches to Multimedia Design

Design Approach	Starting Point	Goal	Issues
Technology-centered	Capabilities of multimedia technology	Provide access to information	How can we use cutting-edge technology in designing multimedia presentations?
Learner-centered	How the human mind works	Aid human cognition	How can we adapt multimedia technology to aid human cognition?

Multimedia Learning as Response Strengthening

Psychology's original view of learning is the response-strengthening view, in which learning involves strengthening or weakening an association between a stimulus and a response. This view entails assumptions about the nature of what is learned, the nature of the learner, the nature of the teacher, and the goals of multimedia presentations. First, it assumes that learning is based on changes in the strength of an association between a stimulus and a response, such as learning that the stimulus "3 + 2 = _____" is associated with the response "5." Second, the learner's job is to make responses and then receive rewards and punishments, such as "right" or "wrong." Thus, the learner is a passive being who is being conditioned by being rewarded or punished for each response. Third, the teacher's job – in this case, the multimedia designer's job – is to present rewards and punishments contingent on the learner's behavior, using reward to strengthen a response or punishment to weaken it. Finally, the goal of multimedia presentations is to enable drill and practice by soliciting responses from the learner and providing reinforcement (i.e., rewards or punishment). The underlying metaphor is that of a drill-and-practice system, so multimedia is a vehicle for rewarding correct responses and punishing incorrect ones.

The response-strengthening view is based on Thorndike's (1911) classic research on how cats learn to pull a loop of string to get out of a puzzle box. Thorndike's research resulted in his famous law of effect: Behaviors that are followed by satisfaction are more likely to occur in the future under the same circumstances; behaviors that are followed by dissatisfaction are less likely to occur in the future under the same circumstances. The law of effect has been a central pillar of learning theory in psychology for 100 years. Yet critics have argued that the law of effect – and the response-strengthening view on which it is based – are not necessarily wrong, but rather are somewhat limited. They may apply to how laboratory animals learn to give a response or even to carry out a procedure, but how can they account for more complex, conceptual learning? As we move from the animal learning laboratory to the study of how humans learn conceptual material in authentic tasks, other views of learning emerge in addition to the response-strengthening view.

Multimedia Learning as Information Acquisition

According to the information-acquisition view, learning involves adding information to one's memory. As with the previous view of learning, the information-acquisition view entails assumptions about the nature of what is learned, the nature of the learner, the nature of the teacher, and the goals of multimedia presentations. First, it assumes that learning is based on information – an objective item that can be moved from place to place (such as from the computer screen to the human mind). Second, the learner's job is to receive information; thus, the learner is a passive being who takes in information from the outside and stores it in memory. Third, the teacher's job is to present information. Fourth, the goal of multimedia presentations is to deliver information as efficiently as possible. The underlying metaphor is that of multimedia as a delivery system; according to this metaphor, multimedia is a vehicle for efficiently delivering information to the learner.

The information-acquisition view is sometimes called the *empty vessel view* because the learner's mind is seen as an empty container that needs to be filled by the teacher pouring in some information. Similarly, the information-acquisition view is sometimes called the *transmission view* because the teacher transmits information to be received by the learner. Finally, this is sometimes called the *commodity view* because information is seen as a commodity that can be moved from one place to another.

What's wrong with the information-acquisition view? If your goal is to help people learn isolated fragments of information, then I suppose nothing is wrong with the information-acquisition view. However, when your goal is to promote understanding of the presented material, the information-acquisition view is not very helpful. Even worse, it conflicts with the research base on how people learn complex material (Bransford, Brown, & Cocking, 1999; Mayer, 2008a). When people are trying to understand presented material – such as a lesson on how a car's braking system works – they are not tape recorders who carefully store each word. Rather, humans focus on the meaning of presented material and interpret it in light of their prior knowledge.

Multimedia Learning as Knowledge Construction

In contrast to the information-acquisition view, the knowledge-construction view is that multimedia learning is a sense-making activity in which the learner seeks to build a coherent mental representation from the presented material. Unlike information – which is an objective commodity that can be moved from one mind to another – knowledge is personally constructed by the learner and cannot be delivered in exactly the same form from one mind to another. This is why two learners can be presented with the same multimedia message and come away with different learning outcomes. Second, according to the knowledge-construction view, the learner's job is to make sense of the presented material; thus, the learner is an active sense-maker who experiences a multimedia presentation and tries to organize and integrate the presented material into a coherent mental representation. Third, the teacher's job is to assist the learner in this sense-making process; thus, the teacher is a cognitive guide who provides needed guidance to support the learner's cognitive processing. Fourth, the goal of multimedia presentations is not only to present information, but also to provide guidance for how to process the presented information – that is, for determining what to pay attention to, how to mentally organize it, and how to relate it to prior knowledge. Finally, the underlying metaphor is that of multimedia as a helpful communicator; according to this metaphor, multimedia is a sense-making guide, that is, an aid to knowledge construction.

Table 1.3 summarizes the differences among the three views of multimedia learning. In this book, I favor a knowledge-construction view because it is more consistent with the research base on how people learn and because it is more consistent with my goal of promoting understanding of presented material. Rather than seeing the goal of multimedia presentations as exposing learners to vast quantities of information, my goal for multimedia is to help people develop an understanding of important aspects of the presented material. For example, the Cognition and Technology Group at Vanderbilt (1996) notes that the conception of learning has changed from being able to

Table 1.3. *Three Metaphors of Multimedia Learning*

Metaphor	Definition	Content	Learner	Teacher	Goal of Multimedia
Response strengthening	Strengthening or weakening an association	Associations	Passive recipient of rewards and punishments	Dispenser of rewards and punishments	Enable drill and practice; act as a reinforcer
Information acquisition	Adding information to memory	Information	Passive information receiver	Information provider	Deliver information; act as a delivery vehicle
Knowledge construction	Building a coherent mental structure	Knowledge	Active sense-maker	Cognitive guide	Provide cognitive guidance; act as a helpful communicator

remember and repeat information to being able to find and use it. Similarly, Bransford, Brown, and Cocking (1999, p. xi) note that "in the last 30 years ... views of how effective learning proceeds have shifted from the benefits of diligent drill and practice to focus on students' understanding and application of knowledge." In short, the knowledge-construction view offers a more useful conception of learning when the goal is to help people to understand and to be able to use what they have learned.

THREE KINDS OF MULTIMEDIA LEARNING OUTCOMES

There are two major goals of learning – *remembering* and *understanding*. Remembering is the ability to reproduce or recognize the presented material, and is assessed by retention tests. The most common retention tests are *recall* – in which learners are asked to reproduce what was presented (for example, writing down all they can remember from a lesson they read) – and *recognition* – in which learners are asked to select what was presented (as in a multiple-choice question) or judge whether a given item was presented (as in a true-false question). Thus, the major issue in retention tests involves quantity of learning – that is, how much was remembered.

Understanding is the ability to construct a coherent mental representation from the presented material; it is reflected in the ability to use the presented material in novel situations, and is assessed by transfer tests. In a transfer test, learners must solve problems that were not explicitly given in the presented material – that is, they must apply what they learned to a new situation. An example is an essay question that asks learners to generate solutions to a problem, which requires going beyond the presented material. The major issue in transfer tests involves the quality of learning – that is, how well someone can use what they have learned. The distinction between remembering and understanding is summarized in Table 1.4. My goal in this book is to promote understanding as well as retention.

Consider the following scenario. Alice turns on a computer, selects an on-line multimedia encyclopedia, and clicks on the entry for "brakes." On the screen appears a passage consisting of on-screen text; it explains the steps in the operation of a car's braking system, beginning with stepping on the brake pedal and ending with the car coming to a stop. Alice reads casually, looking at each word but hardly focusing on the material. When I ask her to explain how a car's braking system works, she performs poorly – recalling almost none of

Table 1.4.   Two Goals of Multimedia Learning

Goal	Definition	Test	Example Test Item
Remembering	Ability to reproduce or recognize presented material	Retention	Write down all you can remember from the passage you just read.
Understanding	Ability to use presented material in novel situations	Transfer	List some ways to improve the reliability of the device you just read about.

the eight steps that were presented. When I ask her to solve some problems based on the presented material, such as diagnosing why a car's braking system might fail, she also performs poorly – generating almost no creative solutions (such as saying that a piston could be stuck or a brake line may have a hole in it). This is an example of a learning outcome that is all too familiar – *no learning*. In the case of no learning, the learner performs poorly on tests of retention and transfer. Alice lacks knowledge about the braking system.

Next, consider Brenda. She reads the same "brakes" passage as Alice, but tries hard to learn the presented material. When I ask her to write an explanation of how a car's braking system works, she performs well – recalling many of the eight steps in the passage. However, when I ask her to solve transfer problems, she performs poorly, like Alice. This is an example of another common kind of learning outcome – *rote learning*. The distinguishing pattern for rote learning outcomes is good retention and poor transfer. In this case, Brenda has acquired what can be called *fragmented knowledge* or *inert knowledge*, knowledge that can be remembered but cannot be used in new situations. In short, Brenda has acquired a collection of *factoids* – isolated bits of information.

Finally, consider a third learner, Cathy. When she clicks on "brakes'" she receives a multimedia presentation consisting of the same on-screen text that Alice and Brenda saw as well as a computer-generated animation depicting the steps in the operation of a car's braking system. When I ask Cathy to write an explanation of how a car's braking system works, she performs well – recalling as many of the steps as Brenda. When I ask her to solve transfer problems, she also performs well, unlike Brenda – generating many creative solutions. Cathy's performance suggests a third kind of learning outcome – *meaningful learning*.

Table 1.5. Three Kinds of Multimedia Learning Outcomes

Learning Outcome	Cognitive Description	Test Performance	
		Retention	Transfer
No learning	No knowledge	Poor	Poor
Rote learning	Fragmented knowledge	Good	Poor
Meaningful learning	Integrated knowledge	Good	Good

Meaningful learning is distinguished by good transfer performance as well as good retention performance. Presumably, Cathy's knowledge is organized into an integrated representation.

The three kinds of learning outcomes are summarized in Table 1.5. My goal in this book is to examine design features of multimedia that foster meaningful learning. In particular, I focus on ways of integrating words and pictures that foster meaningful learning.

TWO KINDS OF ACTIVE LEARNING

What's the best way to promote meaningful learning outcomes? The answer rests in *active learning* – because meaningful learning outcomes occur as a result of the learner's activity during learning. However, does active learning refer to what's going on with the learner's physical behavior – such as the degree of hands-on activity – or to what's going on in the learner's mind – such as the degree of integrative cognitive processing? In short, if the goal is to foster meaningful learning outcomes, should multimedia presentations be designed mainly to prime behavioral activity or cognitive activity?

Consider the following situation. Alan is preparing for an upcoming test in meteorology. He sits in front of a computer and clicks on an interactive tutorial on lightning. The tutorial provides hands-on exercises in which he must fill in blanks by writing words. For example, on the screen appears the sentence: "Each year approximately _____ Americans are killed by lightning." He types in an answer, and the computer then provides the correct answer. In this case, Alan is behaviorally active in that he is typing answers on the keyboard, but he may not be cognitively active in that he is not encouraged to make sense of the presented material.

By contrast, consider the case of Brian, who is preparing for the same upcoming meteorology test. Like Alan, he sits in front of a computer and clicks on a tutorial about lightning; however, Brian's tutorial is a short narrated animation explaining the steps in lightning formation. As he watches and listens, Brian tries to focus on the essential steps in lightning formation and to organize them into a cause-and-effect chain. Wherever the multimedia presentation is unclear about why one step leads to another, Brian uses his prior knowledge to help create an explanation for himself – what Chi and colleagues (Chi, Bassok, Lewis, Reimann, & Glaser, 1989; Roy & Chi, 2005) call a *self-explanation*. For example, when the narration says that positively charged particles come to the surface of the earth, Brian mentally creates the explanation that opposite charges attract. In this scenario, Brian is behaviorally inactive because he simply sits in front of the computer; however, he is cognitively active because he is actively trying to make sense of the presentation.

Which type of active learning promotes meaningful learning? Research on learning shows that meaningful learning depends on the learner's cognitive activity during learning rather than on the learner's behavioral activity during learning. You might suppose that the best way to promote meaningful learning is through hands-on activity, such as a highly interactive multimedia program. However, behavioral activity per se does not guarantee cognitively active learning; it is possible to engage in hands-on activities that do not promote active cognitive processing – such as in the case of people playing some highly interactive computer games. You might suppose that presenting material to a learner is not a good way to promote active learning because the learner appears to sit passively. In some situations, your intuition would be right – presenting a long, incoherent, and boring lecture or textbook chapter is unlikely to foster meaningful learning. However, in other situations, such as the case of Brian, learners can achieve meaningful learning in a behaviorally inactive environment such as a multimedia instructional message. My point is that well-designed multimedia instructional messages can promote active cognitive processing in learners even when they seem to be behaviorally inactive.

Figure 1.1 summarizes the two kinds of active learning – behavioral activity and cognitive activity. If meaningful learning depends on active cognitive processing in the learner, then it is important to design learning experiences that prime appropriate cognitive processing. In this book I focus mainly on learning from multimedia instructional messages in which learners may appear to be behaviorally inactive but which are designed to promote active cognitive learning, as indicated

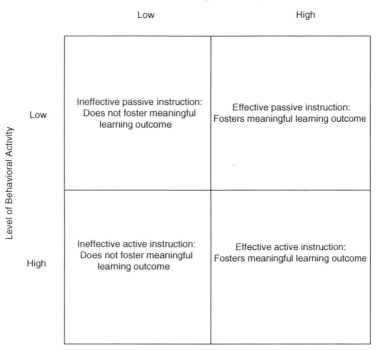

Figure 1.1. Two kinds of active learning.

in the top-right quadrant. This quadrant represents active cognitive learning based on passive instructional methods (Mayer, 2004), such as learning with some well-designed multimedia instructional messages. In addition, the bottom-right quadrant represents active cognitive learning based on active instructional methods (Mayer, 2004), such as interactive games and simulations. Some of the studies on interactive games and simulations reported in this book fall into this quadrant.

TWO GOALS OF MULTIMEDIA RESEARCH

Should you classify multimedia research as basic research or applied research? The goal of basic research is to contribute to theory – for example, a research-based explanation of how people learn (i.e., the science of learning). This goal is represented in the left-side labels of Figure 1.2, in which we ask whether the research contributes to learning

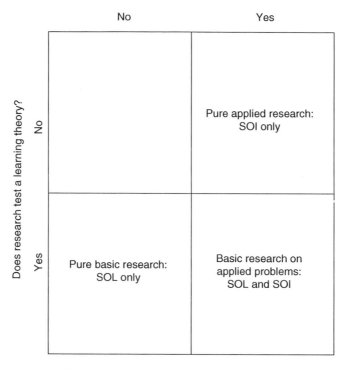

Figure 1.2.   Two kinds of research goals.

theory. The bottom two quadrants contribute to theory, so I have designated them "SOL" (for science of learning). By contrast, the goal of applied research is to contribute to practice – for example, evidence-based principles for how to design effective multimedia instruction (i.e., the science of instruction). This goal is represented in the top labels of Figure 1.2, in which we ask whether the research contributes to instructional practice. The two quadrants on the right contribute to practice, so I have designated them with "SOI" (for science of instruction).

Figure 1.2 presents four quadrants based on these two kinds of research goals, and is inspired by Stokes' (1997) *Pasteur's Quadrant*. The top-left quadrant represents research that does not contribute to learning theory and does not contribute to instructional practice, and thus is not of much interest to anyone. The top-right quadrant represents research that contributes to instructional practice but not to learning theory, which is the hallmark of pure applied research.

This kind of research identifies what works in multimedia instruction, but is of limited value because we do not know how it works or under what conditions we could expect it work. The bottom-left quadrant represents research that contributes to learning theory but not to instructional practice, which is the hallmark of pure basic research. This kind of research is of limited value because it does not test the predictions of learning theory within authentic learning situations.

Finally, the bottom-right quadrant of Figure 1.2 represents research that contributes to learning theory and to instructional practice, which is the hallmark of what Stokes (1997, p. 73) calls "use-inspired basic research" or what I (Mayer, 2008c) call *basic research in applied situations.* In this kind of research, we seek to accomplish two goals – contributing to theory and contributing to practice. Use-inspired basic research challenges learning theory to explain how learning works on authentic tasks and enriches instructional practice by helping us understand the conditions under which the principles can be expected to apply. Although it is customary to view basic research and applied research as opposite ends of a pole, an alternative is to view them as goals that can overlap. In this book, I focus on research that has overlapping goals – to conduct research on multimedia principles that both contribute to learning theory and contribute to instructional practice. In summary, the answer to the question about whether multimedia research should be basic or applied is that it should be both basic and applied. When we are working in the lower-right quadrant with overlapping theoretical and practical goals, successful basic research and successful applied research are the same thing.

In Chapter 2, I focus on the science of instruction, in which I describe the research methodology we used to derive our evidence-based principles of multimedia design. In particular, Chapter 2 includes examples of some of the multimedia instructional messages we used, and overviews of our independent variables, dependent measures, and effect-size methodology. For purposes of conducting research, we have focused on just one kind of multimedia message – instruction aimed at explaining how something works – and we have restricted our studies of multimedia learning to focus on learning from words and pictures. In Chapter 3, I focus on the science of learning, in which I describe the cognitive theory of multimedia learning. In particular, Chapter 3 describes a research-based theory of how people learn from words and pictures, which inspired each of the principles of multimedia design that we tested.

SUGGESTED READINGS

Asterisk (*) indicates that a portion of this chapter was based on this publication.

Section 1 on "What Is Multimedia Instruction?"

Spector, J. M., Merrill, M. D., van Merrienboer, J., & Driscoll, M. P. (2008). *Handbook of research for educational communications and technology* (3rd ed.) New York: Erlbaum.

Mayer, R. E. (Ed.). (2005). *The Cambridge handbook of multimedia learning.* New York: Cambridge University Press.

Section 2 on "The Case for Multimedia Learning"

*Mayer, R. E. (2000). The challenge of multimedia literacy. In A. W. Pailliotet & P. B. Mosenthal (Eds.), *Reconceptualizing literacy in the new age of media, multimedia, and hypermedia* (pp. 363–376). Norwood, NJ: JAI/Ablex.

*Mayer, R. E. (2005). Introduction to multimedia learning. In R. E. Mayer (Ed.), *The Cambridge handbook of multimedia learning* (pp. 1–17). New York: Cambridge University Press.

Section 3 on "Three Views of Multimedia Messages"

*Mayer, R. E. (1997). Multimedia learning: Are we asking the right questions? *Educational Psychologist, 32,* 1–19.

Section 4 on "Two Approaches to Multimedia Design"

Cuban, L. (1986). *Teachers and machines: The classroom use of technology since 1920.* New York: Teachers College Press.

Landauer, T. K. (1995). *The trouble with computers.* Cambridge, MA: MIT Press.

*Mayer, R. E. (1999). Instructional technology. In F. T. Durso, R. S. Nickerson, R. W. Schvaneveldt, S. T. Dumais, D. S. Lindsay, & M. T. H. Chi (Eds.), *Handbook of applied cognition* (pp. 551–569). Chichester, England: Wiley.

Norman, D. A. (1993). *Things that make us smart.* Reading, MA: Addison-Wesley.

Section 5 on "Three Metaphors of Multimedia Learning"

Bransford, J. D., Brown, A. L., & Cocking, R. R. (Eds.). (1999). *How people learn.* Washington, DC: National Academy Press.

*Mayer, R. E. (1992). Cognition and instruction: Their historic meeting within educational psychology. *Journal of Educational Psychology, 84,* 405–412.

Section 6 on "Three Kinds of Multimedia Learning Outcomes"

Anderson, L. W., Krathwohl, D. R., Airasian, P. W., Cruikshank, K. A., Mayer, R. E., Pintrich, R. E., & Raths, J. (2001). *A taxonomy of learning for teaching: A revision of Bloom's taxonomy of educational objectives.* New York: Addison-Wesley-Longman.

*Mayer, R. E. (2008). *Learning and instruction* (2nd ed). Upper Saddle River, NJ: Pearson Prentice Hall Merrill.

Section 7 on "Two Kinds of Active Learning"

*Mayer, R. E. (1999). Designing instruction for constructivist learning. In C. M. Reigeluth (Ed.), *Instructional design theories and models* (pp. 141–159). Mahwah, NJ: Erlbaum.

*Mayer, R. E. (2004). Should there be a three strikes rule against pure discover learning? The case for guided methods of instruction. *American Psychologist, 59*(1), 14–19.

Section 8 on "Two Goals of Multimedia Research"

*Mayer, R. E. (2008). Applying the science of learning: Evidence-based principles of multimedia instruction. *American Psychologist, 63*(8), 760–769.

Stokes, D. E. (1997). *Pasteur's quadrant: Basic science and technological innovation.* Washington, DC: Brookings Institution Press.

2

The Science of Instruction: Determining What Works in Multimedia Learning

The science of instruction is concerned with evidence-based principles for how to help people learn. Evidence-based practice occurs when instructional practice is based on research evidence. A multimedia instructional message is a communication using words and pictures that are intended to promote learning. In our research, examples of multimedia instructional messages include paper-based printed text and illustrations or computer-based narration and animation that explain how lightning storms develop, how car braking systems work, and how bicycle tire pumps work; and interactive computer simulation games that teach topics such as environmental science. In our research, learning outcomes are assessed with transfer tests that provide a quantitative measure of the learner's ability to use what was learned in new situations. An instructional method is a way of presenting a lesson. Overall, we examine the effectiveness of twelve instructional methods for promoting multimedia learning – coherence, signaling, redundancy, spatial contiguity, temporal contiguity, segmenting, pre-training, modality, multimedia, personalization, voice, and image. Our methodology involves conducting scores of experimental comparisons in which we compare the mean transfer test score of students who learned with an instructional feature to the performance of students who learned without the feature. To standardize the comparisons, we compute the effect size. Obtaining large effect sizes across a series of experimental comparisons helps determine what works in multimedia instruction.

▪ ▪ Chapter Outline

As you can see from the previous chapter, my colleagues and I have two overlapping goals in conducting research on multimedia learning – to contribute to the science of instruction by deriving evidence-based principles for the design of effective multimedia instruction (which I examine in this chapter) and to contribute to the science of learning by generating to-be-tested principles of multimedia design that are grounded in the cognitive theory of multimedia learning (which I examine in the next chapter). In short, my goals for this book are to identify principles of multimedia design that are based on research evidence (as described in this chapter) and grounded in learning theory (as described in the next chapter).

THE SCIENCE OF INSTRUCTION

What Is the Science of Instruction?

How can we help people learn? This is the central question in the science of instruction. In short, the science of instruction involves the creation of evidence-based principles for helping people learn. By evidence-based, I mean that the principles are consistent with the results of scientifically rigorous research rather than being based on opinion or dogma.

What Is Evidence-Based Practice?

The goal of the science of instruction is to contribute to *evidence-based practice* – instructional practices that are consistent with research evidence. In this book, I am concerned with "what works" in multimedia learning (O'Neil, 2005, 2008). In Chapters 4–13, I share with you the fruits of our research program carried out over the past twenty years, involving scores of experimental comparisons.

What Is Instruction?

Instruction refers to the instructor's manipulations of the learning environment that are intended to promote learning. This definition has two parts: (a) instruction involves creating a learning environment for the learner, and (b) the goal of the learning environment is to promote experiences in the learner that lead to learning. In multimedia instruction, the manipulations involve the presentation of words and pictures.

In this chapter, you are given an overview of how we conducted research aimed at discovering evidence-based principles for the design of multimedia learning. First, I describe some of the learning materials we used and some of the dependent measures we used to assess learning outcomes. Second, I describe some of the features of the learning materials that we varied in order to determine which features were most effective in promoting learning. Third, I describe how we used experimental methodology to compare the learning outcomes of students who learned under one method of instruction as opposed to another.

MULTIMEDIA INSTRUCTIONAL MESSAGES AND MEASURES

This book is concerned with the design of multimedia instructional messages. A multimedia instructional message is a communication using words and pictures that are intended to promote learning. This definition has three parts: First, the message part of the term reflects the idea that multimedia instructional messages are communications or presentations involving a teacher and learner. Second, the instructional part of the definition reflects the idea that the purpose of the multimedia instructional message is to promote learning (including understanding) in the learner. Third, the multimedia part of the definition reflects the idea that the multimedia instructional message contains both words and pictures.

Let's begin with three examples of multimedia instructional messages: an explanation of how lightning storms develop (Harp & Mayer, 1998; Mayer & Moreno, 1998), an explanation of how car braking systems work (Mayer, 1989a; Mayer & Anderson, 1992), and an explanation of how bicycle tire pumps work (Mayer & Anderson, 1991; Mayer & Gallini, 1990). For each example, I present the explanation in words to show the conventional way the material is presented as a single-medium instructional message. Then, I show how a book-based multimedia instructional message can be constructed using printed text and illustrations, and how a computer-based multimedia instructional message can be constructed using narration and animation. For each multimedia instructional message, I show how learning can be measured by using retention tests – to see how well the learner remembers the explanation – and transfer tests – to see how well the learner understands the explanation. Finally, l give you a brief example of an interactive multimedia computer game designed to help students learn how plants grow (Moreno, Mayer, Spires, & Lester, 2001).

How Lightning Storms Develop

Consider the following scenario. As part of a project, you wish to find out how lightning storms develop. You look up "lightning" in an encyclopedia and come across the following entry:

> Lightning can be defined as the discharge of electricity resulting from the difference in electrical charges between the cloud and the ground.
>
> When the surface of the earth is warm, moist air near the earth's surface becomes heated and rises rapidly, producing an updraft. As the air in these updrafts cools, water vapor condenses into water droplets and forms a cloud. The cloud's top extends above the freezing level. At this altitude, the air temperature is well below freezing, so the upper portion of the cloud is composed of tiny ice crystals.
>
> Eventually, the water droplets and ice crystals in the cloud become too large to be suspended by updrafts. As raindrops and ice crystals fall through the cloud, they drag some of the air from the cloud downward, producing downdrafts. The rising and falling air currents within the cloud may cause hailstones to form. When downdrafts strike the ground, they spread out in all directions, producing the gusts of cool wind people feel just before the start of the rain.
>
> Within the cloud, the moving air causes electrical charges to build, although scientists do not fully understand how it occurs. Most believe that the charge results from the collision of the

cloud's light, rising water droplets and tiny pieces of ice against hail and other heavier, falling particles. The negatively charged particles fall to the bottom of the cloud, and most of the positively charged particles rise to the top.

The first stroke of a cloud-to-ground lightning flash is started by a stepped leader. Many scientists believe that it is triggered by a spark between the areas of positive and negative charges within the cloud. A stepped leader moves downward in steps, each of which is about fifty yards long, and lasts for about one millionth of a second. It pauses between steps for about fifty millionths of a second. As the stepped leader nears the ground, positively charged upward-moving leaders travel up from such objects as trees and buildings to meet the negative charges. Usually, the upward-moving leader from the tallest object is the first to meet the stepped leader and complete a path between cloud and earth. The two leaders generally meet about 165 feet above the ground. Negatively charged particles then rush from the cloud to the ground along the path created by the leaders. It is not very bright and usually has many branches.

As the stepped leader nears the ground, it induces an opposite charge, so positively charged particles from the ground rush upward along the same path. This upward motion of the current is the return stroke, and it reaches the cloud in about seventy microseconds. The return stroke produces the bright light that people notice in a flash of lightning, but the current moves so quickly that its upward motion cannot be perceived. The lightning flash usually consists of an electrical potential of hundreds of millions of volts. The air along the lightning channel is heated briefly to a very high temperature. Such intense heating causes the air to expand explosively, producing a sound wave we call thunder.

You read the words carefully, but if you are like most learners my colleagues and I have studied over the past twenty years, you may not understand the passage. In our research, students who read this 500-word passage do not perform very well on tests of retention and transfer, even when we give the tests immediately after students finish reading the passage. When we ask students to write down an explanation of how lightning storms develop (i.e., a retention test), students typically can remember fewer than half of the main steps in lightning formation. When we ask them to answer questions that require using what was presented to solve novel problems such as figuring out how to reduce the intensity of lightning storms (i.e., a transfer test), students typically are unable to generate many useful solutions. Clearly, the time-honored traditional way of presenting instructional messages – providing an explanation in the form of printed words – does not seem to work so well.

These kinds of results led us to search for ways to make the material more understandable for students. Given our findings of the limitations of verbal forms of presentation, our search led us to the possibilities of visual forms of presentation. Can we help students under-stand better when we add visual representations to verbal ones? What is the best way to combine visual and verbal representations to enhance learning? These are the questions that motivate this book.

The research presented in this book mainly involves two kinds of multimedia learning situations – a book-based environment and a computer-based environment. In a book-based environment, we can focus on the issue of how best to integrate printed text and illustrations. For example, Figure 2.1 presents a book-based multimedia lesson on lightning formation – what I call *annotated illustrations*. The lesson consists of a series of illustrations, each depicting a key step in lightning formation, along with corresponding text segments (or annotations) that each describe a key step in lightning formation. The five illustrations are simple line drawings containing only essential elements such as positive and negative particles, updrafts and downdrafts, and warm and cold air. The text also focuses mainly on the essential elements and events in lightning formation; the 50 words used in the illustrations are selected verbatim from the 500 words used in the longer passage. Importantly, the illustrations and text are coordinated so that corresponding segments of text and illustrations are presented near each other on the page. We place each of these five annotated illustrations next to the corresponding paragraph in the longer 500-word passage that you just read. This is a multimedia lesson because it includes both words (i.e., printed text) and pictures (i.e., illustrations).

The annotated illustrations presented in Figure 2.1 are based on several general design principles adapted from Levin and Mayer's (1993) analysis of illustrations in text:

concentrated – The key ideas (i.e., the steps in lightning formation) are highlighted in both the illustrations and the text.
concise – Extraneous descriptions (e.g., stories about people being struck by lightning) are minimized in the text, and extraneous visual features (e.g., unneeded details or colors) are minimized in the illustrations.

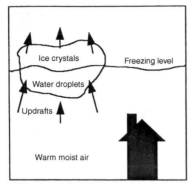

1. Warm moist air rises, water vapor condenses and forms a cloud.

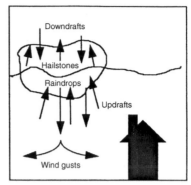

2. Raindrops and ice crystals drag air downward.

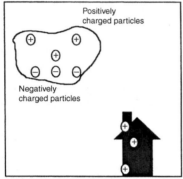

3. Negatively charged particles fall to the bottom of the cloud.

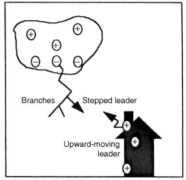

4. Two leaders meet, negatively charged particles rush from the cloud to the ground.

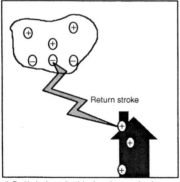

5. Positively charged paticles from the ground rush upward along the same path.

Figure 2.1. Annotated illustrations for the book-based lightning lesson.

correspondent – Corresponding illustrations and text segments are presented near each other on the page.

concrete – The text and illustrations are presented in ways that allow for easy visualization.

coherent – The presented material has a clear structure (e.g., a cause-and-effect chain).

comprehensible – The text and illustrations are presented in ways that are familiar and allow the learner to apply relevant past experience.

codable – Key terms used in the text and key features of the illustrations are used consistently and in ways that make them more memorable.

In short, the annotated illustrations presented in Figure 2.1 constitute an example of a well-constructed multimedia message.

The same approach can be used to produce a multimedia lesson within a computer-based environment. Figure 2.2 presents selected frames from a computer-based multimedia lesson on lightning formation – what I call a *narrated animation*. The lesson consists of a 140-second animation, depicting the key steps in lightning formation, along with a corresponding 300-word narration spoken by a male voice, describing each key step in lightning formation. The animation is adapted from the line drawings used in the illustrations, and the narration is a shortened version of the text. The animation uses simple line drawings consisting of only a few essential elements and events, and the narration also focuses on only a few essential elements and events. Importantly, the words and pictures are coordinated so that when an action takes place in the animation, the learner is given a verbal description of the action at the same time. In this way, the narrated animation summarized in Figure 2.2 is an example of a well-constructed multimedia message. This is a multimedia lesson because it contains both words (i.e., narration) and pictures (i.e., animation).

How can we assess what someone learns from multimedia presentations such as those depicted in Figures 2.1 and 2.2? The traditional measures of learning are retention and transfer. Retention refers to being able to remember what was presented. For example, the top portion of Table 2.1 shows that as a retention test for the lightning lesson we can ask learners to write down an explanation of how lightning storms develop. In our studies, we typically allow students six minutes to write their answers for the retention

"Cool moist air moves over a warmer surface and becomes heated."

"Warmed moist air near the earth's surface rises rapidly."

"As the air in this updraft cools, water vapor condenses into water droplets and forms a cloud."

"The cloud's top extends above the freezing level, so the upper portion of the cloud is composed of tiny ice crystals."

"Eventually, the water droplets and ice crystals become too large to be suspended by the updrafts."

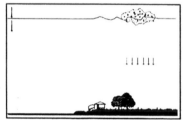

"As raindrops and ice crystals fall through the cloud, they drag some of the air in the cloud downward, producing downdrafts."

"When downdrafts strike the ground, they spread out in all directions, producing the gusts of cool wind people feel just before the start of the rain."

"Within the cloud, the rising and falling air currents cause electrical charges to build."

(Continues)

Figure 2.2. Frames from the narrated animation for the computer-based lightning lesson.

"The charge results from the collision of the cloud's rising water droplets against heavier, falling pieces of ice."

"The negatively charged particles fall to the bottom of the cloud, and most of the positively charged particles rise to the top."

"A stepped leader of negative charges moves downward in a series of steps. It nears the ground."

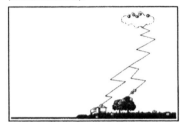

"A positively charged leader travels up from such objects as trees and buildings."

"The two leaders generally meet about 165-feet above the ground."

"Negatively charged particles then rush from the cloud to the ground along the path created by the leaders. It is not very bright."

"As the leaser stroke nears the ground, it induces an opposite charge, so positively charged particles from the ground rush upward along the same path."

"This upward motion of the current is the return stroke. It produces the bright light that people notice as a flash of lighning."

Figure 2.2. Continued.

Table 2.1. Retention and Transfer Questions for the Lightning Lesson

Retention Test
Please write down an explanation of how lightning works.
Transfer Test
What could you do to decrease the intensity of lightning?
Suppose you see clouds in the sky, but no lightning. Why not?
What does air temperature have to do with lightning?
What causes lightning?

test. Some of the key steps in lightning formation, based on our presentation, are:

1. air rises
2. water condenses
3. water and crystals fall
4. wind is dragged downward
5. negative charges fall to the bottom of the cloud
6. the leaders meet
7. negative charges rush down
8. positive charges rush up

To compute a retention score for a learner, I can examine what the learner writes – i.e., the learner's *recall protocol* – and then judge which of the eight main steps are included. In making this judgment, I focus on the meaning of the learner's answer rather than the exact wording. Thus, if the learner wrote "negative parts move to the cloud's bottom" the learner would get credit for idea "5" even though the wording is not exact. To make sure the scoring is objective, the recall protocol is scored by two independent scorers who do not know which instructional message the learner received. In general, there are few disagreements, but all disagreements are resolved by consensus. Thus, the retention performance of each learner is expressed as a percentage – that is, the number of idea units remembered divided by the total possible (i.e., eight).

Although retention measures are important, I am most interested in measures of transfer. I not only want students to be able to remember what was presented, I also want them to be able to use what they have learned to solve problems in new situations. Thus, I did not stop with measuring how much is remembered; in fact, the main focus of my research is on measuring students' understanding by measuring their transfer performance.

The bottom portion of Table 2.1 lists some transfer questions for the lightning lesson. The first question is a redesign question – asking the learner to modify the system to accomplish some function; the second question is a troubleshooting question – asking the learner to diagnose why the system might fail; the third question is a prediction question – asking the learner to describe the role of a particular element or event in the system; and the fourth question is a conceptual question – asking the learner to uncover an underlying principle (such as "opposite charges attract"). The student is given the questions one at a time on a sheet of paper, and allowed 2.5 minutes to write as many acceptable answers as possible. After 2.5 minutes, the question sheet is collected and the next question sheet is handed out.

To compute a transfer score for each learner, I count how many acceptable answers the learner wrote across all the transfer questions. To help in scoring, I construct an answer key, listing the acceptable answers for each question. For example, acceptable answers to the first question about decreasing the intensity of a lightning storm include removing positive particles from the earth's surface or placing positive particles near the cloud; acceptable answers to the second question about lack of lightning include that the top of the cloud may not be above the freezing level or that no ice crystals form; acceptable answers to the third question about the role of temperature include that the earth's surface is warm and the oncoming air is cool or that the top of the cloud is above the freezing level and the bottom of the cloud is below the freezing level; acceptable answers to the fourth question about the causes of lightning include a difference in electrical charge within the cloud and a difference in air temperature within the cloud. Answers based on common knowledge, such as using a lightning rod or not standing under a tree, were not counted as acceptable answers. Students receive credit for a particular answer if they express the idea in their written answer regardless of their writing style or use of terminology. For example, students would receive credit for the fourth question if they wrote "separation of minus and plus charges in the cloud" rather than "separation of negatively charged and positively charged particles." As with the retention test, answers to the transfer test are scored by two raters who do not know which lesson the learner received. Disagreements are rare and are settled by consensus. Overall, there were twelve possible acceptable answers across the four questions, so each learner's transfer performance can be expressed as a percentage – the number of acceptable answers generated divided by the total possible (i.e., twelve).

How Brakes Work

Having explored a physical system – the process of lightning formation – let's move on to a mechanical system – the operation of a car's braking system. Suppose your car's brakes need maintenance, so you look up an article on brakes in an encyclopedia. This article explains how cable brakes work in bicycles, how hydraulic brakes work in cars, and how air brakes work in trucks. Here's what the section on hydraulic brakes says:

Hydraulic brakes use various fluids instead of levers or cables. In automobiles, the brake fluid is in chambers called cylinders. Metal tubes connect the master cylinder with wheel cylinders located near the wheels. *When the driver steps on the car's brake pedal, a piston moves forward inside the master cylinder. The piston forces brake fluid out of the master cylinder and through the tubes to the wheel cylinders. In the wheel cylinders, the increase in fluid pressure makes a set of smaller pistons move. These smaller pistons activate either drum or disk brakes,* the two types of hydraulic brakes. Most automobiles have drum brakes on the rear wheels and disk brakes on the front wheels.

Drum brakes consist of a cast-iron drum and a pair of semicircular brake shoes. The drum is bolted to the center of the wheel on the inside. The drum rotates with the wheel, but the shoes do not. The shoes are lined with asbestos or some other material that can withstand heat generated by friction. *When the brake shoes press against the drum, both the drum and wheel stop or slow down.*

I have added italics to indicate the words that explain how disk brakes work; the italics was not in the original passage.

Did you learn much from this lesson? Did this lesson make sense to you? Admittedly, the basic explanation of how disk brakes work is presented in this passage, as indicated by the words in italic; however, if you are like most students who read this passage in our studies, you remembered less than 20 percent of the italicized material, and you were not able to answer transfer questions. Apparently, people have some difficulty in learning and understanding explanations that are presented in words alone.

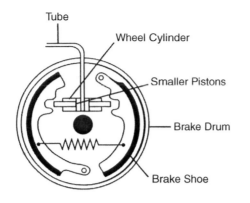

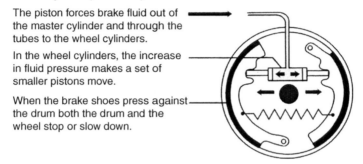

When the driver steps on the car's brake pedal...

A piston moves forward inside the master cylinder (not shown).

The piston forces brake fluid out of the master cylinder and through the tubes to the wheel cylinders.

In the wheel cylinders, the increase in fluid pressure makes a set of smaller pistons move.

When the brake shoes press against the drum both the drum and the wheel stop or slow down.

Figure 2.3. Annotated illustrations for the book-based brakes lesson.

Let's add some illustrations to complement the words. Figure 2.3 presents a portion of the brakes passage that uses words and illustrations to explain how car brakes work. The illustration shows two frames depicting the braking system – one before the driver steps on the brake pedal and one after the driver steps on the brake pedal. The illustrations are annotated with approximately seventy-five words taken from the brakes passage you just read – labels for the main parts (e.g., tube, wheel cylinder, smaller piston, brake drum, and brake shoe) and brief descriptions of each major action as italicized in the passage you read (e.g., "set of smaller pistons move"). The annotated illustrations are placed next to the corresponding paragraphs in the passage; for example, the annotated illustrations about car brakes are placed next to the paragraph that covers this material.

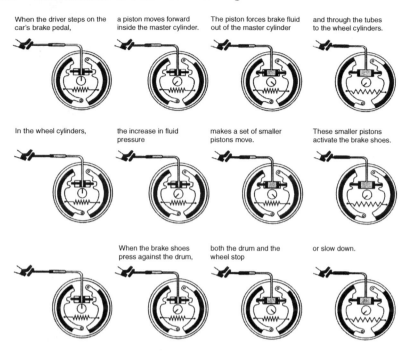

When the driver steps on the car's brake pedal,

a piston moves forward inside the master cylinder.

The piston forces brake fluid out of the master cylinder

and through the tubes to the wheel cylinders.

In the wheel cylinders,

the increase in fluid pressure

makes a set of smaller pistons move.

These smaller pistons activate the brake shoes.

When the brake shoes press against the drum,

both the drum and the wheel stop

or slow down.

Figure 2.4. Frames from the narrated animation for the computer-based brakes lesson.

This is a book-based multimedia lesson because words are presented as printed text and pictures are presented as illustrations. I refer to the lesson in Figure 2.3 as annotated illustrations because the words and pictures are coordinated – that is, the verbal description of an event such as "set of smaller pistons move" is presented next to a visual depiction of smaller pistons moving outward.

Alternatively, let's convert the multimedia lesson on brakes into a computer-based medium consisting of animation and narration. Figure 2.4 presents selected frames from a narrated animation that explains how car brakes work. The narration – spoken by a male voice – is coordinated with the animation so that when an event is depicted in the animation (e.g., the piston moving forward in the master cylinder), the narration concurrently describes the event in words (saying, e.g., "a piston moves forward in the master cylinder"). The presentation lasts about 30 seconds and focuses only on the essential steps in the process. The animation is based on an expanded version of the illustration in Figure 2.3, and the narration is based mainly on a slightly revised version of the italicized portion of

Table 2.2. Retention and Transfer Questions for the Brakes Lesson

Retention Test

Please write down an explanation of how a car's braking system works. Pretend that you are writing to someone who does not know much about brakes. (Used for computer-based version.)

Write down all you can remember from the passage you just read. Pretend that you are writing an encyclopedia for beginners. (Used for book-based version.)

Transfer Test

Why do brakes get hot?

What could be done to make brakes more reliable, that is, to make sure they would not fail?

What could be done to make brakes more effective, that is, to reduce the distance needed to bring a car to a stop?

Suppose you press on the brake pedal in your car but the brakes don't work. What could have gone wrong?

What happens when you pump the brakes (i.e., press the pedal and release the pedal repeatedly and rapidly)?

the brakes passage you read – containing about seventy-five words. As you can see, the narrated animation focuses only on car braking systems in contrast to the annotated illustrations, which focused on several types of braking systems.

How can we measure what a person learns from the multimedia brakes lessons presented in Figures 2.3 and 2.4? As with the lightning lessons, we can measure retention – what a learner remembers from the lesson – and transfer – how well a person can apply the lesson to solving new problems. For example, the top portion of Table 2.2 shows a simple retention test in which learners are asked to explain how car brakes work. Depending on the length of the passage, I allow students five to eight minutes to write their answers for the retention test.

To measure retention, I focus on the main ideas that are presented in the part of the text that explains how car brakes work, that is, the italicized portion of the passage. For example, some of the explanative idea units for the car brakes section are:

1. driver steps on the brake pedal
2. piston moves forward inside the master cylinder
3. piston forces brake fluid out to the wheel cylinder

4. fluid pressure increases in wheel cylinders
5. smaller pistons move
6. smaller pistons activate either drum or disk brakes
7. brake shoes press against the drum
8. drum and wheel stop or slow down

The learner's answer does not need to have the exact wording in order to be counted as correct. For example, if a learner writes "the shoes push on the drum," he or she would get credit for idea unit seven. I compute a percentage by counting the number of explanative idea units in the learner's answer to the retention question and dividing that by the total number of explanative idea units in the presented material.

The focus of our research is on promoting problem-solving transfer. The bottom portion of Table 2.2 lists some transfer questions aimed at evaluating learners' understanding of how braking systems work. The first question is a conceptual question, in which the learner must uncover an underlying principle (such as the idea of friction); the second and third questions are redesign questions, in which the learner is asked to modify the system to accomplish a function; the fourth question is a troubleshooting question, in which the learner diagnoses why the system failed; and the fifth question is a prediction question, in which the learner infers what happens in the system when a certain event occurs. As in the lightning lesson, I give the learner 2.5 minutes to write as many solutions as possible for each question; the learner works on one problem at a time and is not able to go back to previous items.

For each question, I make a list of acceptable answers. For example, acceptable answers for the five questions include: brakes get hot because of friction (for question one); brakes can be made more reliable by adding a back-up system or a cooling mechanism (for question two); brakes can be made more effective by using a more friction-sensitive brake shoe or by having less space between the brake shoe and brake pad (for question three); brakes fail because there is a leak in the tube or because the master cylinder is stuck in one position (for question four); and pumping reduces heat and reduces wearing of the drum in one place (for question five). Answers based on common knowledge, such as saying that brake shoes should be replaced regularly, were not counted as acceptable answers. I give a learner one point for each acceptable answer across all five transfer problems, using the same procedure as for the lightning lesson. Overall, there are fourteen possible acceptable answers across the five questions, so I can express each learner's transfer performance as a percentage, that is, the number of acceptable answers the learner produced divided by the total possible.

How Pumps Work

As a third example of an instructional message, consider a passage that explains how pumps work. The passage uses words to explain several kinds of pumps, including the following excerpt explaining how a bicycle tire pump works:

> Bicycle tire pumps vary in the number and location of the valves they have and in the way air enters the cylinder. Some simple bicycle tire pumps have the inlet valve on the piston and the outlet valve at the closed end of the cylinder. A bicycle tire pump has a piston that moves up and down. Air enters the pump near the point where the connecting rod passes through the cylinder. *As the rod is pulled out, air passes through the piston and fills the areas between the piston and the outlet valve. As the rod is pushed in, the inlet valve closes and the piston forces air through the outlet valve.*

This paragraph seems to present plenty of worthwhile information in a clearly written way. For your information, I have italicized the portion that explains the steps in the operation of a bicycle tire pump, but no italic is included when we use this material in research. In spite of reading this paragraph carefully, you probably did not learn much about how pumps work. For example, students in our research are able to remember less than 20 percent of the main ideas in the passage – in this case, the italicized steps in the operation of the pump. Even worse, students who read the passage do not perform well on transfer tests in which they are asked to use the material to solve new problems; in fact, they generally fail to produce any more correct answers than students who do not read the passage.

These results, like those for the lightning and brake passages, led us to search for better ways to help learners understand how pumps work. The search led us beyond the domain of words to explore the potential of pictures. For example, consider the book-based multimedia lesson in Figure 2.5, which uses printed text and illustrations to explain how pumps work. I refer to this lesson as annotated illustrations because it consists of words that describe the steps in how a

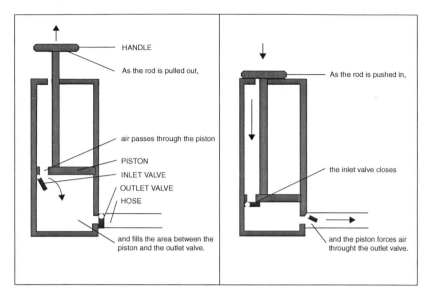

Figure 2.5. Annotated illustration for the book-based pumps lesson.

pump works and pictures that depict the steps in how a pump works. The words are short sentences describing actions such as "the inlet valve closes," and the pictures are frames depicting the pump in two states – with the handle up and with the handle down. Importantly, the words and pictures are coordinated so that the verbal description of an event such as "the inlet valve closes" is placed near a corresponding picture of the inlet valve closing. Each set of annotated illustrations is placed next to its corresponding paragraph, so that the annotated illustrations about bicycle tire pumps (shown in Figure 2.5) are placed next to the paragraph about bicycle tire pumps (shown in the box that you just read). As you can see, the words in the annotated illustrations are taken from the text passage (i.e., the italicized portion of the paragraph).

Similarly, Figure 2.6 summarizes frames from a computer-based multimedia lesson, which uses animation and narration to explain how pumps work. I refer to this lesson as a narrated animation because it contains animation segments depicting steps in the operation of a pump and corresponding speech by a male voice describing the steps in words. The words and pictures are coordinated so that, for example, when the animation shows the inlet valve opening, the narration says "the inlet valve opens." As you can see, the narration is modified slightly from the annotated

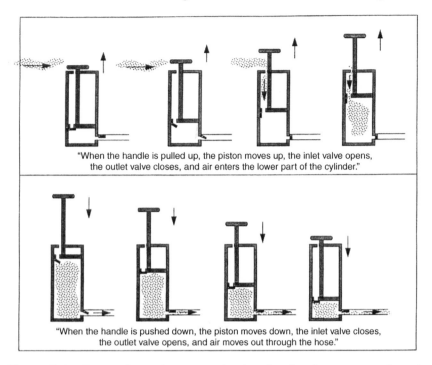

"When the handle is pulled up, the piston moves up, the inlet valve opens, the outlet valve closes, and air enters the lower part of the cylinder."

"When the handle is pushed down, the piston moves down, the inlet valve closes, the outlet valve opens, and air moves out through the hose."

Figure 2.6. Frames from the narrated animation for the computer-based pumps lesson.

illustrations – containing a fuller description of the steps involved in the operation of a bicycle tire pump but no extraneous details – and no other kinds of pumps are presented. The line drawing used in the animation is simple – containing only the parts mentioned in the narration – and the narration is short – containing about fifty words. The entire presentation lasts about thirty seconds.

To measure learning, I use retention and transfer tests as with the lightning and brake lessons. The top of Table 2.3 presents a question for a retention test in which learners are asked to write down all they can remember about how pumps work. Learners are given five minutes to write an answer based on the narrated animation (which contains information about one kind of pump) and ten minutes for the annotated illustration (which contains information about three kinds of pumps). For the narrated animation I focus on how many of the following steps about bicycle tire pumps the learner writes down:

1. handle is pulled up
2. piston moves up

Table 2.3. Retention and Transfer Questions for the Pumps Lesson

Retention Test

Please write down an explanation of how a bicycle tire pump works. Pretend that you are writing to someone who does not know much about pumps. (Used for computer-based version.)

Write down all you can remember from the passage you just read. Pretend that you are writing an encyclopedia for beginners. (Used for book-based version.)

Transfer Test

What could be done to make a pump more reliable, that is, to make sure it would not fail?

What could be done to make a pump more effective, that is, to move more air more rapidly?

Suppose you push down and pull up the handle of a pump several times but no air comes out. What could have gone wrong?

Why does air enter a pump? Why does air exit from a pump?

3.   inlet valve opens
4.   outlet valve closes
5.   air enters cylinder
6.   handle is pushed down
7.   piston moves down
8.   inlet valve closes
9.   outlet valve opens
10. air exits through the hose

For the annotated illustrations, I use a similar procedure based on the steps described in the annotations. As with scoring the lightning and brakes retention tests, I compute a retention score as a percentage of the number of idea units remembered divided by the total number possible.

The bottom of Table 2.3 contains some transfer questions. The first two questions ask the learner to redesign the system to accomplish a new function; the third question asks the learner to troubleshoot the system; and the final question asks the learner to uncover an underlying principle (e.g., "air travels from high- to low-pressure areas"). Acceptable answers for the first question about reliability include using airtight seals or using a back-up system; acceptable answers for the second question about effectiveness include increasing the size of the cylinder or pulling harder; acceptable answers for the troubleshooting question include a hole in the cylinder or a valve stuck in one position; and acceptable answers for the last question include the idea that lower air pressure in the cylinder accounts for air entering and higher air pressure in the cylinder accounts for air exiting. I do not give any credit for answers based on common knowledge, such as improving reliability by using thorn-resistant tire tubes, or for vague answers, such as saying the pump doesn't work because "something is wrong with valves." Based on our answer key, the maximum number of points across all four transfer questions is ten, so I can compute a percentage score for each learner by dividing the number of acceptable answers by the total number possible. For both the retention and transfer tests, I follow the same general scoring procedure as with lightning and brakes.

Other multimedia instructional lessons used in our research include narrated animations on how the respiratory system works (Mayer & Sims, 1994), the process of ocean waves (Mayer & Jackson, 2005), and how airplanes achieve lift (Mautone & Mayer, 2001).

How Plants Grow

Although the majority of our research focuses on multimedia presentations such as computer-based narrated animations and paper-based annotated illustrations, some of our research also involves interactive games and simulations. For example, suppose you got into a space ship and traveled to another planet where the weather is windy and rainy. With the help of your sidekick Herman the Bug (shown in Figure 2.7), you are asked to design a plant that would flourish in these conditions. First, you must choose the type of roots from a set of eight possible root types ranging from deep to shallow and from thick to thin; then, you must choose the stem from a set of eight possible stems ranging from short to tall and from thick to thin; and finally, you must choose the leaves from a set of eight possible leaves ranging from large to small and from thin-skinned to thick-skinned. When you make a decision, you get to see how well your plant survives, and Herman explains the process of plant growth in a narrated animation.

This is the scenario for a desktop computer game called Design-a-Plant, whose goal is to help students learn how the characteristics of plants are adapted to the environmental conditions (Moreno et al., 2001). After traveling to several planets, and learning to design

Figure 2.7.   Herman the Bug in the Design-a-Plant game.

plants with the help of Herman's narrated animations on plant growth, students are given a retention test and a transfer test, as summarized in Table 2.4. On the retention test, students receive one point for each of the eight types of roots, stems, and leaves they remember, for a total of twenty-four possible points. On the transfer test, students are given five problems like the first transfer question in the table and two like the second problem, and after each answer they are asked to explain their choice. Students receive one point for each correctly checked answer and one point for each correct explanation for a total of sixty possible points.

Other interactive games and simulations used in our research include a desktop computer geology simulation game called The Profile Game (Mayer, Mautone, & Prothero, 2002), a desktop computer interactive simulation of how an electric motor works called Dr. Phyz (Mayer, Dow, & Mayer, 2003), a desktop computer simulation game in industrial engineering called Virtual Factory (Wang, Johnson, Mayer, Rizzo, Shaw, & Collins, 2008), a virtual reality simulation of an aircraft's fuel system (O'Neil, Mayer, Herl, Thurman, & Olin, 2000), and a virtual reality version of the Design-a-Plant game (Moreno and Mayer, 2002b).

As you can see, the research reported in this book focuses mainly on multimedia messages aimed at explaining how some system works, including mechanical, physical, and biological systems. The learner's job is to construct a mental model of the cause-and-effect chain. I am mainly interested in whether learners can apply what they have learned to new situations, so I focus on transfer test performance as our main measure of learning outcome.

Table 2.4. Retention and Transfer Questions for the Design-a-Plant Game

Retention Test

Please write down all the types of roots that you can remember from the lesson.

Please write down all the types of stems that you can remember from the lesson.

Please write down all the types of leaves that you can remember from the lesson.

Transfer Test

Design a plant to live in an environment that has low sunlight.

Circle the types of roots (1 or more): (1) branching, deep, thick, (2) branching, deep, thin, (3) branching, shallow, thick, (4) branching, shallow, thin, (5) non-branching, deep, thick, (6) non-branching, deep, thin, (7) non-branching, shallow, thick, (8) non-branching, shallow, thin

Circle the types of stem (1 or more): (1) short, thick, bark, (2) short, thin, bark, (3) short, thick, no bark, (4) short, thin, no bark, (5) long, thick, bark, (6) long, thin, bark, (7) long, thick, no bark, (8) long, thin, no bark

Circle the type of leaves (1 or more): (1) thin, small, thick skin, (2) thin, small, thin skin, (3) thin, large, thin skin, (4) thin, large, thick skin, (5) thick, small, thick skin, (6) thick, small, thin skin, (7) thick, large, thin skin, (8) thick, large, thick skin

[Pictures of each type of roots, stem, and leaves were included.]

In what kind of environment would you expect to see the following plant flourish (i.e., to see the plant grow well)? Please put a check mark next to one or more conditions. [Picture of plant with thick, large, thin-skinned leaves; short, thick, no bark stem; and branching, shallow, thick roots.]

_____ low temperature, _____ high temperature, _____ low rainfall, _____ heavy rainfall, _____ low nutrients, _____ high nutrients, _____ low water table, _____ high water table

MULTIMEDIA INSTRUCTIONAL METHODS

What Is an Instructional Method?

An instructional method is a way of presenting a lesson, such as using spoken versus printed text along with an animation. An instructional method does not change the content of the lesson – the covered material is the same. In short, what is presented stays the same under both instructional methods. Similarly, an instructional method does not change the medium of the lesson (e.g., whether the lesson is presented on a computer screen or on paper). In short, the device usedo to present the material stays the same under both instructional methods.

Twelve Kinds of Methods

In our research on multimedia instructional methods, we vary a feature of the way the lesson is presented, but we teach the same content and use the same medium. In particular, we have examined the effectiveness of twelve features of our multimedia lessons:

coherence – Do people learn better when extraneous material is excluded (concise method) rather than included (elaborated method)?

signaling – Do people learn better when essential material is highlighted (signaled method) rather than not highlighted (non-signaled method)?

redundancy – Do people learn better from animation and narration (nonredundant method) rather than from animation, narration, and on-screen text (redundant method)?

spatial contiguity – Do people learn better when corresponding graphics and printed text are placed near each other (integrated method) rather than far from each other (separated method) on the page or screen?

temporal contiguity – Do people learn better when corresponding graphics and spoken text are presented at the same time (simultaneous method) rather than in succession (successive method)?

segmenting – Do people learn better when a multimedia lesson is presented in learner-paced segments (segmented method) rather than as a continuous presentation (continuous method)?

pre-training – Do people learn better when they receive pre-training in the names and characteristics of key components (pre-training method) rather than without pre-training (no-pre-training method)?

modality – Do people learn better from graphics and narration (narration method) than from graphics and printed text (text method)?

multimedia – Do people learn better from words and pictures (multimedia method) than from words alone (single-medium method)?

personalization – Do people learn better from a multimedia lesson when the words are in conversational style (personalized method) rather than in formal style (nonpersonalized method)?

voice – Do people learn better when the words in a multimedia lesson are spoken by a human voice (human-voice method) rather than a machine voice (machine-voice method)?

image – Do people learn better from a multimedia lesson when the speaker's image is on the screen (image-present method) rather than not on the screen (no-image method)?

As you can see, testing the effectiveness of each of these features involves testing one instructional method against another. By contrast, we are not testing the effectiveness of one medium against another – such as whether desktop computers are more effective than books or whether immersive virtual reality is better than desktop computers. Clark (2001) has eloquently argued that instructional methods cause learning, but instructional media do not cause learning. Similarly, Moreno and Mayer (2002) have shown that the same instructional methods have the same effects on learning regardless of whether the medium is a desktop computer, nonimmersive virtual reality, or immersive virtual reality.

DETERMINING WHAT WORKS IN MULTIMEDIA LEARNING

What Is an Experimental Comparison?

The central requirement of the science of instruction is that educational practice be based on empirical evidence (Mayer, 2008c). How can we tell if one method is more effective than another in promoting learning? In our research, we rely on an experimental comparison – in which an experimental group of learners receives a lesson that contains the to-be-tested feature while a control group of learners receives an otherwise identical lesson that lacks the to-be-tested feature, and subsequently both groups take transfer tests. The transfer test yields a mean score and standard deviation for each group.

Although there are many acceptable research methodologies – including experimental and observational methods – and many acceptable measures – including quantitative and qualitative measures (Shavelson & Towne, 2002), when the goal is to make a causal claim about instructional effectiveness an extremely useful approach is to use experimental methods with quantitative measures (Phye, Robinson, & Levin, 2005). In making this argument for experimental comparisons, I (Mayer, 2005) have emphasized that our goal is simply to determine whether an instructional method is effective. Two important features of an experimental comparison are *random assignment* – the idea that learners are randomly assigned to groups – and *experimental control* – the idea that the only difference between the groups is the instructional method used to present the material (Mayer, 2005).

The core evidence reported in Chapters 4–13 consists of experimental comparisons conducted by my colleagues and me. Here are the criteria I used for including each experimental comparison as core evidence: (a) the comparison involved one of the twelve kinds of methods listed in the previous section and was carried out with appropriate random assignment and experimental control, (b) the dependent measure was problem-solving transfer in which the mean transfer score and standard deviation were reported for both groups, and (c) the research was conducted by my colleagues and me and was published in a peer-reviewed original research journal (or chapter) that is readily available.

What Is Effect Size?

The next step is to determine the strength of the effect. Following Cohen (1988), we compute the effect size (d) by subtracting the mean score of the control group from the mean score of the experimental group, and dividing by the pooled standard deviation. The effect size tells us how many standard deviations of improvement in transfer test performance were obtained by implementing a particular design feature. The effect-size score is useful when we want to examine a set of experimental comparisons that used different materials and tests, because it allows us to use a common metric – answering the question, "The experimental treatment caused how many standard deviations of improvement over the control group on the transfer test?" According to Cohen (1988), an effect size of .8 is considered large, .5 is considered medium, and .2 is considered small.

In our research, we seek to identify instructional methods that cause large effect sizes across many different experimental comparisons. A large effect size indicates that an instructional method has practical significance in addition to statistical significance, because it has a large effect on performance. When we have many experimental comparisons of the same instructional method, we focus on the median effect size – the effect size that has half the scores above it and half the scores below it. When the median effect size is large – or even medium – we have reason to believe that the instructional method is effective for educational practice.

CONCLUSION

The theme of this chapter is that multimedia instructional messages should be designed in ways that are consistent with a scientific research base of empirical evidence. Our research focuses on instructional messages about how things work – such as lightning, brakes, pumps, electrical motors, and plant growth – although the details of the instructional materials, tests, and procedure may vary from study to study. What do all these multimedia instructional messages have in common? First, each is a *message* – that is, a communication to a learner. In particular, I focus on a specific kind of communication, namely, an explanation of how a physical, mechanical, or biological system works. Each explanation takes the form of a cause-and-effect chain in which a change in one part of the system causes a change in another part and so on. I focus on explanations – that is, messages about cause-and-effect systems – because these are at the heart of many educational presentations in subjects ranging from science to history. Second, each is *instructional* – that is, the purpose of the communication is to foster learning. In particular, I measure learning through tests of retention – being able to remember the steps in the explanation – and transfer – being able to use the explanation to solve new problems. I particularly focus on transfer because I am most interested in promoting learners' understanding of instructional messages. Third, each is based on *multimedia* because the communication is presented using both words and pictures. For book-based presentations, the words are in the form of printed text and the pictures are in the form of illustrations. For computer-based presentations, the words are in the form of narration and the pictures are in the form of animation. For interactive games, the material is presented as graphics and narration. I am most interested in discovering productive ways of adding pictures to words – an approach that grows from my interest in exploiting the potential of visual ways of learning.

Overall, our research examines twelve instructional methods aimed at improving the effectiveness of multimedia instructional messages. For each instructional method, we conduct a series of experimental comparisons in which we compare the transfer scores of students who received instruction with the to-be-tested feature (i.e., experimental group) and without the to-be-tested feature (i.e., control group). We look for methods that produce large effect sizes across many experimental comparisons.

This chapter focuses on the science of instruction by showing how we identified evidence-based principles for designing effective multimedia instructional messages. However, determining what works in multimedia learning is only half the job. We also want to know how the instructional methods work, that is, we need to understand how our instructional manipulations affect people's cognitive processing during learning. These issues are addressed in the next chapter, which focuses on the science of learning.

SUGGESTED READINGS

Asterisk (*) indicates that part of this chapter is based on this publication.

"How Lightning Storms Develop"

*Harp, S. F., & Mayer, R. E. (1998). How seductive details do their damage: A theory of cognitive interest in science learning. *Journal of Educational Psychology, 90*, 414–434.

*Mayer, R. E., & Moreno, R. (1998). A split-attention effect in multimedia learning: Evidence for dual processing systems in working memory. *Journal of Educational Psychology, 90*, 312–320.

"How Brakes Work"

*Mayer, R. E. (1989). Systematic thinking fostered by illustrations in scientific text. *Journal of Educational Psychology, 81*, 240–246.

*Mayer, R. E., & Anderson, R. B. (1992). The instructive animation: Helping students build connections between words and pictures in multimedia learning. *Journal of Educational Psychology, 84*, 444–452.

"How Pumps Work"

*Mayer, R. E., & Anderson, R. B. (1991). Animations need narrations: An experimental test of a dual-coding hypothesis. *Journal of Educational Psychology, 83*, 484–490.

*Mayer, R. E., & Gallini, J. K. (1990). When is an illustration worth ten thousand words? *Journal of Educational Psychology, 82*, 715–726.

"How Plants Grow"

*Moreno, R., & Mayer, R. E. (2002). Learning science in virtual reality multimedia environments: Role of methods and media. *Journal of Educational Psychology, 94*, 598–610.

*Moreno, R., Mayer, R. E., Spires, H. A., & Lester, J. C. (2001). The case for social agency in computer-based teaching: Do students learn more deeply when they interact with animated pedagogical agents? *Cognition and Instruction, 19*, 177–213.

3

The Science of Learning: Determining How Multimedia Learning Works

The science of learning is concerned with a theory of how people learn. Theory-grounded practice refers to developing instructional methods that are consistent with how people learn. Multimedia messages that are designed in light of how the human mind works are more likely to lead to meaningful learning than those that are not. A cognitive theory of multimedia learning assumes that the human information-processing system includes dual channels for visual/pictorial and auditory/verbal processing, each channel has limited capacity for processing, and active learning entails carrying out appropriate cognitive processing during learning. Five steps in multimedia learning are selecting relevant words from the presented text or narration, selecting relevant images from the presented illustrations, organizing the selected words into a coherent verbal representation, organizing selected images into a coherent visual representation, and integrating the visual and verbal representations and prior knowledge. Processing of pictures occurs mainly in the visual/pictorial channel; processing of spoken words occurs mainly in the auditory/verbal channel; but processing of printed words takes place initially in the visual/pictorial channel and then moves to the auditory/verbal channel. Three kinds of cognitive load are extraneous cognitive processing, which is cognitive processing that does not serve the instructional goal and is caused by poor instructional design; essential processing, which is cognitive processing that is required to represent the material in working memory and is determined by the complexity of the material; and generative processing, which is deep cognitive processing including organizing and integrating the material. Effective instructional design depends on techniques for reducing extraneous processing, managing essential processing, and fostering generative processing.

▩ ▩ **Chapter Outline**

In line with Stokes's (1997, p. 73) call for "use-inspired basic research" (as described in Chapter 1), this book has two goals – to contribute to practice (i.e., the science of instruction), which is addressed in Chapter 2, and to contribute to theory (i.e., the science of learning), which is addressed in this chapter. Overall, this book is concerned with research on multimedia learning principles that meet two criteria: (a) being *theory-grounded* – the principles are derived from a cognitive theory of multimedia learning – and (b) being *evidence-based* – the principles are consistent with empirical research on multimedia learning.

The first criterion – being theory-grounded – is introduced in this chapter, in which I spell out a cognitive theory of multimedia learning. The second criterion – being evidence-based – is introduced in

Chapter 2, in which I summarize how we developed an empirical research base for multimedia design principles. Both criteria are infused in Chapters 4–13, in which I describe how well twelve instructional design principles work when tested in multimedia learning environments (i.e., evidence-based) and explain how each principle works within the context of a theory of multimedia learning (i.e., theory-grounded).

In particular, in this chapter I spell out a cognitive theory of multimedia learning – that is, a cognitive theory of how people construct knowledge from words and pictures. First, I explore three fundamental assumptions underlying the theory; second, I examine each of five steps in meaningful multimedia learning based on the theory; third, I give examples of how three kinds of materials are processed; and finally, I distinguish among three kinds of cognitive load in multimedia learning.

THE SCIENCE OF LEARNING

What Is the Science of Learning?

How do people learn? This is the central question in the science of learning. The science of learning is concerned with the creation of a theory of learning based on scientific evidence. The cognitive theory of multimedia learning, which I describe in this chapter, is a research-based theory of learning aimed specifically at explaining learning from words and pictures.

What Is Theory-Grounded Practice?

Principles of multimedia instructional design should be based on an understanding of how people learn from words and pictures. This is the premise underlying theory-grounded practice. An advantage of theory-grounded practice is that instead of rigidly following instructional principles, instructors can have a better understanding of how instructional principles work and the conditions under which instructional principles are most likely to be effective.

What Is Learning?

Learning is a change in knowledge attributable to experience. This definition has three parts: (a) learning is a change in the learner; (b) what is changed is the learner's knowledge; and (c) the cause of the change is the learner's experience in a learning environment. Learning is personal, in that it happens within the learner's cognitive system. The change in knowledge cannot be directly observed but must be inferred from a change in the learner's behavior – such as performance on a test. The change may involve reorganizing and integrating knowledge rather than simply adding new knowledge. What is learned may involve five kinds of knowledge (Anderson et al., 2001; Mayer & Wittrock, 2006):

facts – knowledge about characteristics of things or events, such as "Sacramento is the capital of California,"

concepts – knowledge of categories, principles, or models, such as knowing what a dog is or how a pulley system works,

procedures – knowledge of specific step-by-step processes, such as how to enter data into a spreadsheet,

strategies – knowledge of general methods for orchestrating one's knowledge to achieve a goal, such as knowing how to break a problem into subparts, and

beliefs – cognitions about oneself or about how one's learning works, such as the belief that "I am not good at math."

In short, learning always involves a change in what the learner knows. In this chapter, I explore the idea that what is learned depends on the learner's cognitive processing during learning.

THREE ASSUMPTIONS OF A COGNITIVE THEORY OF MULTIMEDIA LEARNING

The guiding criterion for this chapter is that the design of multimedia environments should be compatible with how people learn. In short, principles of multimedia design should be sensitive to what we know about how people process information.

What is the role of a theory of learning in multimedia design? Decisions about how to design a multimedia message always reflect an underlying conception of how people learn – even when the underlying theory of learning is not stated. Designing multimedia messages is always informed by the designer's conception of how the human mind works. For example, when a multimedia presentation consists of a screen overflowing with multicolored words and images – flashing and moving about – this reflects the designer's conception of human learning. The

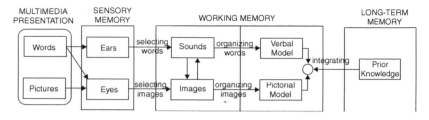

Figure 3.1. Cognitive theory of multimedia learning.

designer's underlying conception is that human learners possess a single-channel, unlimited-capacity, passive-processing system. First, by not taking advantage of auditory modes of presentation, this design is based on a single-channel assumption – all information enters the cognitive system in the same way regardless of its modality. Thus, it does not matter which modality is used to present information – for example, presenting words as sounds or as text – just as long as the information is presented. Second, by presenting so much information, this design is based on an unlimited-capacity assumption – humans can handle an unlimited amount of material. It follows that the designer's job is to present information to the learner. Third, in presenting many isolated pieces of information, this design is based on a passive-processing assumption – humans act as tape recorders who add as much information to their memories as possible. It follows that learners do not need any guidance in organizing and making sense of the presented information.

What's wrong with this vision of learners as possessing a single-channel, unlimited-capacity, passive-processing system? Research in cognitive psychology paints a quite different view of how the human mind works (Bransford, Brown, & Cocking, 1999; Lambert & McCombs, 1998; Mayer, 2008a). Thus, the difficulty with this commonsense conception of learning is that it conflicts with what is known about how people learn.

Figure 3.1 presents a cognitive model of multimedia learning intended to represent the human information-processing system. The boxes represent memory stores, including sensory memory, working memory, and long-term memory. Pictures and words come in from the outside world as a multimedia presentation (indicated on the left side of the figure) and enter sensory memory through the eyes and ears (indicated in the SENSORY MEMORY box). Sensory memory allows for pictures and printed text to be held as exact visual images for a very brief period in a visual sensory memory (at the top) and for spoken words and other sounds to be held as exact auditory images for a very brief period in an auditory sensory memory (at the bottom). The arrow from pictures to eyes corresponds to a picture being registered in the eyes; the arrow from words to ears corresponds to spoken text being registered in the ears; and the arrow from words to eyes corresponds to printed text being registered in the eyes.

The central work of multimedia learning takes place in working memory, so let's focus there. Working memory is used for temporarily holding and manipulating knowledge in active consciousness. For example, in reading this sentence you may be able to actively concentrate on only some of the words at one time, or in looking at Figure 3.1 you may be able to hold the images of only some of the boxes and arrows in your mind at one time. This kind of processing – of which you are consciously aware – takes place in your working memory. The left side of working memory represents the raw material that comes into working memory – visual images of pictures and sound images of words – so it is based on the two sensory modalities, which I called visual and auditory in Chapter 1. By contrast, the right side of working memory represents the knowledge constructed in working memory – pictorial and verbal mental models and links between them – so it is based on the two representation modes, which I called pictorial and verbal in Chapter 1. The arrow from sound images to visual images represents the mental conversion of a sound (such as the spoken word "cat") into a visual image (such as an image of a cat) – that is, when you hear the word "cat" you might also form a mental image of a cat. The arrow from visual images to sound images represents the mental conversion of a visual image (such as a mental picture of a cat or the printed word "cat") into a sound image (such as the sound of the word "cat") – that is, you mentally hear the word "cat" when you see a picture of one.

Finally, the box on the right is labeled LONG-TERM MEMORY and corresponds to the learner's storehouse of knowledge. Unlike working memory, long-term memory can hold large amounts of knowledge over long periods of time, but in order to actively think about material in long-term memory it must be brought into working memory (as indicated by the arrow from long-term memory to working memory).

In this chapter, I explore three assumptions underlying a cognitive theory of multimedia learning – *dual channels, limited capacity*, and *active processing*. These assumptions – which are derived from the learning sciences – are summarized in Table 3.1. In accordance with the dual-channel assumption, I have divided sensory memory and working memory into two channels – the one across the top deals with visual images and eventually with pictorial representations, whereas the one across the bottom deals with auditory sounds and eventually with

Table 3.1. Three Assumptions of a Cognitive Theory of Multimedia Learning

Assumption	Description	Related Citations
Dual channels	Humans possess separate channels for processing visual and auditory information.	Paivio, 1986; Baddeley, 1992
Limited capacity	Humans are limited in the amount of information that they can process in each channel at one time.	Baddeley, 1992; Chandler & Sweller, 1991
Active processing	Humans engage in active learning by attending to relevant incoming information, organizing selected information into coherent mental representations, and integrating mental representations with other knowledge.	Mayer, 2008a; Wittrock, 1989

verbal representations. In this way I try to compromise between the sensory-modality view – which I use to create two channels on the left side of working memory – and the representation-mode view – which I use to create two channels on the right side of working memory.

In accordance with the limited-capacity assumption, working memory is limited in the amount of knowledge it can process at one time – so that only a few images can be held in the visual channel of working memory, and only a few sounds can be held in the auditory channel of working memory. In accordance with the active-processing assumption, I have added arrows to represent cognitive processes for selecting knowledge to be processed in working memory (i.e., arrows labeled *selecting*, which move from the presented material to working memory), for organizing the material in working memory into coherent structures (i.e., arrows labeled *organizing*, which move from one kind of representation in working memory to another), and for integrating the created knowledge with other knowledge, including knowledge brought in from long-term memory (i.e., arrows labeled *integrating*, which move from long-term memory to working memory and between the visual and auditory representations in working memory). The major cognitive processes required for multimedia learning are represented by the arrows labeled *selecting images, selecting sounds, organizing images, organizing sounds,* and *integrating* – which are described in the next section.

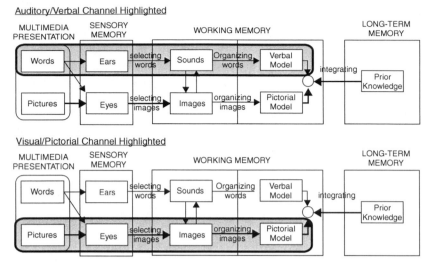

Figure 3.2. The auditory/verbal channel (top frame) and the visual/pictorial channel (bottom frame) in a cognitive theory of multimedia learning.

Dual-Channel Assumption

The dual-channel assumption is that humans possess separate information-processing channels for visually represented material and auditorially represented material. The dual-channel assumption is summarized in Figure 3.2: the top frame shows the auditory/verbal channel highlighted, and the bottom frame shows the visual/pictorial frame highlighted. When information is presented to the eyes (such as illustrations, animations, video, or on-screen text), people begin by processing that information in the visual channel; when information is presented to the ears (such as narration or nonverbal sounds), people begin by processing that information in the auditory channel. The concept of separate information-processing channels has a long history in cognitive psychology and currently is most closely associated with Paivio's dual-coding theory (Clark & Paivio, 1991; Paivio, 1986, 2006) and Baddeley's model of working memory (Baddeley, 1992, 1999).

What Is Processed in Each Channel?

There are two ways of conceptualizing the differences between the two channels – one based on *presentation modes* and the other based on *sensory modalities*. The presentation-mode approach focuses on whether the presented stimulus is verbal (such as spoken or printed words) or nonverbal (such as illustrations, video, animation, or background sounds). According to the presentation-mode approach, one channel processes verbal material, and the other channel processes pictorial material and nonverbal sounds. This conceptualization is most consistent with Paivio's (1986, 2006) distinction between verbal and nonverbal systems.

By contrast, the sensory-modality approach focuses on whether learners initially process the presented materials through their eyes (such as for illustrations, video, animation, or printed words) or ears (such as for spoken words or background sounds). According to the sensory-modality approach, one channel processes visually represented material and the other channel processes auditorially represented material. This conceptualization is most consistent with Baddeley's (1992, 1999) distinction between the visuo-spatial sketchpad and the articulatory (or phonological) loop.

Whereas the presentation-mode approach focuses on the format of the stimulus-as-presented (i.e., verbal or nonverbal), the sensory-modalities approach focuses on the stimulus-as-represented in working memory (i.e., auditory or visual). The major difference concerning multimedia learning rests in the processing of printed words (e.g., on-screen text) and background sounds. On-screen text is initially processed in the verbal channel in the presentation-mode approach but in the visual channel in the sensory-modality approach; background sounds, including nonverbal music, are initially processed in the nonverbal channel in the presentation-mode approach but in the auditory channel in the sensory-mode approach.

For purposes of the cognitive theory of multimedia learning, I have opted for a compromise in which I use the sensory-modalities approach to distinguish between visually presented material (such as pictures, animations, video, and on-screen text) and auditorially presented material (such as narration and background sounds) as well as a representation-mode approach to distinguish between the construction of pictorially based and verbally based models in working memory. However, additional research is needed to clarify the nature of the differences between the two channels.

What Is the Relation Between the Channels?

Although information enters the human information system via one channel, learners may also be able to convert the representation for processing in the other channel. When learners are able to devote adequate cognitive resources to the task, it is possible for information originally presented in one channel to also be represented in the other channel. For example, on-screen text may initially be processed in the visual channel because it is presented to the eyes, but an experienced reader may be able to mentally convert images into sounds, which are processed through the auditory channel. Similarly, an illustration of an object or event, such as a cloud rising above the freezing level, may initially be processed in the visual channel, but the learner may also be able to mentally construct the corresponding verbal description in the auditory channel. Conversely, a narration describing some event, such as "the cloud rises above the freezing level," may initially be processed in the auditory channel because it is presented to the ears, but the learner may also form a corresponding mental image that is processed in the visual channel. Such cross-channel representations of the same stimulus play an important role in Paivio's (1986, 2006) dual-coding theory.

Limited-Capacity Assumption

The second assumption is that humans are limited in the amount of information that can be processed in each channel at one time. When an illustration or animation is presented, the learner is able to hold only a few images in working memory at any one time, reflecting portions of the presented material rather than an exact copy of the presented material. For example, if an illustration or animation of a tire pump is presented, the learner may be able to focus on building mental images of the handle going down, the inlet valve opening, and air moving into the cylinder. When a narration is presented, the learner is able to hold only a few words in working memory at any one time, reflecting portions of the presented text rather than a verbatim recording. For example, if the spoken text is "When the handle is pushed down, the piston moves down, the inlet valve opens, the outlet valve closes, and air enters the bottom of the cylinder," the learner may be able to hold the following verbal representations in auditory working memory: "handle goes up," "inlet valve opens," and "air enters cylinder." The conception of limited capacity in consciousness has a long history in psychology, and some modern examples are Baddeley's (1992, 1999) theory of working memory and Sweller's (1999, 2005a; Chandler and Sweller, 1991) cognitive load theory.

What Are the Limits on Cognitive Capacity?

If we assume that each channel has limited processing capacity, it is important to know just how much information can be processed in each channel. The classic way to measure someone's cognitive capacity is to give the person a memory span test (Miller, 1956; Simon, 1980). For example, in a digit span test, I can read a list of digits at the rate of one digit per second (such as 8–7–5–3–9–6–4) and ask you to repeat them back in order. The longest list that you can recite without making an error is your memory span for digits (or digit span). Alternatively, I can show you a series of line drawings of simple objects at the rate of one per second (such as moon–pencil–comb–apple–chair–book–pig) and ask you to repeat them back in order. Again, the longest list you can recite without making an error is your memory span for pictures. Although there are individual differences, on average memory span is fairly small – approximately five to seven chunks.

With practice, of course, people can learn techniques for chunking the elements in the list, such as grouping the seven digits 8–7–5–3–9–6–4 into three chunks 875–39–64 (i.e., "eight seven five" pause "three nine" pause "six four"). In this way, the cognitive capacity remains the same – that is, five to seven chunks – but more elements can be remembered within each chunk. Researchers have developed more refined measures of verbal and visual working memory capacity, but continue to show that human processing capacity is severely limited.

How Are Limited Cognitive Resources Allocated?

The constraints on our processing capacity force us to make decisions about which pieces of incoming information to pay attention to, the degree to which we should build connections among the selected pieces of information, and the degree to which we should build connections between selected pieces of information and our existing knowledge. *Metacognitive strategies* are techniques for allocating, monitoring, coordinating, and adjusting these limited cognitive resources. These strategies are at the heart of what Baddeley (1992) calls the *central executive* – the system that controls the allocation of cognitive resources – and play a central role in modern theories of intelligence (Sternberg, 1990).

Active-Processing Assumption

The third assumption is that humans actively engage in cognitive processing in order to construct a coherent mental representation of their experiences. These active cognitive processes include paying attention, organizing incoming information, and integrating incoming information with other knowledge. In short, humans are active processors who seek to make sense of multimedia presentations. This view of humans as active processors conflicts with a common view of humans as passive processors who seek to add as much information as possible to memory, that is, as tape recorders who file copies of their experiences in memory to be retrieved later.

What Are the Major Ways in Which Knowledge Can Be Structured?

Active learning occurs when a learner applies cognitive processes to incoming material – processes that are intended to help the learner make sense of the material. The outcome of active cognitive processing is the construction of a coherent mental representation, so active learning can be viewed as a process of model building. A *mental model* (or *knowledge structure*) represents the key parts of the presented material and their relations. For example, in a multimedia presentation of how lightning storms develop, the learner may attempt to build a cause-and-effect system in which a change in one part of the system causes a change in another part. In a lesson comparing and contrasting two theories, construction of a mental model involves building a sort of matrix structure that compares the two theories along several dimensions.

If the outcome of active learning is the construction of a coherent mental representation, it is useful to explore some of the typical ways that knowledge can be structured. Some basic knowledge structures include *process, comparison, generalization, enumeration*, and *classification* (Chambliss & Calfee, 1998; Cook & Mayer, 1980). Process structures can be represented as cause-and-effect chains and consist of explanations of how some system works. An example is an explanation of how the human ear works. Comparison structures can be represented as matrices and consist of comparisons among two or more elements along several dimensions. An example is a comparison of how two competing theories of learning view the role of the learner, the role of the teacher, and useful types of instructional methods. Generalization structures can be represented as a branching tree and consist of a main idea with subordinate supporting details. An example is an outline of a chapter explaining the major causes for the American Civil War. Enumeration structures can be represented as lists and consist of a collection of items. An example is the names of principles of multimedia learning listed in this book. Classification structures can be represented as hierarchies and consist of sets and subsets. An example is a biological classification system for sea animals. These structures are summarized in Table 3.2.

Table 3.2. Five Kinds of Knowledge Structures

Type of Structure	Description	Representation	Example
Process	Explain a cause-and-effect chain	Flow chart	Explanation of how the human ear works
Comparison	Compare and contrast two or more elements along several dimensions	Matrix	Comparison of two theories of learning with respect to the nature of the learner, teacher, and instructional methods
Generalization	Describe main idea and supporting details	Branching tree	Presentation of thesis for the major causes of the American Civil War along with evidence
Enumeration	Present a list of items	List	List of the names of twelve principles of multimedia design
Classification	Analyze a domain into sets and subsets	Hierarchy	Description of a biological classification system for sea animals

Understanding a multimedia message often involves constructing one of these kinds of knowledge structures. This assumption suggests two important implications for multimedia design: (a) the presented material should have a coherent structure, and (b) the message should provide guidance to the learner on how to build the structure. If the material lacks a coherent structure – if it is, say a collection of isolated facts – the learner's model-building efforts will be fruitless. If the message lacks guidance on how to structure the presented material, the learner's model-building efforts may be overwhelmed. Multimedia design can be conceptualized as an attempt to assist learners in their model-building efforts.

What Are the Cognitive Processes Involved in Active Learning?

Three processes that are essential for active learning are selecting relevant material, organizing selected material, and integrating selected material with existing knowledge (Mayer, 2005a, 2008a, 2008b; Mayer & Wittrock, 2006; Wittrock, 1989). Selecting relevant material occurs when a learner pays attention to appropriate words and images in the presented material. This process involves bringing material from the outside into the working-memory component of the cognitive system. Organizing selected material involves building structural relations among the elements – for example, by using one of the five kinds of structures described earlier. This process takes place within the working-memory component of the cognitive system. Integrating selected material with existing knowledge involves building connections between incoming material and relevant portions of prior knowledge. This process involves activating knowledge in long-term memory and bringing it into working memory. For example, in a multimedia message, learners must pay attention to certain words and images, arrange them into a cause-and-effect chain, and relate the steps to prior knowledge such as the principle that hot air rises. These processes are summarized in Table 3.3.

In sum, the implicit theory of learning underlying some multimedia messages is that learning is a single-channel, unlimited-capacity, passive-processing activity. Thus, multimedia design is sometimes based on the empty-vessel view of learning described in Chapter 1 – the idea that the learner lacks knowledge so learning involves pouring information into the learner's empty mind. By contrast, I offer a cognitive theory of multimedia learning that is based on three basic assumptions about how the human mind works – namely, that the human mind is a dual-channel, limited-capacity, active-processing system.

FIVE STEPS IN A COGNITIVE THEORY OF MULTIMEDIA LEARNING

Building on the three assumptions described in the previous section, Figure 3.1 presents a cognitive theory of multimedia learning. For purposes of this book, I define a multimedia environment as one in which material is presented in more than one format – such as in words and pictures. For meaningful learning to occur in a multimedia environment, the learner must engage in five cognitive processes: (1) selecting relevant words for processing in verbal working memory, (2) selecting relevant images for processing in visual

Table 3.3 Three Processes for Active Learning

Name	Description	Example
Selecting	Learner pays attention to relevant words and pictures in a multimedia message in order to create a word base and an image base.	In viewing a narrated animation on lightning formation, learner pays attention to words and pictures describing each of the main steps.
Organizing	Learner builds internal connections among selected words in order to create a coherent verbal model and among pictures in order to create a coherent pictorial model.	Learner organizes the steps into a cause-and-effect chain for the words and for the pictures.
Integrating	Learner builds external connections between the verbal and pictorial models and with prior knowledge.	Learner makes connections between corresponding steps in the verbal chain and in the pictorial chain and justifies the steps on the basis of his or her knowledge of electricity.

working memory, (3) organizing selected words into a verbal mental model, (4) organizing selected images into a visual mental model, and (5) integrating verbal and visual representations. Although I present these processes as a list, they do not necessarily occur in linear order, so a learner might move from process to process in many different ways. Successful multimedia learning requires that the learner coordinate and monitor these five processes. More research is needed to clarify how these processes are monitored and coordinated.

Selecting Relevant Words

The first labeled step shown in Figure 3.1 involves a change in knowledge representation from the external presentation of spoken words (such as a computer-generated narration) to a sensory representation of sounds, and then to an internal working memory representation of word sounds. The input for this step is a spoken verbal message – that is, the spoken words in the multimedia message. The output for this step is a word sound base – a mental representation in the learner's verbal working memory of selected words or phrases.

The cognitive process mediating this change is called *selecting relevant words* and involves paying attention to some of the words that are presented in the multimedia message as they pass through auditory sensory memory. If the words are presented as speech, this process begins in the auditory channel (as indicated by the arrows from "words" to "ears" to "sounds"). If the words are presented as on-screen text or printed text, however, this process begins in the visual channel (as indicated by the arrow from "words" to "eyes") and later may move to the auditory channel if the learner mentally articulates the printed words (as indicated by the arrow from "images" to "sounds" on the left side of working memory). The need for selecting only part of the presented message arises because of capacity limitations in each channel of the cognitive system. If the capacity were unlimited, there would be no need to focus attention on only part of the verbal message. Finally, the selection of words is not arbitrary; the learner must determine which words are most relevant – an activity that is consistent with the view of the learner as an active sense-maker.

For example, in the lightning lesson, one segment of the multimedia presentation contains the words, "Cool, moist air moves over a warmer surface and becomes heated"; the next segment contains the words, "Warmed moist air near the earth's surface rises rapidly"; and the next segment has the words, "As the air in this updraft cools, water vapor condenses into water droplets and forms a cloud." When a learner engages in the selection process, the result may be that some of the words are represented in verbal working memory – for example, "Cool air becomes heated, rises, forms a cloud."

Selecting Relevant Images

The second step involves a change in knowledge representation from the external presentation of pictures (such as an animation segment or an illustration) to a sensory representation of unanalyzed visual images, and then to an internal representation in working memory (such as a visual image of part of the animation or illustration). The input for this step is a pictorial portion of a multimedia message that is held briefly in visual sensory memory. The output for this step is a visual image base – a mental representation in the learner's working memory of selected images.

The cognitive process underlying this change is *selecting relevant images*, which involves paying attention to part of the animation or illustrations presented in the multimedia message. This process begins in the visual channel, but it is possible to convert part of it to the auditory channel (such as by mentally narrating an ongoing animation). The need to select only part of the presented pictorial material arises from the limited processing capacity of the cognitive system. It is not possible to process all parts of a complex illustration or animation, so learners must focus on only part of the incoming pictorial material. Finally, the selection process for images – like the selection process for words – is not arbitrary because the learner must judge which images are most relevant for making sense out of the multimedia presentation.

In the lightning lesson, for example, one segment of the animation shows blue-colored arrows – representing cool air – moving over a heated land surface that contains a house and trees; another segment shows the arrows turning red and traveling upward above a tree; and a third segment shows the arrows changing into a cloud with lots of dots inside. In selecting relevant images, the learner may compress all this into images of a blue arrow pointing rightward, a red arrow pointing upward, and a cloud; details such as the house and tree on the surface, the wavy form of the arrows, and the dots in the cloud may be lost.

Organizing Selected Words

Once the learner has formed a word sound base from the incoming words of a segment of the multimedia message, the next step is to organize the words into a coherent representation – a knowledge structure that I call a *verbal model*. The input for this step is the word sound base – the words and phrases selected from the incoming verbal message – and the output for this step is a verbal model – a coherent (or structured) representation of the selected words or phrases in the learner's working memory.

The cognitive process involved in this change is *organizing selected words*, in which the learner builds connections among pieces of verbal knowledge. This process is most likely to occur in the auditory channel and is subject to the same capacity limitations that affect the selection processes. Learners do not have unlimited capacity to build all possible connections, so they must focus on building a simple structure. The organizing process is not arbitrary, but rather reflects an effort at sense-making – such as the construction of a cause-and-effect chain.

For example, in the lightning lesson, the learner might build causal connections between the selected verbal components: "First: cool air is heated; second: it rises; third: it forms a cloud." In mentally building a causal chain, the learner is organizing the selected words.

Organizing Selected Images

The process for organizing images parallels that for selecting words. Once the learner has formed an image base from the incoming pictures of a segment of the multimedia message, the next step is to organize the images into a coherent representation – a knowledge structure that I call a *pictorial model*. The input for this step is the visual image base – the pictures selected from the incoming pictorial message – and the output for this step is a pictorial model – a coherent (or structured) representation of the selected images in the learner's working memory.

This change from images to a pictorial model requires the application of a cognitive process that I call *organizing selected images*. In this process, the learner builds connections among pieces of pictorial knowledge. This process occurs in the visual channel, which is subject to the same capacity limitations that affect the selection process. Learners lack the capacity to build all possible connections among images in their image base, but rather must focus on building a simple set of connections. Like the process of organizing words, the process of organizing images is not arbitrary. Rather, it reflects an effort toward building a simple structure that makes sense to the learner – such as a cause-and-effect chain.

For example, in the lightning lesson, the learner may build causal connections between the selected images: The rightward-moving blue arrow turns into a rising red arrow that turns into a cloud. In short, the learner builds causal links in which the first event leads to the second and so on.

Integrating Word-Based and Image-Based Representations

Perhaps the most crucial step in multimedia learning involves making connections between word-based and image-based representations. This step involves a change from having two separate representations – a pictorial model and a verbal model – to having an integrated representation in which corresponding elements and relations from one model are mapped onto the other. The input for this step is the pictorial model and the verbal model that the learner has constructed so far, and the output is an integrated model that is based on connecting the two representations. In addition, the pictorial and verbal models are connected with prior knowledge activated from long-term memory.

I refer to this cognitive process as *integrating* because it involves building connections between corresponding portions of the pictorial and verbal models as well as knowledge from long-term memory. This process occurs in visual and verbal working memory, and involves the coordination between them. This is a demanding process that requires the efficient use of cognitive capacity. The process reflects the epitome of sense-making because the learner must focus on the underlying structure of the pictorial and verbal representations. The learner can use prior knowledge to help coordinate the integration process, as indicated by the arrow from long-term memory to working memory.

For example, in the lightning lesson, the learner must see the connection between the verbal chain – "First, cool air is heated; second, it rises; third, it forms a cloud" – and the visual chain – the blue arrow followed by the red arrow followed by the cloud shape. In addition, prior knowledge can be applied to the transition from the first to the second event by remembering that hot air rises.

Each of the five steps in multimedia learning is likely to occur many times throughout a multimedia presentation. The steps are applied segment by segment – not on the entire message as a whole. For example, in processing the lightning lesson, learners do not first select all relevant words and images from the entire passage, then organize them into verbal and visual models of the entire passage, and then connect the completed models with one another at the very end. Rather, learners carry out this procedure on small segments: they select relevant words and images from the first sentence of the narration and the first few seconds of the animation; they organize and integrate them; and then this set of processes is repeated for the next segment, and so on.

In short, multimedia learning takes place in the learner's information-processing system – a system that contains separate channels for visual and verbal processing, a system with serious limitations on the capacity of each channel, and a system that requires coordinated cognitive processing in each channel in order for active learning to occur. In particular, multimedia learning is a demanding process that requires selecting relevant words and images, organizing them into coherent verbal and pictorial representations, and integrating the verbal and pictorial representations with each other and with prior knowledge. The theme of this book is that multimedia messages should be designed to facilitate these multimedia learning processes. Multimedia messages that are designed in light of how the human mind works are more likely to lead to meaningful learning than those that are not. This proposition is tested empirically in the following ten chapters.

EXAMPLES OF HOW THREE KINDS OF PRESENTED MATERIALS ARE PROCESSED IN A COGNITIVE THEORY OF MULTIMEDIA LEARNING

Let's take a closer look at how three kinds of presented materials are processed from start to finish according to the model of multimedia learning summarized in Figure 3.1: pictures, spoken words, and printed words. For example, suppose that Albert clicks on an entry for lightning in a multimedia encyclopedia and is presented with a static picture of a lightning storm accompanied by a paragraph of on-screen text about the number of injuries and deaths caused by lightning each year. Similarly, suppose that Barbara clicks on the entry for lightning in another multimedia encyclopedia and is presented with a short animation along with narration describing the steps in lightning formation. In these examples, Albert's presentation contains static pictures and printed words, whereas Barbara's presentation contains dynamic pictures and spoken words.

Processing of Pictures

The top frame in Figure 3.3 shows the path for processing of pictures – indicated by thick arrows and darkened boxes. The first event – represented by the *pictures* box under MULTIMEDIA PRESENTATION on the left side of Figure 3.3 – is the presentation of Albert's lightning photograph (i.e., a static picture) or Barbara's lighting animation (i.e., a dynamic picture). The second event – represented by the eyes box under SENSORY MEMORY – is that the pictures impinge on the eyes, resulting in a brief sensory image – that is, for a brief time Albert's eyes behold the photograph and Barbara's eyes behold the animation frames. These first two events happen without much effort on the part of the learner, but now the active cognitive processing begins – the processing over which the learner has some conscious control. If Albert pays attention to the fleeting image coming into his eyes (or Barbara attends to the images coming into her eyes), parts of the image will become represented in working memory; this attentional

(a) <u>Processing of Pictures</u>

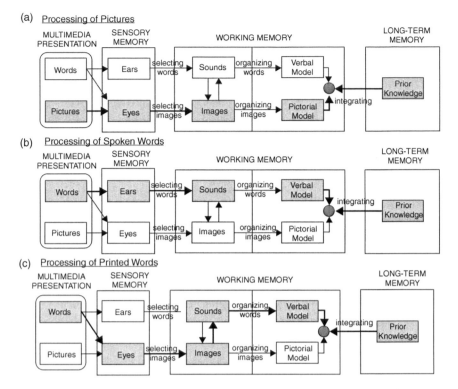

Figure 3.3. Processing of (A) pictures, (B) spoken words, and (C) printed words in a cognitive theory of multimedia learning.

processing corresponds to the arrow labeled *selecting images*, and the resulting mental representation is labeled *images* under WORKING MEMORY. Once the visual base is full of image pieces, the next active cognitive processing involves organizing those pieces into a coherent structure – a process indicated by the *organizing images* arrow. The resulting knowledge representation is a *pictorial model* – that is, Albert builds an organized visual representation of the main parts of a lightning bolt, or Barbara builds an organized set of images representing the cause-and-effect steps in lightning formation. Finally, active cognitive processing is required to connect the new representation with other knowledge – a process indicated by the *integrating* arrow. For example, Albert may use his prior knowledge about electricity to help him include moving positive and negative charges in his mental representation, or Barbara may use her prior knowledge of electricity to help explain why the negative and positive charges are attracted to one another. In addition, if the learners have also produced a verbal mental model, they may try to connect it to the pictorial model – for example, by looking for how a phrase in the text corresponds to a part of the image. This processing results in an integrated learning outcome, as indicated by the circle under WORKING MEMORY.

Processing of Spoken Words

The middle frame in Figure 3.3 shows the path for processing of spoken words – indicated by thick arrows and darkened boxes. When the computer produces spoken narration (as indicated by the *words* box under MULTIMEDIA PRESENTATION), the sounds are picked up by Barbara's ears (as indicated by the *ears* box under SENSORY MEMORY). For example, when the computer says, "The negatively charged particles fall to the bottom of the cloud, and most of the positively charged particles rise to the top," these words are picked up by Barbara's ears and held temporarily in her auditory sensory memory. Next, active cognitive processing can take place. If she pays attention to the sounds coming into her ears (as indicated by the arrow labeled *selecting words*), some of the incoming sounds will be selected for inclusion in Barbara's word sound base (indicated by the *sounds* box under WORKING MEMORY). For example, the resulting collection of words in working memory might include: "positive top, negative bottom." The words in the word base are disorganized fragments, so the next step – indicated by the *organizing words* arrow – is to build them into a coherent mental structure – indicated by the *verbal model* box. In this process, the words change from being represented based on sound to being represented based on word meaning; the result could be a cause-and-effect chain for the steps in lightning formation. Lastly, Barbara may use her prior knowledge to help explain the transition from one step to another and may connect words with pictures – such as connecting "positive top, negative bottom" with an image of positive particles in the top of a cloud and negative charges in the bottom. This process is labeled *integrating*, and the resulting integrated learning outcome is indicated by the circle under WORKING MEMORY.

Processing of Printed Words

So far, cognitive processing of pictures takes place mainly in the visual/pictorial channel (shown in the bottom half of Figure 3.1), whereas the cognitive processing of spoken words takes place mainly in the auditory/verbal channel (shown in the top half of Figure 3.1). However, the arrow from *images* to *sounds* indicates that the learner (such as Barbara) can mentally create sounds corresponding to the visual image – such as mentally saying "wind" when she sees wavy arrows in the animation. Similarly, the arrow from *sounds* to *images* indicates that the learner (such as Barbara) can mentally create images corresponding to the word sound base – such as visualizing a plus sign when the narration says "positively charged particle."

The presentation of printed text in multimedia messages seems to create an information-processing challenge for the dual-channel system portrayed in Figure 3.1. For example, consider the case of Alan, who must read text and view an illustration. The words are presented visually, so they must initially be processed through the eyes – as indicated by the arrow from *words* to *eyes*. Then, Alan may attend to some of the incoming words (as indicated by the *selecting images* arrow) and bring them into working memory as part of the visual image base. Then, by mentally pronouncing the images of the printed words Alan can get the words into the word sound base – as indicated by the arrow from *images* to *sounds*. Once the words are represented in the auditory/ verbal channel they are processed like spoken words, as described earlier. This path is presented in the bottom frame of Figure 3.3. As you can see, when verbal material must enter through the visual channel, the words must take a complex route through the system, and must also compete for attention with the illustration that Alan is also processing via the visual channel. The consequences of this problem are addressed in more detail in Chapter 11 on the modality principle.

THREE KINDS OF COGNITIVE LOAD IN A COGNITIVE THEORY OF MULTIMEDIA LEARNING

A central tenet of the cognitive theory of multimedia learning (Mayer, 2005a, 2008b; Mayer & Moreno, 2003) and cognitive load theory (Chandler & Sweller, 1991; Clark, Nguyen, & Sweller, 2006; Sweller, 1999, 2005a) from which it was derived is that learners can engage in three kinds of cognitive processing during learning, each of which draws on the learner's available cognitive capacity. Table 3.4 summarizes the three kinds of cognitive load, which DeLeeuw and Mayer (2008) refer to as the triarchic model of cognitive load.

Extraneous Cognitive Processing

As indicated in the first row of Table 3.4, *extraneous cognitive processing* (which Sweller [1999] calls *extraneous cognitive load*) refers to

Table 3.4. Three Kinds of Cognitive Load

Type	Definition	Processes
Extraneous	Cognitive processing that does not serve the instructional goal; caused by confusing instructional design.	None
Essential	Cognitive processing required to represent the essential material in working memory; caused by the complexity of the material.	Selecting
Generative	Cognitive processing required for deeper understanding; caused by the motivation of the learner.	Organizing and integrating

cognitive processing during learning that does not serve the instructional goal and that is caused by confusing instructional design. For example, if captions are printed at the bottom of the screen and an animation is presented above, the learner will have to visually scan back and forth between words at the bottom of the screen and the corresponding portion of the animation. This visual scanning is a form of extraneous processing because it wastes precious cognitive capacity due to poor design. The poor design can be corrected by placing words next to the portion of the graphic they describe. If extraneous processing consumes all of the learner's available cognitive capacity, then the learner is not able to engage in cognitive processes for learning such as selecting, organizing, and integrating. The result is no learning, which is reflected in poor retention and poor transfer performance.

Essential Cognitive Processing

As indicated in the second row of Table 3.4, *essential cognitive processing* (which Sweller [1999] calls *intrinsic cognitive load*) is cognitive processing during learning that serves to represent the essential material in working memory and that is determined by the inherent complexity of the material. For example, for a learner who is unfamiliar with the material, the lightning lesson shown in Figure 2.2 is so complex – consisting of many steps and underlying processes – that it could overload the learner's cognitive capacity. One way to help learners process complex material is to provide pre-training in the names and characteristics of the key elements. Essential processing corresponds to the *selecting* arrows in Figure 3.1, which indicate that the learner is building a representation of the material in working memory. If learners engage mainly in essential cognitive processing during learning, the result will be rote learning, as reflected in good retention and poor transfer performance.

Generative Cognitive Processing

As indicated in the third line of Table 3.4, *generative cognitive processing* (which Sweller [1999] calls *germane cognitive load*) is cognitive processing during learning that is aimed at making sense of the essential material and that can be attributed to the learner's level of motivation. Generative processing corresponds to the *organizing* and *integrating* arrows in Figure 3.1, which indicate deeper processing. Generative processing may be primed by creating an engaging learning environment in which the narrator uses a conversational style and polite wording. If learners are able to engage in essential and generative processing, they are more likely to construct a meaningful learning outcome that enables both good retention and good transfer performance.

According to this triarchic model of cognitive load, a major challenge of instructional design is that cognitive capacity is limited, so there is only a limited capacity for extraneous, essential, and generative processing. You can see that each of the three kinds of demands on cognitive capacity leads to a different problem for instructional design: problems attributable to confusing design of the physical layout of the material, problems attributable to the inherent complexity of the material, and problems attributable to unmotivating communication style (Mayer, 2008b).

The three kinds of problems respectively require three kinds of instructional design solutions: reduce extraneous cognitive processing, manage essential cognitive processing, and foster generative cognitive processing. The first kind of problem occurs when confusing instructional design encourages the learner to engage in extraneous cognitive processing, thereby limiting the amount of cognitive capacity available for essential and generative processing. To combat this problem, instructional designers should design lessons that reduce extraneous processing in learners. The next section of this book (Chapters 4–8) reviews five techniques for reducing extraneous cognitive processing – the coherence, signaling, redundancy, spatial contiguity, and temporal contiguity principles.

The second kind of problem occurs when essential processing consumes all or most of the learner's cognitive capacity, leaving insufficient capacity available for generative processing. To address this problem, we need lessons that manage essential processing. The third section of the book (Chapters 9–11) reviews three techniques for managing essential processing – the segmenting, pre-training, and modality principles.

Finally, even if capacity is available for generative processing, we have a problem if learners are not motivated to use that capacity. To address this problem, we need to design lessons that foster generative processing. The fourth section of this book (Chapters 12–13) examines two techniques aimed at fostering generative processing – the multimedia principle and the personalization principle. It also examines the role of the narrator's voice and image on learning (i.e., the voice and image principles).

CONCLUSION

The theme of this chapter is that the design of multimedia messages should be consistent with a research-based theory of how people learn. In this chapter, I presented a cognitive theory of multimedia learning based on three well-established ideas in cognitive science – what I call the dual-channel, limited-capacity, and active-learning processing assumptions. I showed how multimedia learning occurs when the learner engages in five kinds of processing – selecting words, selecting images, organizing words, organizing images, and integrating. I gave examples of how pictures, spoken words, and printed words are processed according to the cognitive theory of multimedia learning. Finally, I showed how instructional designers need to reduce extraneous processing, manage essential processing, and foster generative processing. In the remainder of this book, I use the cognitive theory of multimedia learning to suggest design principles that my colleagues and I have tested.

SUGGESTED READINGS

Asterisk (*) indicates that a portion of this chapter was based on this publication.

Baddeley, A. D. (1986). *Working memory*. Oxford, England: Oxford University Press.

Clark, J. M., & Paivio, A. (1991). Dual coding theory and education. *Educational Psychology Review*, 3, 149–210.

*Mayer, R. E. (2005a). Cognitive theory of multimedia learning. In R. E. Mayer (Ed.), *Cambridge handbook of multimedia* learning (pp. 31–48). New York: Cambridge University Press.

*Mayer, R. E., & Moreno, R. (2003). Nine ways to reduce cognitive load in multimedia learning. *Educational Psychologist, 38*, 43–52.

Sweller, J. (1999). Instructional design in technical areas. Camberwell, Australia: ACER Press.

Wittrock, M. C. (1989). Generative processes of comprehension. *Educational Psychologist, 24*, 345–376.

Section II

Principles for Reducing Extraneous Processing In Multimedia Learning

Consider the following situation. You are interested in how lightning storms develop, so you go to an online encyclopedia and click on a movie icon labeled "How Lightning Works." You watch a three-minute narrated animation that explains the steps in lightning formation. The lesson includes many interesting facts about lightning, such as the fact that each year 150 Americans die from being struck by lightning, and has many interesting video clips, such as ten-second segments showing various lightning storms. To increase your enjoyment, the lesson has an instrumental music loop playing in the background. Your attention is drawn to the many interesting features of the lesson, such as the interesting facts and video clips, so you do not pay much attention to some of the essential information about the steps in lightning formation. On a subsequent retention test, you can remember parts of some of the sentences about lightning formation, and on a transfer test, you are not able to apply what was presented to solving new problems.

What is extraneous processing overload? This situation is an example of extraneous processing overload – that is, a situation in which the cognitive processing of extraneous material in the lesson is so demanding that there is little or no remaining cognitive capacity to engage in essential or generative processing. Extraneous processing overload is likely to occur when the lesson contains attention-grabbing extraneous material or when the lesson is designed in a confusing way. Box 2.1 summarizes two types of essential overload situations – one in which the lesson contains extraneous material and one in which the lesson is presented in a confusing way.

What is extraneous material? Extraneous material is information from the lesson that is not needed to achieve the instructional goal. If the goal is to understand how lightning works, then extraneous material

85

Box 2.1.   What Is Extraneous Processing Overload?

*Scenario 1: Extraneous processing (caused by extraneous material) +
essential processing > cognitive capacity*
Description: Lesson contains attention-grabbing extraneous material.
Example: Interesting but irrelevant facts or graphics, redundant captions
Principles: Coherence, signaling, redundancy

*Scenario 2: Extraneous processing (caused by confusing layout) +
essential processing > cognitive capacity*
Description: Lesson layout creates confusion.
Example: Printed words are far from corresponding graphics; spoken words are not presented simultaneously with corresponding graphics.
Principles: Spatial contiguity, temporal contiguity

---

consists of interesting but irrelevant verbal statements and graphics (such as statistics about lightning fatalities or video of lightning strikes).

What is extraneous processing? Extraneous processing is cognitive processing during learning that does not serve the instructional goal – such as attending to irrelevant information or trying to make up for confusing layout of the lesson.

How can we reduce extraneous processing? In this section of the book, I address the problem of extraneous processing overload. In particular, as summarized in Box 2.2, I explore five principles for reducing

---

Box 2.2.   Five Ways to Reduce Extraneous Processing

Principle	*Description*
Coherence:	Delete extraneous words, sounds, or graphics.
Signaling:	Highlight essential words or graphics.
Redundancy:	Delete redundant captions from narrated animation.
Spatial contiguity:	Place essential words next to corresponding graphics on the screen or page.
Temporal contiguity:	Present corresponding words and pictures simultaneously.

---

extraneous processing – coherence (Chapter 4), signaling (Chapter 5), redundancy (Chapter 6), spatial contiguity (Chapter 7), and temporal contiguity principles (Chapter 8). Coherence techniques involve deleting extraneous words, sounds, and pictures from a multimedia lesson. Signaling involves highlighting the essential words and pictures in a multimedia lesson. Redundancy techniques involve removing redundant captions from narrated animations. Spatial contiguity involves placing words next to corresponding graphics on the screen or page. Temporal contiguity involves presenting corresponding narration and graphics simultaneously. These techniques are intended to reduce extraneous processing so that learners can use their cognitive capacity for essential and generative processing.

4

Coherence Principle

Coherence Principle: *People learn better when extraneous material is excluded rather than included. The coherence principle can be broken into three complementary versions: (1) Learning is improved when interesting but irrelevant words and pictures are excluded from a multimedia presentation; (2) learning is improved when interesting but irrelevant sounds and music are excluded from a multimedia presentation; and (3) learning is improved when unneeded words and symbols are eliminated from a multimedia presentation. Each version of the coherence principle is addressed in turn in this chapter.*

Example: *A learner receives a concise narrated animation (concise group) or the same lesson along with interesting but irrelevant video clips or photos, interesting but irrelevant facts or stories, background music, or specific details (expanded group).*

Theoretical Rationale: *Extraneous material competes for cognitive resources in working memory and can divert attention from the important material, disrupt the process of organizing the material, and prime the learner to integrate the material with an inappropriate theme.*

Empirical Rationale: *In thirteen out of fourteen tests, learners who received concise multimedia presentations performed better on tests of transfer than did learners who received multimedia messages that contained extraneous material. The median effect size is $d = 0.97$.*

Boundary Conditions: *The coherence principle may be particularly important for learners with low working-memory capacity or low domain knowledge.*

■ ■ Chapter Outline

COHERENCE PRINCIPLE 1: LEARNING IS IMPROVED WHEN
INTERESTING BUT IRRELEVANT WORDS OR PICTURES ARE EXCLUDED
FROM A MULTIMEDIA PRESENTATION

The coherence principle is that people better understand an explanation from a multimedia lesson containing essential material (concise lesson) than from a multimedia lesson containing essential material and additional material (expanded lesson). In this chapter I examine three variations of this theme: (a) excluding interesting but irrelevant text or interesting but irrelevant illustrations improves learning; (b) excluding extraneous sounds or music improves learning; and (c) removing nonessential words and symbols improves learning.

COHERENCE PRINCIPLE 1: LEARNING IS IMPROVED WHEN INTERESTING BUT IRRELEVANT WORDS AND PICTURES ARE EXCLUDED FROM A MULTIMEDIA PRESENTATION

Introduction to Coherence Principle 1

How Can We Improve Multimedia Presentations?

Figure 4.1 presents a short lesson on how lightning storms develop – including illustrations depicting the major steps and corresponding text describing the major steps. It is a multimedia presentation because

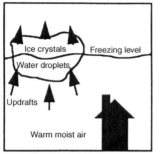

Warm moist air rises, water vapor condenses and forms a cloud.

When the surface of the earth is warm, moist air near the earth's surface becomes heated and rises rapidly, producing an updraft. As the air in these updraft cools, water vapor condenses into water droplets and forms a cloud. The cloud's top extends above the freezing level. At this altitude, the air temperature is well below freezing, so the upper portion of the cloud is composed of tiny ice crystals.

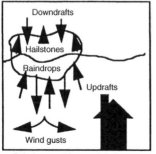

Raindrops and ice crystals drag air downward.

Eventually, the water droplets and ice crystals in the cloud become too large to be suspended by updrafts. As raindrops and ice crystals fall through the cloud, they drag some of the air from the cloud downward, producing downdrafts. The rising and falling air currents within the cloud may cause hailstones to form. When downdrafts strike the ground, they spread out in all directions, producing gusts of cool wind people feel just before the start of the rain.

(Continues)

Figure 4.1. A portion of a multimedia lesson on lightning.

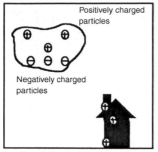

Negatively charged particles fall
to the bottom of the cloud.

Within the cloud, the moving air causes electrical charges to build, although scientists do not fully understand how it occurs. Most believe that the charge results from the collision of the cloud's light, rising water droplets and tiny pieces of ice against hail and other heavier, falling particles. The negatively charged particles fall to the bottom of the cloud, and most of the positively charged particles rise to the top.

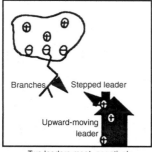

Two leaders meet, negatively
charged particles rush from the
cloud to the ground.

The first stroke of a cloud-to-ground lightning flash is started by a stepped leader. Many scientists believe that it is triggered by a spark between the areas of positive and negative charges within the cloud. A stepped leader moves downward in a series of steps, each of which is about 50-yards long, and lasts for about 1 millionth of a second. It pauses between steps for about 50 millionths of a second. As the stepped leader nears the ground, positively charged upward-moving leaders travel up from such objects as trees and buildings, to meet the negative charges. Usually, the upward moving leader from the tallest object is first to meet the stepped leader and complete a path between the cloud and earth. The two leaders generally meet about 165-feet above the ground. Negatively charged particles then rush from the cloud to the ground along the path created by the leaders. It is not very bright and usually has many branches.

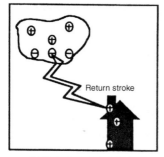

Positively charged particles from
the ground rush upward along the
same path.

As the stepped leader nears the ground, it induces an opposite charge, so positively charged particles from the ground rush upward along the same path. This upward motion of the current is the return stroke and it reaches the cloud in about 70 microseconds. The return stroke produces the bright light that people notice in a flash of lightning, but the current moves so quickly that its upward motion cannot be perceived. The lightning flash usually consists of an electrical potential of hundreds of millions of volts. The air along the lightning channel is heated briefly to a very high temperature. Such intensse heating causes the air to expand explosively, producing a sound wave we call thunder.

Figure 4.1. Continued.

the explanation is presented in both words and pictures. The lesson is consistent with many of the design principles suggested in this book because it combines words and pictures in an integrated way. What can you do to improve on this lesson – so that students will be able to use it to solve problems?

One seemingly reasonable suggestion is to spice up the lesson by adding some text and pictures intended to make the lesson more interesting. For example, let's add a short story about a high school football player who was struck by lightning during football practice, and show a picture of the hole it produced in his helmet and uniform. Also, let's add a description of what happens when lightning strikes a swimming pool and show a picture of swimmers as "sitting ducks." Figure 4.2 shows some interesting material that can be added to the lesson – including sentences and pictures.

Garner and her colleagues coined the term *seductive details* to refer to interesting but irrelevant material that is added to a passage in order to spice it up (Garner, Brown, Sanders, & Menke, 1992; Garner, Gillingham, & White, 1989). In order to distinguish between the use of words and pictures, Harp and Mayer (1997, 1998) used the term *seductive text* to refer to interesting but irrelevant text that is added to a passage and the term *seductive illustrations* to refer to interesting but irrelevant illustrations that are added to a passage. The seductive text and seductive illustrations in Figure 4.2 are *interesting* because readers rate them as entertaining and interesting. The seductive text and seductive illustrations in Figure 4.2 are *irrelevant* because they are not related to the cause-and-effect explanation of how lightning works.

The Case for Adding Interesting Words and Pictures

The major theoretical justification for adding seductive details (such as the seductive text and seductive illustrations in Figure 4.2) is *arousal theory* – the idea that students learn better when they are emotionally aroused by the material. Weiner (1990, 1992) has shown how arousal theories have dominated the field of motivation in the past, and Kintsch (1980) refers to the idea as *emotional interest*. According to arousal theory, adding interesting but irrelevant material energizes learners so that they pay more attention and learn more overall. In this case emotion affects cognition, that is, a high level of enjoyment induced by the seductive details causes the learner to pay more attention and encode more material from the lesson. We can predict that students who learn from lessons containing seductive details will perform better on tests of transfer than students who learn without seductive details.

What's wrong with arousal theory? In spite of its commonsense approach, arousal theory is based on an outmoded view of learning as *knowledge transmission* – the idea that learning involves taking information from the teacher and putting it into the learner. By contrast, the

Actual picture of
airplane being struck
by lightning

Metal airplanes conduct lightning, but
sustain little damage.

When the surface of the earth is warm, moist air near the earth's surface becomes heated and rises rapidly, producing an updraft. As the air in these updrafts cools, water vapor condenses into water droplets and forms a cloud. When flying through updrafts, an airplane ride can become bumpy. Metal airplanes conduct lightning very well, but they sustain little damage because the bolt, meeting no resistance, passes right through. The cloud's top extends above the freezing level. At this altitude, the air temperature is well below freezing, so the upper portion of the cloud is composed of tiny ice crystals.

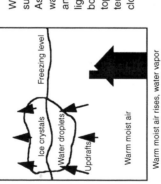

Freezing level

Ice crystals

Water droplets

Updrafts

Warm moist air

Warm moist air rises, water vapor
condenses and forms a cloud.

Figure 4.2. A portion of a multimedia lesson on lightning with interesting but irrelevant words and pictures added.

cognitive theory of multimedia learning is based on the view of learning as *knowledge construction* – the idea that learners actively build mental representations based on what is presented and what they already know. It follows that seductive details may interfere with the process of knowledge construction – an idea that is spelled out in the next section.

The Case Against Adding Interesting Words and Pictures

In his classic book *Interest and Effort in Education*, Dewey (1913) argued against viewing interest as an ingredient that could be added to spice up an otherwise boring lesson. In particular, Dewey noted: "When things have to be made interesting, it is because interest itself is wanting. Moreover, the phrase is a misnomer. The thing, the object, is no more interesting than it was before" (Dewey, 1913, p. 11–12). More recently, Kintsch (1980) used the term *cognitive interest* to refer to the idea that students enjoy lessons that they can understand. According to this view, cognition affects emotion – that is, when students can make sense out of a lesson they tend to enjoy the lesson.

In contrast to arousal theory, the cognitive theory of multimedia learning suggests that adding seductive details can interfere with the process of knowledge construction in several ways – involving selecting relevant information, organizing the information into a coherent structure, and integrating material with existing knowledge. First, the presence of seductive details may direct the learner's attention away from the relevant material about the steps in lightning formation. Second, the insertion of seductive details within the explanation may disrupt the learner's ability to build a cause-and-effect chain among the main steps in lightning formation. Third, the learners may assume that the theme of the passage comes from the seductive details – such as stories about people being injured by lightning – and therefore try to integrate all incoming information into a general framework about lightning injuries. Harp and Mayer (1998) provide some evidence favoring the third hypothesis, but additional research is needed. According to the cognitive theory of multimedia learning, adding seductive details will result in poorer performance on tests of transfer.

Research on Coherence Principle 1

Core Evidence Concerning Coherence Principle 1

Does adding interesting but irrelevant words and/or pictures to a multimedia explanation affect student learning? In order to answer

Table 4.1a. Core Evidence Concerning the Coherence Principle –
Type 1: Exclude Interesting but Irrelevant Words and Pictures

Source	Content	Format	Effect Size
Harp & Mayer (1997, Expt. 1)	Lightning	Paper	1.67
Harp & Mayer (1998, Expt. 1)	Lightning	Paper	2.59
Harp & Mayer (1998, Expt. 2)	Lightning	Paper	1.65
Harp & Mayer (1998, Expt. 3)	Lightning	Paper	1.17
Harp & Mayer (1998, Expt. 4)	Lightning	Paper	1.85
Mayer, Heiser, & Lonn (2001, Expt. 3)	Lightning	Computer	0.70
Median			1.66

this question, my colleagues and I conducted six separate comparisons in which we compared the transfer performance of students who received a multimedia presentation such as shown in Figure 4.1 with the performance of students who received an expanded version that also contained added words and/or pictures such as shown in Figure 4.2 (Harp & Mayer, 1997, Experiment 1; Harp & Mayer, 1998, Experiments 1, 2, 3, and 4; Mayer, Heiser, & Lonn, 2001, Experiment 3). Five of the tests involved a paper-based environment, whereas one involved a computer-based environment. All lessons explained the steps in the formation of lightning, and the transfer test involved writing as many answers as possible to questions such as, "How can you decrease the intensity of a lightning storm?" According to the interest hypothesis, adding interesting but irrelevant words and/or pictures should result in improved transfer performance, whereas the cognitive theory of multimedia learning yields the opposite prediction.

Table 4.1a summarizes the results of six experimental tests of the first version of the coherence principle. In the first set of five studies (Harp & Mayer, 1997, 1998), students read a booklet about lightning formation and then took a transfer test. The concise booklet included five paragraphs and five corresponding illustrations (to the left of each paragraph) explaining the process of lightning formation, whereas the expanded booklet contained identical words and illustrations along with five interspersed photos with captions (to the right of each paragraph) and inserted sentences concerning interesting stories about lightning within each paragraph. For example, in the expanded version, to the right of the first paragraph was a photo of swimmers sitting in inner tubes in a swimming pool along with the caption, "Swimmers are sitting ducks for lightning." Inserted within the text of the first paragraph was the statement, "Every year approximately 150

Americans are killed by lightning. Swimmers are sitting ducks for lightning, because water is an excellent conductor of this electrical charge." Students performed better on a subsequent transfer test after reading the concise rather than the expanded booklet, yielding effect sizes above 1 in all five comparisons.

The sixth line of Table 4.1a is based on a computer-based study (Mayer, Heiser, & Lonn, 2001) in which students viewed a narrated animation on lightning formation (concise group) or viewed the identical narrated animation along with six eight-to-ten-second video clips inserted throughout the lesson with accompanying narration (expanded group). For example, the first clip showed several different flashes of lightning in the open sky, near clouds, and above a cluster of trees, along with the narration, "Lightning can occur in virtually any season and potentially can strike anywhere at any time." Interspersing the short narrated video clips resulted in poorer transfer test performance, yielding an effect size in the medium-to-large range.

Overall, adding interesting but irrelevant pictures and words had a strong negative effect on people's understanding of the explanation presented in the lesson. In all six cases, students who received the concise version generated more solutions to transfer problems than did students who received the expanded version. The median effect size favoring the concise group was 1.66, which is a strong effect. These results provide strong and consistent evidence for the *coherence principle*: People learn more deeply from a multimedia message when extraneous material is excluded rather than included.

Overall, the first version of the coherence principle is consistent with the cognitive theory of multimedia learning and inconsistent with the interest hypothesis. In the case of adding interesting words and pictures, this research shows that less is more – that is, learning how a system works can be improved when less material is presented.

Related Evidence Concerning Coherence Principle 1

In general, research on seductive details shows that adding interesting text that is irrelevant to the theme of a passage either reduces or does not enhance students' remembering of the main ideas in the passage (Garner et al., 1989; Garner et al., 1992; Hidi & Baird, 1988; Mohr, Glover, & Ronning, 1984; Shirey, 1992; Shirey & Reynolds, 1988; Wade, 1992; Wade & Adams, 1990). In addition, students tend to be able to remember the seductive details better than they can remember the central ideas in the passage (Garner, Alexander, Gillingham,

Kulikowich, & Brown, 1991; Garner et al., 1992; Hidi & Anderson, 1992; Hidi & Baird, 1986). More recently, Lehman, Schraw, McCrudden, and Hartley (2007) found that adding seductive details to a text passage on lightning formation resulted in poorer performance on a transfer test. The research summarized in Table 4.1a goes beyond other related research on seductive details by focusing on the role of seductive details in multimedia presentations – including text-based and computer-based environments – rather than in text passages alone, by examining the effects of adding interesting words and pictures rather than words alone, and by evaluating learning outcomes with transfer tests rather than tests of retention alone.

Boundary Conditions for Coherence Principle 1

Sanchez and Wiley (2006) examined students' eye movements as they read a multimedia lesson that included interesting but irrelevant illustrations. Students who were low in working-memory capacity tended to spend more time looking at the irrelevant illustrations than did students who were high in working-memory capacity. This finding suggests that seductive details may be particularly distracting for learners who have difficulty controlling their information processing in working memory. Thus, the coherence principle may apply particularly strongly to learners who have low working-memory capacity – and who generally are less able learners.

COHERENCE PRINCIPLE 2: LEARNING IS IMPROVED WHEN INTERESTING BUT IRRELEVANT SOUNDS AND MUSIC ARE EXCLUDED FROM A MULTIMEDIA PRESENTATION

Introduction to Coherence Principle 2

How Can We Improve Multimedia Presentations?

The foregoing section showed the detrimental effects of adding interesting but irrelevant words and pictures to a multimedia presentation. Our valiant effort to spice up the lesson failed – perhaps because the added material (i.e., words and pictures) was too much like the target material. Undaunted, let's try another way to make the lesson more interesting. Let's return to the concise narrated animation on lightning formation, as summarized in Figure 2.2 in Chapter 2, and see if there is some other way to make it more enjoyable.

One tempting technique for making a multimedia lesson more interesting is to add some "bells and whistles" in the form of background music or environmental sounds. For example, we can add a short instrumental music loop that plays continuously in the background. The music does not interfere with the narration but provides a gentle musical background to the presentation. In addition, we can add environmental sounds that correspond to events in the process of lightning formation, such as the sound of blowing wind when the program mentions gusts of cool wind or the sound of ice cubes crackling when the program mentions the formation of ice crystals. Again, the environmental sounds do not interfere with the narration but rather provide appropriate sound effects for the presentation.

The Case for Adding Interesting Music and Sounds

The rationale for adding background music and sounds is based on arousal theory, similar to the rationale for adding interesting words and pictures. According to arousal theory, music and sound effects make the multimedia presentation more enjoyable for the learner, thereby increasing the learner's level of emotional arousal. This increase in arousal results in increased attention to the presented material, and therefore leads to more learning. Based on arousal theory, we can predict that adding interesting music and sounds will result in improved performance on tests of transfer.

What's wrong with this straightforward approach to improving multimedia presentations? As in the first section of this chapter, the major problem is that the rationale for adding interesting music and sounds is based on an outmoded view of learning as information transmission. According to this view, information is simply transferred from teachers to learners, and background music and sounds can speed up this delivery process. However, my approach in this book is based on the knowledge-construction view of learning – the idea that learners seek to actively build mental representations that make sense. Unfortunately, adding music and sounds can interfere with this sense-making process; this hypothesis is examined in the next section.

The Case Against Adding Interesting Music and Sounds

According to the cognitive theory of multimedia learning, learners process multimedia messages in their visual and auditory channels – both of which are limited in capacity. In the case of a narrated animation, the

When Sound/Music Is Added: Spoken Words and Sounds/Music Compete for
Processing Capacity in the Auditory Channel

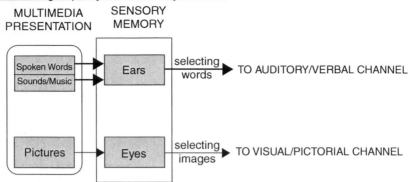

When No Sound/Music Is Added: Spoken Words Do Not Compete for Processing
Capacity in the Auditory Channel

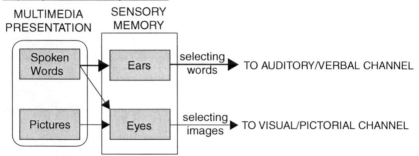

Figure 4.3.   A cognitive analysis of how adding irrelevant sounds or music can
disrupt learning: multimedia presentations with sound or music and multimedia
presentations without sound or music.

animation is processed in the visual channel and the narration is
processed in the auditory channel. As is shown in Figure 4.3, when
additional auditory information is presented, it competes with the
narration for limited processing capacity in the auditory channel. When
processing capacity is used to process the music and sounds, there is less
capacity available for paying attention to the narration, organizing it into
a coherent cause-and-effect chain, and linking it with the incoming visual
information. Based on this theory, we can predict that adding interesting
music and sounds to a multimedia presentation will result in poorer
performance on transfer tests. In short, the cognitive theory of multimedia
learning predicts a coherence effect in which adding interesting material –
in the form of music and sounds – hurts student learning.

Table 4.1b. Core Evidence Concerning the Coherence Principle –
Type 2: Exclude Interesting but Irrelevant Sounds

Source	Content	Format	Effect Size
Moreno & Mayer (2000a, Expt. 1)	Lightning	Computer	1.27
Moreno & Mayer (2000a, Expt. 2)	Brakes	Computer	0.96
Median			1.11

Research on Coherence Principle 2

Core Evidence Concerning Coherence Principle 2

Does adding interesting music and sounds to a multimedia explanation affect student learning and understanding? In order to answer
this question, we conducted two separate comparisons in which we
compared the transfer performance of students who received a narrated animation with the performance of students who received an
expanded version that also contained background music or environmental sounds (Moreno & Mayer, 2000a, Experiments 1 and 2). Both
comparisons involved a computer-based environment – one involved
a narrated animation explaining the steps in lightning formation, and
the other involved a narrated animation explaining how a car's
braking systems works. The background music and background
sounds were soft enough that they did not interfere with the learner's
ability to clearly hear the narration. According to the arousal
hypothesis, adding background music and sounds should result in
improved transfer performance, whereas the cognitive theory of
multimedia learning yields the opposite prediction.

Table 4.1b shows that adding background music and environmental
sounds (expanded group) resulted in poorer transfer test performance
than not having the added music and sounds (concise group), yielding
large effect sizes for both comparisons. The median effect size was
1.11, which is a large effect. These results show that the coherence
principle also applies to extraneous sounds. Overall, this second version of the coherence effect is consistent with the cognitive theory of
multimedia learning and inconsistent with the interest hypothesis.

Related Research on Coherence Principle 2

Research on children's television viewing examines how viewers'
attention can be guided through the use of audio features (Anderson &
Lorch, 1983; Kozma, 1991). For example, sound effects generally cause

children to pay attention – albeit momentarily – to a TV presentation (Alwitt, Anderson, Lorch, & Levin, 1980; Calvert & Scott, 1989). Kozma (1991, p. 194) summarizes this line of research as follows: "This research paints a picture of television viewers who monitor a presentation at a low level of engagement, their moment-to-moment visual attention periodically attracted by salient audio cues. . . ." As you can see, this line of research does not focus on multimedia learning, but it does suggest that auditory features of a presentation may guide the learner's attention toward specific content.

Boundary Conditions for Coherence Principle 2

Adults may be better able to ignore irrelevant sounds than are children, but this hypothesis needs to be subjected to experimental research. Music and background sounds may support certain kinds of instructional materials, such as those with emotional content or in cases where the music and sounds are part of the essential content, but this hypothesis needs testing.

COHERENCE PRINCIPLE 3: STUDENT LEARNING IS IMPROVED WHEN UNNEEDED WORDS AND SYMBOLS ARE REMOVED FROM A MULTIMEDIA PRESENTATION

Introduction to Coherence Principle 3

How Can We Improve Multimedia Presentations?

In the first two sections of this chapter, we attempted to spice up a multimedia lesson by adding interesting words and pictures or by adding background music and sound effects. In both cases, the added material – which was intended to improve the multimedia lesson – turned out to hurt student learning and understanding. The theme of our results – which we call the coherence principle – is that students are better able to make sense out of a multimedia lesson when interesting but irrelevant material is not included.

In this section, we take this "less-is-more" theme one step further. Let's begin with a text passage and captioned illustrations such as those shown in Figure 4.1. The text passage contains approximately 550 words, many of which are not directly relevant to the theme of the lesson – namely, a description of the steps in the cause-and-effect chain leading to lightning formation. In fact, the central steps from the text are reproduced in the captions of the illustrations. In order to make the lesson more concise, we could eliminate the text passage, and present learners only with the captioned illustrations. The captioned illustrations constitute a highly concentrated summary of the main steps in lightning formation – presented in both words and pictures.

The Case for Retaining Unneeded Words and Symbols

At first blush, it seems obvious that students will learn more from a full presentation than from a summary. The theoretical rationale is straightforward: In the full version, the words describing the steps in lightning formation are presented twice – within the text passage in elaborated form and within the captions in abbreviated form. In the summary version, the words describing the steps in lightning formation are presented only once – within the captions. Two ways of delivering the words are better than one, so students should learn more from the full presentation than from the summary presentation. This argument is consistent with the information-delivery hypothesis – namely, the idea that students learn more when they receive information via more routes.

The Case Against Retaining Unneeded Words and Symbols

Why would a summary result in better learning than the full presentation? According to the cognitive theory of multimedia learning, learners seek to actively make sense out of the presented material by selecting relevant information, organizing it into a coherent representation, and linking it with other knowledge. The summary greatly facilities these processes because the key words are in the captions, they are presented in order, and they are presented near the corresponding illustrations. Thus, the cognitive processes involved in sense-making can be facilitated by a clear and concise summary. This argument is consistent with the cognitive theory of multimedia learning. Based on this theory, we can predict that students given a multimedia summary will perform as well or better on tests of transfer than students given the summary along with the regular text passage.

Research on Coherence Principle 3

Core Evidence Concerning Coherence Principle 3

Do students learn better from a multimedia summary than from a full lesson? In the case of the lightning passage, the multimedia summary

Table 4.1c. Core Evidence Concerning the Coherence Principle –
Type 3: Exclude Extraneous Words and Symbols

Source	Content	Format	Effect Size
Mayer et al. (1996, Expt. 1)	Lightning	Paper	−0.17
Mayer et al. (1996, Expt. 2)	Lightning	Paper	0.70
Mayer et al. (1996, Expt. 3)	Lightning	Paper	0.98
Mayer & Jackson (2005, Expt. 1a)	Ocean waves	Paper	0.94
Mayer & Jackson (2005, Expt. 1b)	Ocean waves	Paper	0.97
Mayer & Jackson (2005, Expt. 2)	Ocean waves	Computer	0.69
Median			0.82

presents a concise statement of the cause-and-effect chain in words and illustrations, as shown in the captioned illustrations in Figure 4.1. The full lesson contains the same illustrations along with 550 words of text, as shown in Figure 2.2. We compared the transfer performance of students who read a multimedia summary with the performance of students who read a full lesson on lightning.

In the first set of three comparisons listed in Table 4.1c (Mayer et al., 1996), students read a booklet explaining lightning formation and then took a transfer test. The concise booklet was a summary of the main steps in lightning formation, in the form of a series of annotated illustrations. The expanded booklet contained the same printed words and illustrations along with additional text providing details about lightning. As you can see, in the first three lines in the bottom portion of Table 4.1c, students performed better on transfer tests after reading the summary than after reading the longer lesson in two out of three tests. The first study, in which no strong effect was found, contained a verbal summary that may have been so short that it excluded some essential material.

Let's explore Coherence Principle 3 in a slightly different way. Do students learn better from a lesson that includes quantitative details (such as measurements and computations) or from a lesson that focuses solely on the essential material without quantitative details? The last three lines of Table 4.1c summarize three comparisons between a concise and expanded lesson explaining three steps in how ocean waves work, including paper-based and computer-based lessons. The concise paper-based lesson described how ocean waves are created, how they move across the ocean, and how waves break near the shore, using both words and illustrations; whereas the expanded version contained the identical material along with inserted sentences and illustrations that provided quantitative measurements and computations related to each of the three steps. The computer-based versions of the concise and expanded lessons used narrated graphics based on the paper-based lessons. The transfer test questions required understanding how ocean waves work, but did not involve quantitative measurements or calculations. For example, one question was, "What can you do to make sure waves break about fifty feet from shore?" In all three comparisons, the concise group performed better on generating acceptable answers to transfer questions than did the expanded group, yielding medium and large effect sizes.

These six comparisons provide additional support for the coherence principle, particularly when the extraneous material consists of related but unnecessary details. The median effect size favoring the concise group for the third version of the coherence effect was $d = 0.82$, which is a large effect. Overall, this third version of the coherence effect is consistent with the cognitive theory of multimedia learning and inconsistent with the information-delivery hypothesis.

Related Research on Coherence Principle 3

Our findings are consistent with earlier research showing that college students remember more important material from reading chapter summaries than from reading entire textbook chapters (Reder & Anderson, 1980). However, our research extends earlier work by also examining students' problem-solving transfer performance. Thus, our research shows not only that students remember more of the important material when it is presented as a summary, but that they also better understand the material.

Boundary Conditions for Coherence Principle 3

The learners in our experiments were relatively inexperienced in the domains of the lesson; for example, in the ocean wave experiment, learners lacked extensive prior knowledge about ocean waves. Ploetzner, Fehse, Kneser, and Spada (1999) suggest that more experienced learners may be more able to build connections between qualitative and quantitative representations. If students had been more knowledgeable, they may have been better able to benefit from the quantitative details in the ocean waves lessons – a pattern that Kalyuga (2005) refers to as the expertise reversal effect. Research is needed to determine whether the coherence principle applies mainly to low-knowledge learners rather than high-knowledge learners.

Implications of the Coherence Principle

Implications for Multimedia Learning

The overarching theme of research on coherence is that adding extraneous material to a lesson – even if it is interesting – can sometimes result in poorer understanding. In short, in the case of multimedia lessons, students tend to learn more when less is presented. The cognitive theory of multimedia learning helps to explain this apparent paradox. Learners are actively trying to make sense of the presented material by building a coherent mental representation, and adding extraneous information gets in the way of this structure-building process. In particular, when learners are processing extraneous material they are engaging in extraneous processing. Given the limits on working memory, cognitive resources must be diverted to process the extraneous material and therefore are not available for processing the essential material. In addition, when extraneous information is highly salient, learners may organize incoming material around the theme of the extraneous material – such as lightning injuries – rather than around the author's intended theme – a cause-and-effect explanation of lightning formation.

Implications for Multimedia Instruction

The implications for multimedia design are clear: Do not add extraneous words and pictures to a multimedia presentation. Do not add unneeded sounds and music to a multimedia presentation. Keep the presentation short and to the point. A concise presentation allows the learner to build a coherent mental representation – that is, to focus on the key elements and to mentally organize them in a way that makes sense. In short, our results show that multimedia designers should resist the temptation to add unneeded bells and whistles to an instructional presentation. The coherence design guideline is to avoid seemingly interesting words, pictures, and sounds that are not relevant to the lesson's main message. Needed elaboration should be presented after the learner has constructed a coherent mental representation of the concise cause-and-effect system. For example, after a concise multimedia presentation helps the learner understand the major steps in the process of lightning formation, additional material can be presented to elaborate on each step.

Limitations and Future Directions

The rationale for providing extraneous material is to promote learner interest, that is, we want to make the lesson more interesting in order to motivate the learner. Although the added material investigated in this chapter tended to hurt learning, you still might be wondering what can be done to motivate learners. When is learner interest a good thing? One aspect of this issue is addressed in the fourth section of this book, on principles for fostering generative processing. However, additional research on motivation is needed before we can arrive at any complete theory of multimedia learning.

SUGGESTED READINGS

Asterisk (*) indicates that a portion of this chapter is based on this publication.

Section 1 on Coherence Principle 1

*Harp. S. F., & Mayer, R. E. (1998). How seductive details do their damage: A theory of cognitive interest in science learning. *Journal of Educational Psychology*, *90*, 414–434.

*Harp, S. F., & Mayer, R. E. (1997). The role of interest in learning from scientific text and illustrations: On the distinction between emotional interest and cognitive interest. *Journal of Educational Psychology*, *89*, 92–102.

*Mayer, R. E., Heiser, J., & Lonn, S. (2001). Cognitive constraints on multimedia learning: When presenting more material results in less understandings. *Journal of Educational Psychology*, *93*, 187–198.

Section 2 on Coherence Principle 2

*Moreno, R., & Mayer, R. E. (2000a). A coherence effect in multimedia learning: The case for minimizing irrelevant sounds in the design of multimedia messages. *Journal of Educational Psychology*, *92*, 117–125.

Section 3 on Coherence Principle 3

*Mayer, R. E., Bove, W., Bryman, A., Mars, R. & Tapangco, L. (1996). When less is more: Meaningful learning from visual and verbal summaries of science textbook lessons. *Journal of Educational Psychology*, *88*, 64–73.

*Mayer, R. E., & Jackson, J. (2005). The case for coherence in scientific explanations: Quantitative details can hurt qualitative understanding. *Journal of Experimental Psychology: Applied*, *11*, 13–18.

5

Signaling Principle

Signaling Principle: *People learn better when cues that highlight the organization of the essential material are added.*

Example: *In a narrated animation on how airplanes achieve lift, signaling involves adding an introductory sentence that names the three main sections (using the same words as in the lesson), a heading for each of the three sections (using the same words as in the lesson), and vocal emphasis on key words.*

Theoretical Rationale: *Signaling reduces extraneous processing by guiding the learner's attention to the key elements in the lesson and guiding the learner's building of connections between them.*

Empirical Rationale: *In five out of six tests, learners who received a signaled multimedia lesson performed better on transfer tests than did learners who received a nonsignaled multimedia lesson, yielding a median effect size of 0.52.*

Boundary Conditions: *Signaling may be particularly useful when the signals are used sparingly, when the learner has low reading skill, and when the multimedia lesson is disorganized or contains extraneous material.*

▪ ▪ Chapter Outline

108

INTRODUCTION TO THE SIGNALING PRINCIPLE

How Can We Help Learners Process Multimedia Lessons?

In the previous chapter, we examined a straightforward way of minimizing extraneous processing during multimedia learning – namely, deleting extraneous material from the multimedia lesson. Extraneous material can draw the learner's attention and thereby cause the learner to engage in cognitive processing during learning that does not support the learning goal. In some situations, however, it may not be possible to eliminate extraneous material from a lesson, so in this chapter we explore another solution to the problem of having too much extraneous material in a multimedia lesson. The solution is to insert cues that direct the learner's attention toward the essential material, which is a technique that can be called *signaling*. As summarized in Table 5.1, signaling the verbal material involves adding cues such as (1) an outline or outline sentence at the start of the lesson, (2) headings that are keyed to the outline, (3) vocal emphasis on key words, and (4) pointer words such as "first . . . second . . . third."

For example, suppose we present a narrated animation explaining how an airplane achieves lift, using the script shown in Table 5.2 (without the italicized sentences and without emphasizing the bolded words). This script contains some material that is not essential to understanding the process of lift, so we can direct the learner's attention to the essential material by using signals such as an outline sentence that lists the main steps (indicated by the italicized sentences inserted at the end of the first paragraph in Table 5.2), headings for each step (as shown in the italicized phrases before the second, third, and fifth paragraphs in Table 5.2), and spoken emphasis on key words (indicated by the words in bold font in Table 5.2). As you can see, the signals do not add any new information but rather highlight (or repeat) the essential material in the lesson. These are examples of verbal signaling because they help the reader attend to and mentally organize the essential words in the incoming narration.

Table 5.1.   Common Features of Verbal Signaling

Feature	Example
Outline	A sentence at the start of the lesson saying that airplane lift depends on wing shape, air flow, and air pressure.
Headings	A phrase or short sentence inserted at the start of each section, keyed to the outline, such as: "Wing Shape: Curved Upper Surface Is Longer."
Vocal emphasis	Saying key words in a louder and slower voice, such as for the bolded words in "the surface on the **top** of the wing is **longer** than on the **bottom**."
Pointer words	Inserted words such as "first...second...third," as in "First, how the top of the wing is shaped differently than the bottom."

We might not only signal the verbal material, but also signal the pictorial material. That is, we might want to draw the learner's attention to specific parts of the graphic. As shown in Table 5.3, visual signaling involves adding visual cues such as arrows, distinctive colors, flashing, pointing gestures, or graying out of nonessential areas. For example, in the narrated animation on airplanes achieving lift we could add blue arrows above the wing and red arrows below the wing to represent differences in wing shape, airflow, and air pressure. The arrows draw the learner's attention to differences in air pressure between the top and bottom of the wing.

The Case Against Adding Signaling

Signaling adds no new information, so it should have no effect on learning. This assertion is consistent with the information-delivery view of learning, in which learning involves adding presented material to memory. The signals might even disrupt learning because they are redundant. In short, according to the information-delivery view, signaling adds nothing to the lesson except to make it longer than it needs to be.

The Case for Adding Signaling

By contrast, the knowledge-construction view of learning holds that the learner is trying to construct a cognitive representation based on the multimedia lesson. Thus, the instructor's job is not just to present the essential information, but also to help guide the way the

Table 5.2. Portion of Script for Lessons on Airplane Lift (Signaling Consists of Added Outline and Headings Indicated by Italic and Spoken Emphasis Indicated by Boldface)

What is needed to cause an aircraft, which is heavier than air, to climb into the air and stay there? An aerodynamic principle formulated by Daniel Bernouille in 1738 helps explain it. Bernouille's Principle explains how upward forces, called lift, act upon the plane when it moves through the air. *To understand how lift works, you need to focus on differences between the top and bottom of the airplane's wing. First, how the top of the wing is **shaped** differently than the bottom; second, how quickly **air flows** across the top surface, compared to across the bottom surface; and third, how the **air pressure** on the wing compares to that on the bottom of the wing.*

Wing shape: Curved upper surface is longer. A cross section of a bird's wing, a boomerang, and a Stealth bomber all share a shape similar to that of an airplane wing. The upper surface of the wing is curved more than the bottom surface. The surface on the **top** of the wing is **longer** than on the **bottom**. This is called an airfoil.

Air flow: Air moves faster across top of wing. In order to achieve lift, air must flow over the wing. The wingspan of a 747 is more than 200 feet; that's taller than a fifteen-story building. When the airplane moves forward, its wings cut through the air. As the air moves across the wing, it will push against it in all directions, perpendicular to the surface of the wing.

When an airplane is in flight, air hitting the front of the wing separates. Some air flows over the wing and some flows under the wing. The air meets up again at the back of the wing. The air flowing over the top of the wing has a longer distance to travel in the same amount of time. Air traveling over the curved **top** of the wing **flows faster** than air that flows under the **bottom** of the wing.

Air pressure: Pressure on the top is less. When air moves faster, its pressure decreases. You have probably noticed that when you turn on the water in the shower, the curtain moves in. The running water makes the air in the shower move faster, and since it exerts less pressure against the curtain than the still air outside the curtain does, the curtain is pushed in. A similar principle is at work on airplane wings.

Since the air over the top of the wing is moving faster, it gets more spread out, and therefore pressure on the top part of the wing decreases. The **top** surface of the wing now has **less pressure** exerted against it than the **bottom** surface of the wing. The downward force of the faster-moving air on the top of the wing is not as great as the upward force of the slower-moving air under the wing, and as a result, there is a net upward force on the wing – a lift.

learner processes the presented information. Signaling can help guide what the learner pays attention to (i.e., the process of *selecting* in Figure 3.1) and can help the learner to mentally organize the key material (i.e., the process of *organizing* in Figure 3.1). Without

Table 5.3.   Common Features of Visual Signaling

Feature	Example
Arrows	Arrows point to the bottom and top of the wing in the animation as the voice says, "how air pressure on the top of the wing compares to that on the bottom of the wing."
Distinctive colors	In an animation on air flight, the airplane is drawn with black lines but arrows representing airflow are drawn in red (below the wing) and blue (above the wing).
Flashing	A particular component on the system flashes, such as the bottom of the wing.
Pointing gestures	An onscreen agent points to a part of the system, such as the bottom of the wing.
Graying out	When a particular component is being described, it is shown in a "magnifying glass" and the rest of the picture is grayed out.

guidance on how to carry out appropriate cognitive processing, the learner is more likely to engage in extraneous cognitive processing – such as processing extraneous material and trying to organize it with the rest of the material.

RESEARCH ON THE SIGNALING PRINCIPLE

Core Evidence Concerning the Signaling Principle

According to the cognitive theory of multimedia learning, signaling is another technique for reducing extraneous processing because it provides cues to the learner about what to attend to and how to organize it. Table 5.4 lists six tests of the signaling principle. In the first study (Harp & Mayer, 1998), some students (nonsignaled group) read a paper-based lesson on lightning such as the one described in the previous chapter and then took a transfer test. For other students (signaled group), the text was modified by adding an organizational sentence listing the main steps (using the same words as in the text) and then inserting numbers such as "(1)" to correspond to each step as it was described in the lesson. As shown in the first line of Table 5.4, this modest form of signaling produced a small effect size.

In the second set of two studies (Mautone & Mayer, 2001), some students (nonsignaled group) received a narrated animation explaining how an airplane achieves lift and then took a transfer test. Other

Table 5.4. Core Evidence Concerning the Signaling Principle

Source	Content	Format	Effect Size
Harp & Mayer (1998, Expt. 3a)	Lightning	Paper	0.34
Mautone & Mayer (2001, Expt. 3a)	Airplane	Computer	0.60
Mautone & Mayer (2001, Expt. 3b)	Airplane	Computer	0.70
Stull & Mayer (2007, Expt. 1)	Biology	Paper	−0.03
Stull & Mayer (2007, Expt. 2)	Biology	Paper	0.58
Stull & Mayer (2007, Expt. 3)	Biology	Paper	0.45
Median			0.52

students (signaled group) received the same instruction and test, except that the narration was signaled – that is, the narrator began by listing the three main steps (using the same words as in the script), the narrator inserted a heading sentence before each section (using the same words as in the introductory sentence), and the narrator gave vocal emphasis to the key words in the script. Then learners took a transfer test in which they were asked to write solutions to problems such as, "How could an airplane be designed to achieve lift more rapidly?" or "Using what you've learned about how airplanes achieve lift, explain how helicopters achieve lift." Signaling benefited the students on the transfer test, yielding medium effect sizes as shown in the next two lines of Table 5.4.

Finally, the last three lines of Table 5.4 summarize experimental comparisons reported by Stull and Mayer (2007) in which students read a ten-paragraph biology lesson on reproductive barriers that contained words and illustrations (nonsignaled group) or the same lesson along with graphic organizers showing the structure of the passage and of each paragraph using the same words as used in the lesson (signaled group). For example, Figure 5.1 shows some graphic organizers used for the signaled group. On a transfer test, students were asked to write answers to several questions about reproductive barriers. In Experiment 1, twenty-seven graphic organizers were used (i.e., approximately three per paragraph, as shown in Figure 5.1) and there was no signaling effect. In Experiments 2 and 3, eighteen and ten graphic organizers were used respectively (i.e., approximately two or one per paragraph respectively) and there was a medium-sized signaling effect. Thus, it appears that graphic organizers can serve as effective signals when they are not overused.

Overall, the evidence summarized in Table 5.4 provides preliminary support for the *signaling principle*: People learn better from a multimedia message when the text is signaled rather than nonsignaled. The

Reproductive Barriers

Reproductive barriers keep species separate

Clearly, a fly will not mate with a frog or a fern. But what prevents species that are closely related from interbreeding? While geographic barriers may prevent similar species from interbreeding, geography is not intrinsic to organisms. It takes a reproductive barrier – a biological feature of the organisms themselves – to prevent populations belonging to closely related species from interbreeding even when their ranges overlap. The various types of reproductive barriers that isolate the gene pool of species can be categorized as either prezygotic or postzygotic, depending on whether they function before or after zygotes (fertilized eggs) form.

Prezygotic Barriers

Prezygotic barriers actually prevent mating or fertilization between species. There are five main types of prezygotic barriers. One type, called temporal isolation, occurs when two species breed at different times – during different seasons, at different times of the day, or even in different years. For example, the geographic ranges of the western spotted skunk and the eastern spotted skunk overlap in the Great Plains, but the western species breeds in the fall and the eastern species in the late winter. Many plants also exhibit seasonal differences in breeding time. Two species of pine tree, the Monterey pine (*Pinus radiate*) and Bishop's pine (*P. mauricata*), inhabit some of the same area of central California. The two species are reproductively isolated, however: The Monterey pine releases pollen in February, while the Bishop's pine does so in April. Some plants are temporally isolated because their flowers open at different times of the day, so pollen cannot be transferred from one to another.

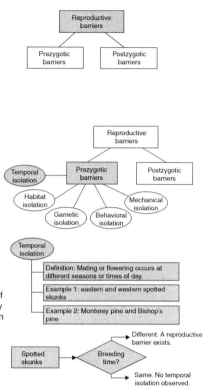

Figure 5.1.   Examples of graphic organizers used in biology lesson.

signaling principle was supported in five out of six tests, yielding a median effect size of 0.52. Given that the effects are not strong and are based on only six tests, support for the signaling principle in multimedia learning should be considered promising but preliminary. In addition, Mautone and Mayer (2001) did not find any evidence that visual signaling aided student learning. One explanation may be that learners use the verbal script to guide them when looking at the graphic, so the visual signaling is not needed. Additional research is needed to determine the effects of signaling techniques on multimedia learning, including verbal and visual signaling.

Related Evidence Concerning the Signaling Principle

One of the reasons we were encouraged to study the effects of signaling on multimedia learning – for example, text and illustrations or narration and animation – is that signaling has been shown to be effective in improving learning from text. For example, in a series of experiments conducted over the past thirty years, verbal signaling improved learners' retention of a text passage (Loman & Mayer, 1983; Lorch, 1989; Lorch & Lorch, 1996; Lorch, Lorch, & Inman, 1993; Meyer, 1975; Meyer, Brandt, & Bluth, 1980). The new contribution of the evidence in Table 5.4 is that the focus is on using signaling in lessons involving words and pictures (rather than words alone) and on measuring the effects of signaling on transfer performance (rather than retention performance alone).

Hypertext learning environments can be particularly confusing because learners have difficulty seeing the structure of the lesson (Dillon & Jobst, 2005). To address this problem, researchers have applied a form of signaling to hypertext learning environments – providing the learner with a spatial outline showing the structure of the material. For example, Naumann, Richter, Flender, Christmann, and Groeben (2007) asked German university students to read a hypertext on visual perception with 504 cross-referenced links (non-signaled group) or the same hypertext along with graphic organizers showing the overall structure of the lesson as a hierarchy (signaled group), and then to write an essay on the material. The signaled group outperformed the nonsignaled group on transfer measures such as the number of appropriate inferences in the essay, yielding an effect size of 1.13. Apparently, signals in the form of organizational graphic organizers can help students learn more deeply from a hypertext lesson.

Consistent with Mautone and Mayer (2001), Hegarty and Kriz (2007) reported that adding arrows to an unnarrated animation on how a toilet tank flushes did not aid learning. Although Mautone and Mayer (2001) and Hegarty and Kriz (2007) did not find any positive effects for visual signals, are there situations in which visual signals help? Consider an online mathematics lesson in which you see a worked-out problem and hear a voice that explains each step. Atkinson (2002) found that adding an onscreen agent who pointed to the step being described by the voice resulted in better transfer test performance in some circumstances, but not in others. Thus, pointing gestures may be an effective form of visual signaling when the learner might not otherwise know where to look on the screen.

In a similar learning task, Jeung and Sweller (1997) provided online instruction in solving geometry problems that involved narration and on-screen worked-out examples. In the signaled group, the part of the problem being described in the narration was flashing on the screen, whereas in the nonsignaled group there was no flashing. This form of signaling was effective in improving problem-solving test performance when the visual display was complex.

Boundary Conditions for the Signaling Principle

The previously reported set of studies by Stull and Mayer (2007) shows that signals – in the form of graphic organizers – promote learning when they are used sparingly (e.g., one per paragraph) but not when they are overused (three per paragraph). In short, too much highlighting adds confusion rather than guiding attention. Thus, an important boundary condition for signaling is that the signals be used sparingly.

There is some evidence that the signaling principle applies mainly to low-skill readers rather than high-skill readers. For example, Meyer, Brandt, and Bluth (1980) were the first to report that signaling of expository text had strong effects for underachieving readers but not for high-performing readers. In a more recent study, Naumann and colleagues (2007) found that signaling of a hypertext lesson on visual perception tended to improve the transfer performance of low-skill readers but not high-skill readers. Presumably, high-skill readers are better able to adjust their reading strategies to compensate for disorganized text.

Jeung, Chandler, and Sweller (1997) also reported that visual signaling – in the form of flashing a part of the display – was effective when the display was complex but not when it was simple. Thus, another important boundary condition for signaling is that the presented material be so disorganized that the learner does not know where to look. Each of these suggested boundary conditions warrants further study.

IMPLICATIONS

Implications for Multimedia Learning

Signals are intended to reduce extraneous processing in learning situations where a learner might be tempted to process extraneous material in a multimedia lesson. In particular, signals are intended to guide learners' attention to essential material and to guide learners' organization of the essential material into a coherent structure. According to the cognitive theory of multimedia learning, this kind of appropriate processing should lead to meaningful learning, as indicated by performance on transfer tests. The evidence reported in Table 5.4 supports the claim that verbal signals can be used to guide appropriate cognitive processing during multimedia learning.

Implications for Multimedia Instruction

When a learner might otherwise be tempted to focus on extraneous material in a multimedia lesson, signaling should be used to guide the learner's cognitive processing. An important design implication is that verbal signaling – including outlines, headings, vocal emphasis, and pointer words – should be incorporated into the scripts of multimedia lessons. In short, people learn better when cues that highlight the organization of the essential material are added.

Limitations and Future Directions

In our research we found evidence for the effectiveness of verbal signaling but not of visual signaling. Research is needed to determine whether some forms of visual signaling (such as highlighting portions of the graphic that correspond to the ongoing narration) have positive effects on learning. In addition, we found preliminary evidence that too much signaling can be a detriment to learning, so research is needed to determine how much signaling to use. Finally, some research on signaling of verbal material suggests that signaling may be most effective for lower-skilled learners, so more research is needed to determine who benefits most from signaling.

SUGGESTED READINGS

Asterisk (*) indicates that part of this chapter is based on this publication.

*Harp, S. F., & Mayer, R. E. (1998). How seductive details do their damage: A theory of cognitive interest in science learning. *Journal of Educational Psychology, 90*, 414–434.

*Mautone, P. D., & Mayer, R. E. (2001). Signaling as a cognitive guide in multimedia learning. *Journal of Educational Psychology, 93*, 377–389.

*Stull, A., & Mayer, R. E. (2007). Learning by doing versus learning by viewing: Three experimental comparisons of learner-generated versus author-provided graphic organizers. *Journal of Educational Psychology, 99*, 808–820.

6

Redundancy Principle

Redundancy Principle: *People learn better from graphics and narration than from graphics, narration, and printed text.*

Example: *A learner views a narrated animation on lightning formation (nonredundant group) or a narrated animation along with concurrent onscreen captions that contain the same words as in the narration (redundant group).*

Theoretical Rationale: *Redundancy creates extraneous processing (a) because the visual channel can become overloaded by having to visually scan between pictures and on-screen text, and (b) because learners expend mental effort in trying to compare the incoming streams of printed and spoken text.*

Empirical Rationale: *In five out of five tests, learners who received graphics and narration performed better on tests of transfer than did learners who received graphics, narration, and printed text. The median effect size was d = 0.72.*

Boundary Conditions: *The redundancy principle may be less applicable when (a) the captions are shortened to a few words and placed next to the part of the graphic they describe, (b) the spoken text is presented before the printed text rather than concurrently, and (c) there are no graphics and the verbal segments are short. In each of these cases, extraneous processing is diminished.*

▪ ▪ Chapter Outline

INTRODUCTION

How Can We Improve Concise Narrated Animations?

Suppose there is a multimedia encyclopedia that contains entries based on the principles outlined in this book. For example, for each scientific explanation in the encyclopedia – such as how car brakes work, how the pumps work, or how lightning storms develop – the computer presents a short animation depicting the main steps in the process along with concurrent narration describing the main steps in the process. Thus, the multimedia explanations consist of *concise narrated animations* (or CNAs) – *concise* refers to a focus on the essential steps in the process; *narrated* refers to the words being presented as speech; and *animations* refers to the pictures being presented as an animation. The top of Figure 6.1 shows a selected frame from a concise narrated animation for lightning formation: as the animation segment containing this frame appears on the screen, the spoken words shown in quotation marks come out of the speaker (or headphone) but are not printed on the screen.

What can be done to improve on the concise narrated animations that have been created, that is, to help all students understand the explanations? One seemingly helpful suggestion is to add on-screen text that corresponds to the narration. An example is shown at the bottom of Figure 6.1. In this case, the narrated animation of lightning formation is augmented with on-screen text presented at the bottom of the screen. The on-screen text contains the same words as in the narration, and each sentence is on the screen during the same period that the corresponding narration is being spoken.

The Case for Adding On-Screen Text to Narrated Animations

The rationale for adding on-screen text to concise narrated animations is based on what can be called the *learning preferences hypothesis*:

Animation with Narration

A

"As the air in this updraft cools, water vapor
condenses into water droplets and forms a cloud."

Animation with Narration
and On-Screen Text

As the air in this updraft cools, water vapor
condenses into water droplets and forms a cloud.

B

"As the air in this updraft cools, water vapor
condenses into water droplets and forms a cloud."

Figure 6.1.   Frame from lightning lesson with (A) animation and narration or
with (B) animation, narration, and on-screen text.

Different people learn in different ways, so it is best to present
information in many different formats. For example, if a student
prefers to learn from spoken words, the student can pay attention to
the narration; and if a student prefers to learn from printed words,
the student can pay attention to the on-screen text. By using multiple
presentation formats, instructors can accommodate each student's
preferred learning style.

The learning preferences hypothesis is represented in Figure 6.2. The top frame shows just one delivery path from the presented information to the learner – so information may have a hard time getting through. Even worse, the one available path may be blocked if the learner is not efficient in processing material in that form. When two paths are available, as shown in the middle frame, more information can get to the learner; if there is a blockage in one path, information can still get through on the other. However, there still may be some blockage in the flow of incoming information if the learner is unable to use one of the paths. For example, the spoken-word path may be blocked if the learner is not efficient in processing auditory information. The bottom frame shows three delivery paths from the presented material to the learner; this arrangement allows the learner to receive more information than is available using just two paths. Importantly, the information can get through even if some of the paths are blocked – if the spoken-word path is blocked (such as for learners who are inefficient in auditory processing), verbal information can still get through via the printed-word path; and if the printed-word path is blocked (such as for learners who are poor at visual processing), verbal information can still get through via the spoken-word path.

The role of individual differences in learning has long been recognized in educational psychology (Cronbach & Snow, 1977; Jonassen & Grabowski, 1993). For example, Jonassen and Grabowski (1993, p. xii) have shown how "individual differences are learning filters." In the case of multimedia explanations, students who prefer auditory learning will have difficulty if material is presented solely as printed text, and students who prefer text-based learning will have difficulty if material is presented solely as narration. One solution to this problem is to adapt instruction to better fit the ways in which individual students learn: "It is possible and desirable to adapt the nature of instruction to accommodate differences in ability, style, or preferences among individuals to improve learning outcomes" (Jonassen & Grabowski, 1993, p. 19). When customized lessons are not feasible, a possible alternative is to incorporate multiple instructional methods and formats into a single lesson. Thus, the suggestion to present words as both narration and on-screen text is a somewhat modest implementation of this general principle.

The premise underlying the learning preferences hypothesis is that learners should be allowed to choose the method of instruction that best suits the way they learn – including being able to choose the format in which information is presented. If the same material is presented in many formats – such as pictures, printed text, and spoken

A   Narration Only: One Delivery Path to The Learner

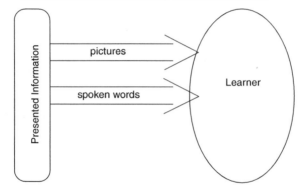

B   Narrated Animation: Two Delivery Paths to The Learner

C   Narrated Animation with Redundant Text: Three Delivery Paths to The Learner

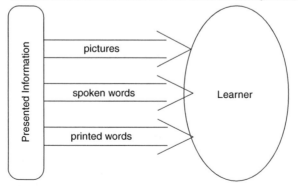

Figure 6.2. Why the information-delivery hypothesis predicts that a combination of animation, narration, and on-screet text (C) is better than animation with narration only (B) or narration alone (A).

text – then learners can focus on the format that best suits their learning preferences. When a student's preferred presentation mode is not included, that student will have more difficulty in learning – consistent with the *learning filter* metaphor. Based on this theory we can predict that adding on-screen text to a concise animated narration will result in improved learning as measured by tests of transfer.

The Case Against Adding On-Screen Text to Narrated Animations

What's wrong with the learning preferences hypothesis? At the most fundamental level, it is based on the information-delivery theory of multimedia learning, in which learning is viewed as transmitting information from the teacher to the learner. According to this conception, learning occurs when information is presented by the instructor and received by the student. It follows that the reception will be better when more rather than fewer delivery paths are used, particularly when some of the paths are blocked. This view conflicts with the cognitive theory of multimedia learning presented in Chapter 3, in which learners actively build mental representations within their information-processing systems.

The case against adding on-screen text is based on the *capacity limitation hypothesis:* People have limited capacity to process visually presented material and limited capacity to process auditorily presented material. The limited-capacity hypothesis is based on the cognitive theory of multimedia learning described in Chapter 3, and is summarized in Figure 6.3. When words are presented visually – as on-screen text – this places an additional load on the visual information-processing channel. This increased cognitive load in the visual channel reduces the amount of processing that people can apply to the animation, which also enters through the visual channel. The top frame in Figure 6.3 shows that both pictures and printed words must enter the learner's information processing through the eyes and must initially be represented as images in working memory (thus, both compete for resources within the visual channel); by contrast, the bottom frame in Figure 6.3 shows that pictures enter through the eyes (and are processed in the visual channel), whereas spoken words enter through the ears (and are processed in the verbal channel).

According to the cognitive theory of multimedia learning, meaningful learning occurs when people can attend to relevant portions of the incoming visual and auditory information, organize the material into coherent verbal and pictorial representations, and integrate the

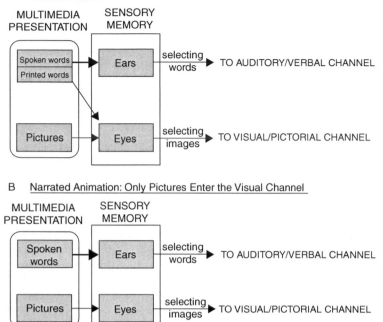

Figure 6.3. Why the cognitive theory of multimedia learning predicts that (A) animation with both narration and on-screen text is worse than (B) animation with narration only.

two representations. When pictures, printed words, and spoken words are all presented, the system can become overloaded by extraneous processing in two ways. First, pictures and printed words compete for limited cognitive resources in the visual channel because both enter the learner's information processing through the eyes. When the learner's eyes are scanning between printed words and pictures, extraneous processing is created. Second, when verbal information is presented both visually and auditorially, learners may be tempted to attend to both in an attempt to reconcile the two information streams; this extraneous processing requires cognitive resources that consequently are not available for the essential and generative processing needed for meaningful learning. By contrast, the most efficient way to present verbal material is through the verbal channel – that is, as spoken text only – because in this way it does not compete with pictures for cognitive resources in the visual channel. Based on this theory, we can predict a *redundancy effect* in which adding on-screen text to a concise narrated animation will result in poorer learning as indicated by transfer test performance.

Understanding the Redundancy Effect

Kalyuga, Chandler, and Sweller (1998, p. 2) have used the term *redundancy effect* in a broad sense to refer to any multimedia situation in which "eliminating redundant material results in better performance than when the redundant material is included." For example, in some situations, student learning is hurt when text is added to a multimedia instructional presentation, presumably because the text is redundant with the same information that has already been presented via diagrams or other sources (Bobis, Sweller, & Cooper, 1993; Chandler & Sweller, 1991; Kalyuga, Chandler, & Sweller, 1998; Sweller & Chandler, 1994). By contrast, in this book I use the term *redundancy effect* in a more restricted sense to refer to any multimedia situation in which learning from animation (or illustrations) and narration is superior to learning from the same materials along with printed text that matches the narration.

The learning preferences hypothesis and the capacity limitation hypothesis differ in their views about redundancy and in their conceptions of learning. First, the learning preferences hypothesis is based on the commonsense notion that presenting words in two ways (e.g., spoken and printed) is better than presenting words in only one way (e.g., spoken only). Tindall-Ford, Chandler, and Sweller (1997, p. 257) summarize this conventional view as "two sensory modalities are better than one." By contrast, the limited-capacity hypothesis holds that in some situations presenting words in one sense modality (e.g., as spoken words) is better than presenting words in two modalities (e.g., as spoken words and printed words). In short, redundancy is not necessarily a virtue when it comes to the design of multimedia explanations.

Second, the learning preferences hypothesis is based on the information delivery theory of multimedia learning, in which the instructor's job is to present information and the student's job is to receive it. Each presentation format is a delivery system for information, so having two deliveries of the same words is better than having only one delivery. If one delivery is blocked – perhaps because the learner does not learn well from that format – then the information still gets through via another route. By contrast, the capacity limitation hypothesis is based on the cognitive theory of multimedia learning, in which the learner actively builds a mental representation that makes

Table 6.1. Core Evidence Concerning the Redundancy Principle

Source	Content	Format	Effect Size
Mayer, Heiser, & Lonn (2001, Expt. 1)	Lightning	Computer	0.88
Mayer, Heiser, & Lonn (2001, Expt. 2)	Lightning	Computer	1.21
Moreno & Mayer (2002a, Expt. 2)	Lightning	Computer	0.72
Moreno & Mayer (2002b, Expt. 2a)	Environmental science game	Computer	0.19
Moreno & Mayer (2002b, Expt. 2b)	Environmental science game	Computer	0.25
Median			0.72

sense to the learner. The process of knowledge construction requires that the learner select, organize, and integrate relevant visual and verbal information subject to limitations in visual and auditory processing. Presentation modes that overload a channel – such as presenting animation and words through the visual channel – hinder the process of knowledge construction.

RESEARCH ON THE REDUNDANCY PRINCIPLE

Core Evidence Concerning the Redundancy Principle

Does adding concurrent on-screen text to narrated animations affect student learning? In order to answer this question we conducted a set of five studies in which we compared the transfer performance of students who received multimedia explanations consisting of animation and narration (nonredundant group) to the performance of students who received animation, narration, and concurrent on-screen text that was identical to the narration (redundant group). According to the learning preferences hypothesis, the redundant group should outperform the nonredundant group on tests of transfer, but the capacity limitation hypothesis makes the opposite prediction.

Table 6.1 shows the source, content, format, and effect size (favoring the nonredundant group) for each of five experimental tests conducted in our lab. In the first three comparisons listed in Table 6.1, learners received a narrated animation explaining how lightning storms develop or the same narrated animation along with concurrent on-screen text presented as a caption at the bottom of the screen

(Mayer, Heiser, & Lonn, 2001; Moreno & Mayer, 2002a). The top panel of Figure 6.1 exemplifies the narrated animation treatment for the lightning lesson, whereas the bottom panel of Figure 6.1 exemplifies the same narrated animation with on-screen text treatment. The transfer test involved writing answers to essay questions such as, "What could be done to reduce the intensity of a lightning storm?" and was scored by tallying the number of acceptable answers. The top three rows of Table 6.1 shows large effect sizes favoring the nonredundant group (narration and animation) over the redundant group (narration, animation, and on-screen text).

Finally, the last two lines of Table 6.1 summarize studies by Moreno and Mayer (2002b) involving an environmental science game in which the game was presented on a desktop computer (fourth line) or via a head-mounted display in virtual reality (fifth line). As part of the game, some students viewed animations and heard concurrent explanations about plant growth (nonredundant group), whereas others viewed animations, heard concurrent explanations, and also saw on-screen text that was identical to the spoken explanations (redundant group). The nonredundant group performed better on transfer tests than the redundant group, but the effect sizes were small. In this study, the narrated animation was a small part of the overall lesson, so perhaps it played a smaller role in learning.

Across all five comparisons there is consistent evidence that learners perform more poorly on problem-solving transfer when they learn with animation, narration, and text than when they learn with animation and narration. We refer to this pattern as a *redundancy effect* because adding on-screen text that is identical to the narration tends to hurt student understanding. As shown in Table 6.1, the median effect size favoring the nonredundant treatment is $d = 0.72$, which is in the medium-to-large range. Overall, the redundancy effect is consistent with the capacity limitation hypothesis and inconsistent with the learning preferences hypothesis. These results support the *redundancy principle:* People learn more deeply from graphics and narration than from graphics, narration, and printed text.

Related Evidence Concerning the Redundancy Principle

The redundancy principle also has been supported in experimental tests conducted by other researchers. Table 6.2 summarizes the source, content, format, and effect size for seven related experimental comparisons between the transfer test performance of people who

Table 6.2. Related Evidence Concerning the Redundancy Principle

Source	Content	Format	Effect Size
Mousavi, Low, & Sweller (1995, Expt. 1)	Math problems	Paper	0.65
Mousavi, Low, & Sweller (1995, Expt. 2)	Math problems	Paper	0.49
Kalyuga, Chandler, & Sweller (1999, Expt. 1)	Electrical engineering	Computer	1.38
Kalyuga, Chandler, & Sweller (2000, Expt. 1)	Electrical engineering	Computer	0.86
Craig, Gholson, & Driscoll (2002, Expt. 2)	Lightning	Computer	0.67
Leahy, Chandler, & Sweller (2003, Expt. 2)	Temperature graphs	Paper	1.13
Jamet & Bohec (2007)	Human memory	Computer	0.63

learned with redundant and nonredundant multimedia lessons. The first two lines are based on studies by Mousavi, Low, and Sweller (1995) in which secondary school students learned to solve geometry problems through worked examples. Some students (redundant group) received worked examples in the form of a sheet with printed diagrams and printed words as well as an audio message with spoken words that were identical to the printed words. Other students (nonredundant group) received worked examples in the form of a sheet with printed diagrams and an audio message with spoken words. On a subsequent test of problem-solving transfer, the nonredundant group outperformed the redundant group, yielding effect sizes in the medium range.

The next two lines of Table 6.2 are based on studies by Kalyuga, Chandler, and Sweller (1999, 2000) in which trainees learned engineering topics. Students were given a computer presentation containing a printed diagram on the screen and an audio message with spoken words (nonredundant group) or a computer presentation containing a printed diagram and printed text on the screen along with an audio message with spoken words that were identical to the printed words (redundant group). On a subsequent problem-solving transfer test, the nonredundant group outperformed the redundant group, yielding high effect sizes. In the study shown on the fourth line of Table 6.2, the results were obtained for low-experience learners only. High-experience learners may have so much free processing capacity that they did not suffer any ill effects from processing redundant materials.

The fifth line of Table 6.2 summarizes a study (Craig, Gholson, & Driscoll, 2002) in which students who viewed a narrated animation on lightning formation (nonredundant group) performed better on a problem-solving transfer test than did students who viewed the same narrated animation along with redundant on-screen text (redundant group). This study provides a direct replication of the redundancy effect reported by Mayer, Heiser, and Lonn (2001).

The sixth line of Table 6.2 summarizes a study by Leahy, Chandler, and Sweller (2003) in which elementary school students learned to use temperature graphs to answer questions. Some students viewed the graph along with printed text on the same page and concurrent auditory commentary that was identical to the text (redundant group), whereas others viewed the same graph and printed text without concurrent auditory commentary (nonredundant group). Consistent with previous research, students in the nonredundant group performed better than students in the redundant group on transfer questions, yielding a high effect size. In this case a redundancy effect was obtained even though the nonredundant group received graphics with printed text (rather than graphics with spoken text). Students had unlimited time to study the graph and text, thus eliminating difficulties associated with modality.

The seventh line of Table 6.2 summarizes a study by Jamet and Bohec (2007) in which college students viewed a multimedia lesson on how human memory works consisting of diagrams with spoken text (nonredundant group) or diagrams, spoken text, and concurrent on-screen text (redundant group). On a subsequent transfer test, the nonredundant group outperformed the redundant group, yielding a medium-to-large effect size.

Overall, there is consistent support for the redundancy principle: People learn more deeply from graphics and narration than from graphics, narration, and on-screen text. In all twelve tests reported in Tables 6.1 and 6.2, the nonredundant group outperformed the redundant group on tests of problem-solving transfer.

The redundancy principle described in this chapter represents a subset of Sweller's (2005) redundancy principle. Sweller (2005) defines redundancy as occurring when "the same information is presented in multiple forms or is unnecessarily elaborated" (p. 159). This definition includes what I call redundancy (in this chapter) and coherence (in Chapter 4) as well as situations in which words and graphics convey the same information (which I do not address). In short, the redundancy principle described in this chapter involves a specific situation in which the narration (i.e., the spoken words) and the on-screen text (i.e., the printed words) are identical.

Boundary Conditions for the Redundancy Principle

Although the redundancy effect has been replicated across twelve experimental tests, you may be tempted to ask: Are there any situations in which the redundancy principle does not apply, or in which its effect is diminished? To date, the research literature suggests that the redundancy principle may be less applicable (a) when the captions are shortened to a few words and placed next to the part of the graphic they describe, (b) when the spoken text is presented before the printed text rather than concurrently, or (c) when there are no graphics and the verbal segments are short. In each of these cases, the need to engage in extraneous processing is lessened.

First, consider what happens when the redundant on-screen text is shortened to just a few key words (rather than a long caption) and the words are placed next to the corresponding part of the graphic (rather than at the bottom of the screen). For example, Mayer and Johnson (2008) presented sixteen slides from the lightning passage, each with concurrent narration (nonredundant group), or sixteen slides each with concurrent narration and a few words from the narration printed next to the corresponding part of the graphic (redundant group). For the redundant group, for example, the slide with the narration "Cool moist air moves over a warmer surface and becomes heated" also contained the redundant on-screen text "Air becomes heated," which was placed next to wavy lines representing the air on the slide.

Mayer and Johnson (2008, Experiments 1 and 2) found that when the redundant on-screen text is just a few words that are placed next to the corresponding part of the graphic, the redundancy effect for transfer test performance disappeared, both for a multimedia lesson on lightning ($d = -.04$ favoring the redundant group) and a multimedia lesson on braking systems ($d = .15$ favoring the nonredundant group). Thus, an important boundary condition for the redundancy principle is that the effect is minimized when the text contains a few key words rather than a long passage and when the on-screen text is placed near the corresponding part of the graphic to help guide attention.

This boundary condition for the redundancy principle is consistent with the cognitive theory of multimedia learning. Redundancy hinders learning when it creates extraneous processing (by placing text far from the corresponding graphics) and when it detracts from essential processing (by highlighting the entire text rather than highlighting key portions of the text). Redundancy may help learning when it minimizes extraneous processing (by placing text near corresponding graphics) and fosters essential processing (by highlighting key portions of the text).

Second, consider a situation in which adult trainees learn about mechanical engineering in a computer-based lesson containing concurrent diagrams, spoken text, and printed text. Kalyuga, Chandler, and Sweller (2004) found a large improvement in transfer performance when the spoken text was presented before the printed text. Thus, even though the printed text and spoken text were redundant in both situations, students learned more deeply when the spoken words were presented before the printed words rather than concurrently. Again, this boundary condition for the redundancy principle is consistent with the cognitive theory of multimedia learning, because separating the printed and spoken text helps reduce extraneous processing (e.g., trying to reconcile the two incoming verbal strings).

Third, consider what happens when a lesson consists of redundant printed words and spoken words – that is, a lesson in which printed words are read aloud for the learner – but no graphics are presented. Moreno and Mayer (2002) refer to this situation as *verbal redundancy*. In situations where the verbal segments are short – such as a sentence at a time – verbal redundancy tends to result in better transfer performance as compared to receiving printed words alone (Moreno & Mayer, 2002). In situations where the verbal material is long – such as an entire passage – verbal redundancy tends to result in worse transfer performance as compared to receiving printed words alone (Diao & Sweller, 2007). This pattern is also consistent with the cognitive theory of multimedia learning, in which longer segments are more likely to create extraneous processing that interferes with learning.

Overall, these boundary conditions for the redundancy principle suggest that principles of instructional design are not intended as universal rules but rather should be applied in ways that are consistent with how the human information-processing system works.

IMPLICATIONS OF THE REDUNDANCY PRINCIPLE

Implications for Multimedia Learning

In five separate tests carried out in our lab, learning a scientific explanation from a concise narrated animation was hurt by the addition of on-screen text that contained the same words as the narration. We refer to this finding as the *redundancy priciple*: Adding redundant on-screen text to a narrated animation detracts from multimedia learning.

The redundancy principle provides important support for the cognitive theory of multimedia learning and its capacity limitation hypothesis. In particular, the redundancy principle is consistent with the capacity limitation hypothesis, in which visual working memory becomes overloaded when animation and on-screen text are presented concurrently (as in the narration–animation–text treatment). In this case, fewer cognitive resources are available for making connections between corresponding words and pictures, thus decreasing the chances for meaningful learning. By contrast, when words are presented in the auditory channel and pictures are presented in the visual channel (as in the narration–animation treatment), the load on these systems is minimized. In this case, more cognitive resources are available for making connections between corresponding words and pictures, so the chances for meaningful learning are increased.

The redundancy principle is not consistent with the learning preferences hypothesis, in which adding redundant on-screen text to a narrated animation is supposed to allow learners to choose the mode of presentation for words – visual or auditory – that best fits their learning style. The learning preferences hypothesis predicts that redundancy will enhance student learning, but our results were the opposite. We caution, however, that the redundancy principle does not invalidate the idea that allowing learners some choice in adjusting multimedia presentations to fit their learning preferences can be effective in some situations. For example, Plass, Chun, Mayer, and Leutner (1998) found that allowing students to choose between pictorial and verbal definitions of words helped them learn the words while reading a story in a second-language-learning multimedia environment.

What is the relation between the redundancy principle and the multimedia principle (as described in Chapter 12)? The redundancy principle seems to suggest that two modalities are worse than one, whereas the multimedia principle seems to suggest that two modalities are better than one. The apparent discrepancy can be resolved by applying the cognitive theory of multimedia learning. The redundancy principle is based on a situation in which presenting words in two sense modalities – as print and speech – is worse than presenting words solely in one modality – as speech. A distinguishing feature in this situation is that the added on-screen text serves to overload the visual channel, which must also process the incoming animation. By contrast, the multimedia principle is based on the idea that learning can be improved when a narration is supplemented with corresponding animation. In this case, load on the visual channel is not increased because words are presented in the auditory channel.

What is the relation between the redundancy principle and the modality principle (as described in Chapter 11)? According to the cognitive theory of multimedia learning, not all techniques for removing redundancy are equally effective. For example, when a multimedia explanation is presented using animation, narration, and text, one effective way to remove redundancy is to remove the on-screen text – yielding the redundancy principle described in this chapter. However, an alternative method of removing redundancy is to remove the narration. According to the cognitive theory of multimedia learning, this situation can overload the visual channel because words and pictures are both presented visually. In Chapter 11, I use the term *modality principle* to refer to the situation in which learning from animation and narration is more effective than learning from animation and on-screen text. In both cases – the redundancy principle and the *modality principle* – learning is more efficient when words are presented in spoken form and not in printed form; however, in the redundancy principle learning is hurt by starting with a concise narrated animation and adding on-screen text, whereas in the modality principle learning is hurt by starting with a concise narrated animation and substituting on-screen text for narration.

Implications for Multimedia Design

Research on redundancy allows us to add another principle of multimedia design to our collection: When making a multimedia presentation consisting of a concise narrated animation, do not add on-screen text that duplicates words that are already in the narration. This design principle has been demonstrated in situations in which the animated narration runs at a fast pace without learner control of the presentation. Overall, the research reviewed in this chapter suggests that it is harmful to present printed and spoken text together when pictorial information is also presented visually and when the material is presented at a rapid pace without opportunity for learner control of the presentation.

This chapter began with the question, "How can we improve concise narrated animations?" The answer is that adding redundant on-screen text is not an effective way to improve a concise narrated animation. Based on the research reviewed in this chapter, the best approach to redesigning a concise narrated animation may simply be to leave it as is.

Limitations and Future Directions

The redundancy principle should not be taken as justification for never presenting printed and spoken text together. As indicated by the boundary conditions reviewed in this chapter, multimedia design principles should not be applied as unbending commandments but rather should be interpreted in light of theories of how people learn, such as the cognitive theory of multimedia learning. Presenting words in spoken and printed form may be harmful in some situations – as reflected in the studies described in this chapter – but not in other situations, such as when the rate of presentation is slow or when no pictorial material is concurrently presented. For example, it might be useful to present summary slides (or to write key ideas on a chalkboard) in the course of a verbal presentation or lecture. Similarly, redundant on-screen text might be useful when the text contains unfamiliar or technical terms, when the learners are non-native speakers, or when the text passages are long and complex. The negative effects of redundancy may be eliminated when the presentation is slow-paced or under learner control. These are research questions that warrant further study.

SUGGESTED READINGS

Asterisk (*) indicates that part of this chapter is based on this publication.

Kalyuga, S., Chandler, P., & Sweller, J. (1999). Managing split-attention and redundancy in multimedia instruction. *Applied Cognitive Psychology*, *13*, 351–371.

*Mayer, R. E., Heiser, H., & Lonn, S. (2001). Cognitive constraints on multimedia learning: When presenting more material results in less understanding. *Journal of Educational Psychology*, *93*, 187–198.

*Moreno, R., & Mayer, R. E. (2002a). Verbal redundancy in multimedia learning: When reading helps listening. *Journal of Educational Psychology*, *94*, 156–163.

7

Spatial Contiguity Principle

Spatial Contiguity Principle: *Students learn better when corresponding words and pictures are presented near rather than far from each other on the page or screen.*

Example: *In an animation on lightning formation, captions are presented at the bottom of the screen (separated presentation) or are placed next to the event they describe in the animation (integrated presentation). In a booklet on lightning formation, the text is presented on a different page than the illustrations (separated presentation), or each paragraph is placed next to the illustration it describes (integrated presentation).*

Theoretical Rationale: *When corresponding words and pictures are near each other on the page or screen, learners do not have to use cognitive resources to visually search the page or screen, and learners are more likely to be able to hold them both in working memory at the same time. When corresponding words and pictures are far from each other on the page or screen, learners have to use cognitive resources to visually search the page or screen, and learners are less likely to be able to hold them both in working memory at the same time.*

Empirical Rationale: *In five out of five tests, learners performed better on transfer tests when corresponding text and illustrations were placed near each other on the page (or when corresponding on-screen text and animation segments were placed near each other on the screen) than when they were placed far away from each other, yielding a median effect size of $d = 1.09$.*

Boundary Conditions: *The spatial contiguity principle is most applicable when (a) the learner is not familiar with the material, (b) the diagram is not fully understandable without words, and (c) the material is complex.*

■ ■ **Chapter Outline**

INTRODUCTION TO THE SPATIAL CONTIGUITY PRINCIPLE

Space as an Economic Resource

When it comes to presenting multimedia material – words and pictures – on a computer screen or textbook page, the amount of available space is limited. A screen or page can hold only a finite amount of verbal or visual material. Therefore, screen space or page space can be viewed as a limited resource that is in great demand. Decisions about multimedia design can be viewed as economic decisions concerning how to allocate space on a page or screen among alternative uses. For example, our analysis of science textbooks has shown that about half the space in textbooks is used for graphics, and about half is used for words (Levin & Mayer, 1993).

In addition to deciding how much space to allocate to words and how much to allocate to pictures, multimedia designers need to determine how to arrange the word-dominated space and the picture-dominated space on the available pages or screen frames. Suppose, for example, that you had a passage on lightning formation that contained 600 words and 5 illustrations. Further, suppose that the space you have for presenting this material is two pages of paper.

On the one hand, you could place all the words on one page and all the illustrations on another page – as is shown in Figure 7.1. This is an

The Process of Lightning

Lightning can be defined as the discharge of electricity resulting from the difference in electrical charges between the cloud and the ground.

Warm moist air near the earth's surface rises rapidly. As the air in the updraft cools, water vapor condenses into water droplets and forms a cloud. The cloud's top extends above the freezing level. At this altitude, the air temperature is well below freezing, so the upper portion of the cloud is composed of tiny ice crystals.

Eventually, the water droplets and ice crystals become too large to be suspended by updrafts. As raindrops and ice crystals fall through the cloud, they drag some of the air in the cloud downward, producing downdrafts. The rising and falling air currents within the cloud may cause hailstones to form. When downdrafts strike the ground, they spread out in all directions, producing gusts of cool wind people feel just before the start of the rain.

Within the cloud, the moving air causes electrical charges to build, although scientists do not fully understand how it occurs. Most believe that the charge results from the collision of the cloud's light, rising water droplets and tiny pieces of ice against hail and other heavier, falling particles. The negatively charged particles fall to the bottom of the cloud, and most of the positively charged particles rise to the top.

The first stroke of a flash of ground-to-cloud lightning is started by a stepped leader. Many scientists believe that it is triggered by a spark between the areas of positive and negative charges. A stepped leader moves downward in a series of steps, each of which is about 50 yards long and lasts for about 1 millionth of a second. It pauses between steps for about 50 millionths of a second. As the stepped leader nears the ground, positively charged upward-moving leaders travel up from such objects as trees and buildings to meet the negative charges. Usually, the upward-moving leader from the tallest object is the first to meet the stepped leader and complete a path between the cloud and earth. The two leaders generally meet about 165 feet above the ground. Negatively charged particles then rush from the cloud to the ground along the path created by the leaders. It is not very bright and usually has many branches.

As the leader stroke nears the ground, it induces an opposite charge, so positively charged particles from the ground rush upward along the same path. This upward motion of the current is the return stroke and it reaches the cloud in about 70 microseconds. A return stroke produces the bright light that people notice in a flash of lightning, but the current travels so quickly that its upward motion cannot be perceived. The lightning flash usually consists of an electrical potential of several million volts. The air along the lightning channel is heated briefly to a very high temperature. Such intense heating causes the air to expand explosively, producing a sound wave we call thunder.

A flash of lightning may end after one return stroke. In most cases, however, dart leaders, which are similar to stepped leaders, carry more negative charges from the cloud down the main path of the previous stroke. Each dart leader is followed by a return stroke. This process commonly occurs 3 or 4 times in one flash, but can occur more than 20 times. People can sometimes see the individual strokes of a flash. At such times the lightning appears to flicker.

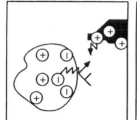
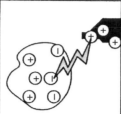
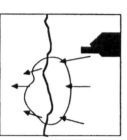
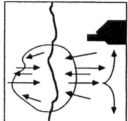
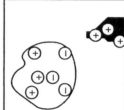
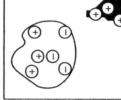

Figure 7.1. Separated book-based multimedia presentation: words separated from pictures.

137

The Process of Lightning

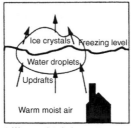

Lightning can be defined as the discharge of electricity resulting from the difference in electrical charges between the cloud and the ground.

Warm moist air near the earth's surface rises rapidly. As the air in this updraft cools, water vapor condenses into water droplets and forms a cloud. The cloud's top extends above the freezing level. At this altitude, the air temperature is well below freezing, so the upper portion of the cloud is composed of tiny ice crystals.

1. Warm moist air rises, water vapor condenses and forms cloud.

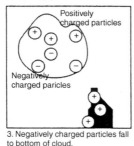

Eventually, the water droplets and ice crystals become too large to be suspended by updrafts. As raindrops and ice crystals fall through the cloud, they drag some of the air in the cloud downward, producing downdrafts. The rising and falling air currents within the cloud may cause hailstones to form. When downdrafts strike the ground, they spread out in all directions, producing gusts of cool wind people feel just before the start of the rain.

2. Raindrops and ice crystals drag air downward.

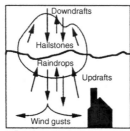

Within the cloud, the moving air causes electrical charges to build, although scientists do not fully understand how it occurs. Most believe that the charge results from the collision of the cloud's light, rising water droplets and tiny pieces of ice against hail and other heavier, falling particles. The negatively charged particles fall to the bottom of the cloud, and most of the positively charged particles rise to the top.

3. Negatively charged particles fall to bottom of cloud.

(Continues)

Figure 7.2. Integrated book-based multimedia presentation: words integrated with pictures.

example of a separation design because your strategy is to place graphics in a different place than text.

On the other hand, you could place each illustration next to the paragraph that describes it. To provide even better integration, you could copy some of the key words from the paragraph as a caption for the corresponding illustration. This does not add any new words, but simply places the most relevant words very close to the corresponding illustration. Figure 7.2 shows an integrated way to present words and illustrations. This is an example of an integration design because your strategy is to place graphics close to the words that describe them.

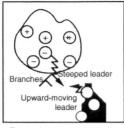

The first stoke of a flash of ground-to-cloud lightning is started by a stepped leader. Many-scientists believe that it is triggered by a spark between the areas of positive and negative charges. A stepped leader, moves downward in a series of steps, each of which is about 50 yards long and lasts for about 1 millionth of a second. It pauses between steps for about 50 millionths of a second. As the stepped leader nears the ground, positively charged upward-moving leaders travel up from such objects as trees and buildings to meet the negative charges. Usually, the upward-moving leader from the tallest object is the first to meet the steeped leader and complete a path between the cloud and earth. The two leaders generally meet about 165 feet above the ground. Negatively charged particles then rush from the cloud to the ground along the path created by the leaders. It is not very bright and usually has many branches.

4. Two leaders meet, negatively charged particles rush from cloud to ground.

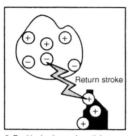

As the leader stroke nears the ground. it induces an opposite charge, so positively charged particles from the ground rush upward along the same path. This upward motion of the current is the return stroke and it reaches the cloud in about 70 microseconds. A return stroke produces the bright light that people notice in a flash of lightning. but the current travels so quickly that its upward motion cannot be perceived. the lightning flash usually consists of an electrical potential of several million volts. The air along the lightning channel is heated briefly to a very high temperature. Such intense heating causes the air to expand explosively, producing a sound wave we call thunder.

A flash of lightning may end after one return stroke. In most cases, however, dart leaders which are similar to stepped leaders, carry more negative charges from the cloud down the main path of the previous stroke. Each dart leader is followed by a return stroke. This process commonly occurs 3 or 4 times in one flash, but can occur more than 20 times. People can sometimes see the individual strokes of a flash. At such times the lightning appears to flicker

5. Positively charged particles from the ground rush upward along the same path.

Figure 7.2. Continued

As you can see, the multimedia lessons in Figures 7.1 and 7.2 contain the same illustrations and the same words, and both require two pages of space. The major difference between the two multimedia lessons is that in the first one the words and illustrations are separated from one another on the pages, and in the second one the words and illustrations are integrated with one another on the pages.

Suppose, instead, that you have a 2.5-minute animation depicting the formation of lightning – based on animating the illustrations from Figures 7.1 and 7.2 – and you have a few hundred words of on-screen text – based on shortening the text from Figures 7.1 and 7.2. The animation depicts about sixteen actions (such as cool, moist air moving over the earth's surface) and the text describes the same sixteen actions. How should you present the animation and text on the computer screen?

If you followed a separation strategy, you might place the text describing an action in a different place than the corresponding animation segment. For example, the top of Figure 7.3 shows a selected frame from an annotated animation on lightning formation in which a sentence describing the movement of air is separated from a

Separated Presentation

As the air in this updraft cools, water vapor
A   condenses into water droplets and forms a cloud.

Integrated Presentation

B

Figure 7.3. Example frames from (A) separated and (B) integrated computer-based multimedia presentation.

corresponding animation segment depicting the movement of air. As
you can see, the text about movement of air is printed at the bottom of
the screen, whereas the action takes place in areas away from the text.

On the other hand, an integration strategy is to place graphics and
corresponding words as near to each other as possible. For example,
the bottom of Figure 7.3 shows a selected frame from an annotated
animation on lightning formation in which sentences describing the
steps in lightning formation are integrated with corresponding animation segments depicting the same steps. As can be seen, the text
about the movement of air is printed next to the corresponding animation action – that is, the wavy lines moving from left to right.

In both cases, the learner is presented with the same words and the
same graphics, but corresponding animation segments and on-screen
text sentences are far apart in the separated version and near one
another in the integrated version. Which arrangement is more successful

in fostering learning? In the next two sections, I explore the case for separating words and pictures and the case for integrating words and pictures, respectively.

The Case for Separating Words and Pictures

Common sense (and a long history of research on verbal learning) dictates that presenting the same material twice will result in students learning more than presenting it once. This is what happens in the separated version of the lightning lesson: The learner first studies the words that describe steps in lightning formation and then studies the pictures that depict the same steps. By separating the words and pictures, we can expose learners to each step twice.

The case for separating words and pictures is based on an information-delivery theory of multimedia learning in which visual and verbal modes of presentation are posited to be separate routes for delivering information to the learner. When the same information is delivered at different times – as in the case of separated lessons – it has a greater effect, because the learner has two chances to store it in memory. By contrast, when words and pictures describing the same information are delivered at the same time – as in the case of integrated lessons – it has less effect, because the learner has only one chance to store it.

Based on the information-delivery theory, we can predict that separated presentations will result in more learning than integrated presentations – as measured by tests of transfer. In short, two separate exposures to the same material are better than one.

The Case for Integrating Words and Pictures

What's wrong with this straightforward, commonsense case for separating words and pictures in multimedia presentations? My major objection is that it is based on an incomplete view of how people learn – the idea that learning involves adding presented information to one's memory. By contrast, the cognitive theory of multimedia learning is based on the idea that learning is an active process in which the learner strives to make sense of the presented material. This sense-making effort is supported when corresponding words and pictures can be mentally integrated in the learner's working memory.

In the integrated version of the lesson, words and pictures are presented in a way that encourages learners to build mental connections between them. Learners do not have to search the screen or page to find a graphic that corresponds to a printed sentence; therefore, they can devote their cognitive resources to the processes of active learning, including building connections between words and pictures. According to the cognitive theory of multimedia learning, meaningful multimedia learning depends on building connections between mental representations of corresponding words and pictures. Thus, integrated presentations foster understanding that is reflected in performance on transfer tests.

In separated versions of the lesson, words and pictures are presented in a way that discourages learners from building mental connections between them. Learners must search the screen or page to try to find a graphic that corresponds to a printed sentence; this process requires cognitive effort – what we call *extraneous processing* – that could have been used to support the processes of active learning. Thus, separated presentations are less likely to foster understanding than are integrated presentations.

Based on this analysis, the cognitive theory of multimedia learning predicts better transfer test performance from integrated presentations than from separated presentations. In short, the case for integrated presentations is that they minimize extraneous processing and serve as aids for building cognitive connections between words and pictures.

RESEARCH ON THE SPATIAL CONTIGUITY PRINCIPLE

Core Evidence Concerning the Spatial Contiguity Principle

In a multimedia presentation consisting of printed text and graphics, should corresponding text and graphics be near or far from each other on the page or screen? My colleagues and I addressed this question in a series of five experimental tests (Mayer, 1989a, Experiment 1; Mayer et al., 1995, Experiments 1, 2, and 3; Moreno & Mayer, 1999, Experiment 1). In each test, we compared the transfer test performance of learners who received separated multimedia presentations with the performance of learners who received integrated multimedia presentations. In some studies the separated and integrated presentations were in book-based environments (Mayer, 1989, Experiment 1; Mayer et al., 1995, Experiments 1, 2, and 3), and in another study (Moreno & Mayer, 1999, Experiment 1) they were in a computer-based environment. In all cases, learning outcomes were assessed by asking students to generate as many solutions as possible to a series of problem-solving

Table 7.1 Core Evidence Concerning the Spatial Contiguity Principle

Source	Content	Format	Effect Size
Mayer (1989, Expt. 2)	Brakes	Paper	1.36
Mayer et al. (1995, Expt. 1)	Lightning	Paper	1.09
Mayer et al. (1995, Expt. 2)	Lightning	Paper	1.35
Mayer et al. (1995, Expt. 3)	Lightning	Paper	1.12
Moreno & Mayer (1999, Expt. 1)	Lightning	Computer	0.82
Median			1.12

transfer questions. According to the information-delivery theory, students who learned from the separated presentation will perform better on transfer tests than students who learned from the integrated presentation. The cognitive theory of multimedia learning makes the opposite prediction because placing words next to the part of the graphic they describe can reduce extraneous processing.

Table 7.1 summarizes the source, content, format, and effect size for five experimental comparisons of integrated versus separated presentations carried out in our lab. In the first line of Table 7.1, the integrated group read a page containing an explanation of how a car's braking system works printed next to frames of a diagram showing the braking system, whereas the separated group read the words on one page and saw the diagrams on another page. On a subsequent transfer test, the integrated group performed much better than the separated group, yielding a large effect size, even though both groups received exactly the same words and pictures.

In the next three rows of Table 7.1, the integrated group read a booklet about lightning formation in which each of five paragraphs was placed next to the illustration it described and key words from the paragraph were embedded in the illustration (as shown in Figure 7.2), whereas the separated group read the entire passage on one page and saw the five illustrations (without any embedded words) on the next page (as shown in Figure 7.1). In all three comparisons, the integrated group outperformed the separated group on a transfer test, yielding large effect sizes, even though exactly the same words and pictures were given to both groups.

Finally, in the last row of Table 7.1, the integrated group viewed an animation about lightning formation in which on-screen text was placed next to the part of the animation it described (as shown at the top of Figure 7.3), whereas the separated group viewed an animation about lightning formation in which on-screen text was placed at the bottom of the screen as a caption (as shown at the bottom of Figure 7.3). As in the other experimental tests, the integrated group performed much better on a transfer test than did the separated group, yielding a large effect size, even though the same animation and captions were presented to both groups.

The same pattern of transfer results was obtained in a book-based environment (Mayer, 1989, Experiment 2; Mayer et al., 1995, Experiments 1, 2, and 3) as in a computer-based environment (Moreno & Mayer, 1999, Experiment 1), and the effect sizes were large in both venues. The effect appears to be stronger in the book-based environment, but this may be attributable to methodological differences. In particular, in the separated presentation the words and pictures are farther apart in the book-based materials (i.e., on separate pages) than in the computer-based material (i.e., a few inches apart on the computer screen). Further research may be needed to create equivalent kinds of separated presentations for books and computers.

Overall, in five out of five tests, students in the integrated group generated more solutions to the problem-solving transfer questions than did students in the separated group. This pattern constitutes support for the *spatial contiguity principle* because placing corresponding words and pictures in spatial contiguity – that is, next to each other on the page or screen – resulted in better performance on transfer tests. The spatial contiguity principle is that students learn more deeply when corresponding words and pictures are presented near rather than far from each other. Table 7.1 shows that the effect sizes are in the large range, with a median effect size of $d = 1.12$.

Related Evidence Concerning the Spatial Contiguity Principle

Similar evidence for the spatial contiguity principle has been reported by other researchers. In a recent meta-analysis of thirty-seven experimental comparisons, Ginns (2006) found an average effect size of $d = 0.72$ favoring integrated presentation rather than separated presentation. However, Ginns's review included unpublished papers, studies that defined separated presentation more broadly than I do in this chapter (e.g., presenting material in a booklet and on a computer versus only in a booklet), and studies that did not include transfer tests. The median effect size in Ginns's analysis is $d = 1.07$, when we focus only on published experiments comparing the transfer test performance of students who learned with words integrated with illustrations versus words separated from illustrations. Ginns (2006, p. 511) concludes

Table 7.2. Related Evidence Concerning the Spatial Contiguity Principle

Source	Content	Format	Effect Size
Sweller, Chandler, Tierney, & Cooper (1990, Expt. 1)	Mathematics	Paper	0.71
Chandler & Sweller (1991, Expt. 1)	Engineering	Paper	1.41
Chandler & Sweller (1991, Expt. 6)	Heart	Paper	0.60
Chandler & Sweller (1992, Expt. 1)	Engineering	Paper	1.19
Tindall-Ford, Chandler, & Sweller (1997, Expt. 1)	Engineering	Paper	1.08
Bodemer, Ploetzner, Feuerlein, & Spada (2004, Expt. 1)	Tire pump	Computer	0.56
Bodemer, Ploetzner, Feuerlein, & Spada (2004, Expt. 2)	Statistics	Computer	0.22
Kester, Kirschner, & van Merrienboer (2005)	Physics	Computer	0.88

that "increasing ... spatial ... contiguity of related elements of information can lead to substantial learning gains."

Table 7.2 lists eight additional tests of the spatial contiguity principle, including the source, content, format, and effect size. The first line in Table 7.2 summarizes a study by Sweller, Chandler, Tierney, and Cooper (1990) in which students learned to solve geometry problems by examining worked examples. In the integrated booklet, the text and symbols describing each step were placed next to the corresponding part of the geometry diagram, whereas in the separated booklet, the text and symbols describing each step were placed below the geometry diagram. The time required to solve a transfer problem was less for students who learned with the integrated rather than the separated booklet, yielding a medium-to-high effect size. Although Sweller, Chandler, Tierney, and Cooper (1990) found similar results in other experiments as well, these experiments are not included in Table 7.2 because means and standard deviations were not reported.

The second line in Table 7.2 summarizes a study in which trainees learned about topics in electrical engineering from an integrated or separated booklet, and later were asked to solve practical problems (Chandler & Sweller, 1991). In the integrated booklet, text describing each step in a procedure was placed next to the corresponding element in a diagram, whereas in the separated booklet the words were at the top of the sheet and the diagram was at the bottom. The integrated group outperformed the separated group, yielding an effect size greater than 1. In a related study (Chandler & Sweller, 1991), students learned about the human heart by viewing a diagram with twelve numbered steps, each printed next to its corresponding part of the diagram (integrated group), or with the twelve numbers embedded in the diagram along with a key at the bottom listing the twelve steps (separated group). As shown in the third line of Table 7.2, the integrated group outperformed the separated group on a series of test problems, including using the material to solve new problems, yielding an effect size of .60. Chandler and Sweller (1991) also reported several other experiments in which students learned faster and remembered more from integrated booklets than from separated booklets, but it is not possible to calculate effect sizes based on the presented data.

In a similar study, summarized in the fourth line of Table 7.2, Chandler and Sweller (1992) taught engineering procedures to trainees using printed diagrams and text. For example, some learners received pages containing a diagram with twelve numbered steps, each placed next to the part of the diagram it described (integrated group), whereas others received all the text presented in a paragraph above the diagram (separated group). The integrated group outperformed the separated group on a set of ten transfer test items, yielding a large effect size according to Ginns's (2006) analysis.

As summarized in the fifth line in Table 7.2, Tindall-Ford, Chandler, and Sweller (1997) asked apprentices to read a booklet on topics in electrical engineering and then solve some practical problems. Some apprentices read an integrated booklet in which text describing each step in a procedure was placed next to the corresponding part of a diagram; others read a separated booklet in which the text was presented below the corresponding diagram. As you can see, the integrated group performed better in solving practical problems than did the separated group, yielding an effect size greater than 1.

The sixth line of Table 7.2 summarizes a study by Bodemer, Ploetzner, Feuerlein, and Spada (2004) in which students received a computer-based lesson on how a bicycle tire pump works. The lesson consisted of diagrams showing the pump when the handle is up and when the handle is down along with fifteen numbered captions, each placed next to the part of the diagram it described (integrated group) or with just the number on the diagram along with a key that listed the captions for each number (separated group). The integrated group outperformed the separated group on a transfer test, yielding an effect size of $d = .56$. As shown in the seventh line of Table 7.2, a similar pattern was found in a follow-up experiment involving a computer-based statistics lesson, yielding an effect size of $d = .22$ favoring the integrated group (Bodemer, Ploetzner, Feuerlein, & Spada, 2004, Experiment 2). The authors explain the relatively weaker effect size in Experiment 2 by noting, "even the integrated format still required a considerable amount of visual search" (p. 336).

The bottom line of Table 7.2 summarizes a study by Kester, Kirschner, and van Merrienboer (2005) in which students learned to solve electrical circuit problems in a computer-based physics lesson consisting of worked-out examples. Students received worked examples with procedural comments placed next to the corresponding parts of a circuit diagram (integrated group) or placed in a key on the right side of the screen away from the diagram (separated group). On a transfer test, the integrated group outperformed the separated group, yielding an effect size of $d = .80$.

In all eight cases listed in Table 7.2, integrated presentations produced better transfer performance than did separated presentations, yielding effect sizes mainly in the medium-to-large range. Thus, there is strong and consistent support for the spatial contiguity principle: People learn more deeply from a multimedia message when corresponding text and pictures are presented near rather than far from each other on the page or screen.

Ayres and Sweller (2005) reviewed similar results concerning spatial contiguity, often using retention tests as the main dependent measure. For example, in a set of related experiments, Purnell, Solman, and Sweller (1991, Experiments 1, 2, 3, and 4) asked students to study a map with the names of various locations printed on the map (integrated presentation) or with the numbers printed on the map along with a numbered key at the bottom (separated presentation). Students in the integrated group tended to perform better on a retention test than students in the separated group, but I did not include this data in Table 7.2 because the article did not report means and standard deviations for the groups on a transfer test. Similar results were obtained using worked examples (Chandler & Sweller, 1992; Cooper & Sweller, 1987; Sweller & Chandler, 1994; Sweller & Cooper, 1985; Tarmizi & Sweller, 1988; Ward & Sweller, 1990).

The spatial contiguity principle represents a subset of what Sweller and his colleagues call the *split-attention principle* (Ayres & Sweller, 2005; Sweller, 1999). The split-attention principle refers to "avoiding formats that require learners to split their attention between, and mentally integrate, multiple sources of information" (Ayres & Sweller, 2005, p. 135) and includes what I refer to as spatial contiguity (described in this chapter), temporal contiguity (described in Chapter 8), and situations in which students must use different multiple delivery systems, such as both a computer-based lesson and a paper-based lesson (which I do not cover). For example, students learn better when words and diagrams are both presented on a computer screen rather than having some material in a manual and some on a computer screen (Bobis, Sweller, & Cooper, 1993).

Boundary Conditions for the Spatial Contiguity Principle

Ayres and Sweller (2005) note that the spatial contiguity principle is most applicable when (a) the learner is not familiar with the material, (b) the diagram is not fully understandable without words, and (c) the material is complex.

First, Kalyuga (2005) summarized evidence for an expertise reversal effect in which instructional methods that help less-experienced learners – such as integrated diagrams and text – do not help more-experienced learners. Similarly, Mayer and colleagues (1995, Experiment 2) reported that integrated presentations were better than separated presentations for low-knowledge learners but not for high-knowledge learners. Thus, a possible boundary condition for the spatial contiguity principle is that the principle applies mainly to less-experienced learners. The explanation for this pattern is that more-experienced learners are able to generate their own verbal commentary for graphics that they study.

Second, Ayres and Sweller (2005, p. 145) note, "the principle only applies when multiple sources of information are unintelligible in isolation." If words are not needed for understanding a graphic, then it is not effective to place words close to rather than far from the corresponding parts of the graphic. The explanation is that learners can learn from the diagram alone and mentally add the needed verbal explanation from their long-term memory.

Third, Ayres and Sweller (2005) found that integrating words and pictures is less likely to be effective when the material is very simple, in which case it "can be easily learned even when presented in split-source format" (p. 145). The explanation is that learners will have adequate cognitive capacity to engage in appropriate cognitive processing even though some extraneous processing is caused by separated presentation.

Finally, Bodemer and colleagues (2004) identified a situation that could increase the effectiveness of the spatial contiguity principle. They found that the spatial contiguity effect could be strengthened if learners actively created an integrated presentation by placing the description of each step in the process of how a pump works at the appropriate location on a diagram of a bicycle tire pump. Thus, another possible boundary condition for the spatial contiguity principle is that the effects of integrating words and pictures may be enhanced through interactivity.

IMPLICATIONS OF THE SPATIAL CONTIGUITY PRINCIPLE

Implications for Multimedia Learning

What makes an effective multimedia message? Research on the *spatial contiguity principle* helps to pinpoint one of the conditions under which multimedia instruction helps people understand a scientific explanation – namely, when the corresponding printed words and illustrations (or animations) are near each other on the page or screen. The spatial contiguity principle can be summarized as follows: Presenting corresponding words and illustrations (or animations) near each other on the page or screen results in better learning than presenting them far from each other.

These results conflict with the predictions of the information-delivery theory, which assumes that two separate presentations of the same material are better than one. For example, when a page containing a text passage on lightning formation is followed by a page containing illustrations depicting lightning formation, the learner is essentially exposed to the same explanation two times. The premise of the information-delivery theory is that verbal and visual presentations are simply routes for delivering information to a learner. According to this view, separated multimedia presentations allow for delivering information via one route and then delivering the same information via another route.

Given the failure to support the predictions based on information-delivery theory, is it possible to revive the information-delivery theory? Perhaps the interpretation of the theory was too strong, so let's consider a somewhat milder interpretation of the information-delivery theory. It is important to note that the same materials – the same words and pictures – were presented in the integrated and separated presentations, so the same information was delivered under both treatments. Therefore, we can conclude that students in the integrated and separated groups should perform at equivalent levels on tests of retention and transfer. Even if we take this somewhat more relaxed approach to the information-delivery theory, the results conflict with our predictions because students consistently performed better on transfer tests when they received the integrated rather than the separated presentation.

Why did the information-delivery theory – in its strong or mild form – fail to generate supportable predictions? One problem is that it is based on an incomplete view of how people learn scientific explanations. According to the information-delivery view, presented material is simply information that learners add to their memories. This account may be accurate when the learning task is a collection of arbitrary fragments, such as a list of unrelated nonsense syllables, but it does not provide a complete explanation of how people learn conceptually deeper material.

By contrast, the results presented in this chapter are consistent with the cognitive theory of multimedia learning. According to this view, learners engage in active cognitive processing in an attempt to make sense out of the presented material. When they read an explanation of how lightning works and see illustrations depicting how lightning works, they are not simply trying to add the information to memory for storage. They are also trying to understand the material by actively selecting relevant words and images, organizing them into coherent verbal and visual mental models, and integrating the models. We refer to this as the active learning assumption of the cognitive theory of multimedia learning.

When corresponding words and pictures are placed near rather than far from each other on the page or screen, the learner experiences less extraneous cognitive processing than when corresponding words and pictures are far apart. The rationale follows from the dual-channel assumption – the idea that humans possess separate verbal and visual information-processing channels – and from the limited-capacity assumption – the idea that each channel has a limited amount of cognitive capacity. Consider how the limited cognitive capacity is used for separated and integrated presentations: For separated presentations, cognitive capacity is used to visually search for words or graphics on the page or screen, so less cognitive processing can be devoted to the integration process; for integrated presentations, the learner is guided in how to integrate corresponding words and pictures, so the integration process is more likely to occur.

In sum, our results are consistent with the three major assumptions underlying the cognitive theory of multimedia learning – dual channels, limited capacity, and active processing. By contrast, the information-delivery view appears to be inadequate in our quest for a design principle for multimedia messages.

Implications for Multimedia Instruction

Our results show that meaningful learning from multimedia presentations depends not just on presenting the necessary information – both the separated and integrated messages presented the same material – but rather on presenting the necessary information along with guidance to the learner on how to mentally process it. The fact that integrated presentation resulted in deeper learning than separated presentation encourages us to consider ways to arrange words and pictures that are most compatible with ways in which people learn.

The research presented in this chapter allows us to offer an important principle for the design of multimedia explanations: Present words and pictures near rather than far from each other. In book-based contexts, this means that illustrations should be placed next to the sentences that describe them, or better, the most relevant phrases may be placed within the illustrations themselves. In computer-based contexts, this means that on-screen words should be presented next to the part of the graphic that they describe.

This spatial contiguity principle provides a step in pinpointing the conditions that lead to deeper learning from multimedia presentations. It focuses mainly on the contiguous spatial arrangement of printed text and illustrations on a textbook page or on a computer screen. In the next chapter, I explore an analogous principle concerning the contiguous temporal arrangement of spoken text and animation in a computer-based context. Thus, whereas this chapter focuses on contiguous arrangement of words and pictures in space, the following chapter (Chapter 8) focuses on their contiguous arrangement in time.

Limitations and Future Directions

Future research is needed to pinpoint the boundary conditions of the spatial contiguity principle, particularly the role of the learner's prior knowledge. In particular, it would be useful to know how the learner's prior knowledge mitigates poor instructional design. Unobtrusive techniques for measuring prior knowledge would also be helpful.

Future research is also needed to determine how many words to put into segments that are embedded within graphics. Based on the coherence principle (in Chapter 4), I predict that the embedded text would be most effective when it is very short – just a few words – but empirical research is needed to address this issue.

Finally, the use of printed text conflicts with the modality principle (discussed in Chapter 11), so research is needed to determine when to use printed text rather than spoken text. In situations where printed text is called for, the spatial contiguity principle comes into play.

SUGGESTED READINGS

Asterisk (*) indicates that part of this chapter is based on this publication.

Ayres, P., & Sweller, J. (2005). The split-attention principle in multimedia learning. In R. E. Mayer (Ed.), *The Cambridge handbook of multimedia learning* (pp. 135–146). New York: Cambridge University Press.

Ginns, P. (2006). Integrating information: A meta-analysis of spatial contiguity and temporal contiguity effects. *Learning and Instruction, 16*, 511–525.

*Mayer, R. E. (1989). Systematic thinking fostered by illustrations in scientific text. *Journal of Educational Psychology, 81*, 240–246.

*Mayer, R. E., Steinhoff, K., Bower, G., & Mars, R. (1995). A generative theory of textbook design: Using annotated illustrations to foster meaningful learning of science text. *Educational Technology Research and Development, 43*, 31–43.

*Moreno, R., & Mayer, R. E. (1999). Cognitive principles of multimedia learning: The role of modality and contiguity. *Journal of Educational Psychology, 91*, 358–368.

8

Temporal Contiguity Principle

Temporal Contiguity Principle: *Students learn better when corresponding words and pictures are presented simultaneously rather than successively.*

Example: *The learner first views an animation on lightning formation and then hears the corresponding narration, or vice versa (successive group), or the learner views an animation and hears the corresponding narration at the same time (simultaneous group).*

Theoretical Rationale: *When corresponding portions of narration and animation are presented at the same time, the learner is more likely to be able to hold mental representations of both in working memory at the same time, and thus, the learner is more likely to be able to build mental connections between verbal and visual representations. When corresponding portions of narration and animation are separated in time, the learner is less likely to be able to hold mental representations of both in working memory at the same time, and thus, the learner is less likely to be able to build mental connections between verbal and visual representations.*

Empirical Rationale: *In eight out of eight tests, learners performed better on transfer tests when corresponding portions of animation and narration were presented simultaneously rather than successively. The median effect size is $d = 1.31$.*

Boundary Conditions: *The temporal contiguity principle may be less applicable when the successive lesson involves alternations between short segments rather than a long continuous presentation or when the lesson is under learner control rather than under system control.*

▨ ▨ Chapter Outline

INTRODUCTION TO THE TEMPORAL CONTIGUITY PRINCIPLE

What Is Temporal Contiguity?

Suppose you want to find out how lightning storms develop, so you go to a multimedia encyclopedia and click on a speaker icon, which describes the steps in lightning formation in spoken text. Then you click on a movie icon, which launches an animation depicting the steps in lightning formation. What is wrong with this scenario? According to the cognitive theory of multimedia learning, it can create cognitive overload in which the requirements for essential processing and extraneous processing (caused by confusing presentation) exceed the learner's cognitive capacity. In this case the learner must hold the words in working memory until the animation is presented – creating an excessive amount of extraneous cognitive processing.

The solution to this problem is the *temporal contiguity principle* – that is, the idea that corresponding words and pictures should be presented at the same time. For example, in a narrated animation of lightning formation, as the narrator says, "Negatively charged particles fall to the bottom of the cloud," the animation should show little negative signs moving from the top to the bottom of the cloud. In short, temporal contiguity refers to the idea that the learner hears narration that describes an event at the same time the learner sees an animation (or static graphic) that depicts the same event.

Suppose you have been asked to create a short multimedia presentation on the formation of lightning to be included as an entry in a multimedia encyclopedia. You can use words such as narration or

Table 8.1. Sixteen Segments of Narration Script for Lightning Lesson

1. Cool, moist air moves over a warmer surface and becomes heated.
2. Warmed moist air near the earth's surface rises rapidly.
3. As the air in this updraft cools, water vapor condenses into water droplets and forms a cloud.
4. The cloud's top extends above the freezing level, so the upper portion of the cloud is composed of tiny ice crystals.
5. Within the cloud, the rising and falling air currents cause electrical charges to build.
6. The charge results from the collision of the cloud's rising water droplets against heavier, falling pieces of ice.
7. The negatively charged particles fall to the bottom of the cloud, and most of the positively charged particles rise to the top.
8. Eventually, the water droplets and ice crystals become too large to be suspended by the updrafts.
9. As raindrops and ice crystals fall through the cloud, they drag some of the air in the cloud downward, producing downdrafts.
10. When downdrafts strike the ground, they spread out in all directions, producing the gusts of cool wind people feel just before the start of the rain.
11. A stepped leader of negative charges moves downward in a series of steps. It nears the ground.
12. A positively charged leader travels up from such objects as trees and buildings.
13. The two leaders generally meet about 165 feet above the ground.
14. Negatively charged particles then rush from the cloud to the ground along the path created by the leaders. It is not very bright.
15. As the leader stroke nears the ground, it induces an opposite charge, so positively charged particles from the ground rush upward along the same path.
16. This upward motion of the current is the return stroke. It produces the bright light that people notice as a flash of lightning.

on-screen text, and you can use pictures such as animation or illustrations. Let's assume that you have developed a narration describing the major steps in lightning formation – consisting of 300 words broken down into 16 segments such as shown in Table 8.1. Let's also assume that you have developed a series of 16 animation segments depicting these same steps in lightning formation – lasting a total of 140 seconds. Some selected frames are shown in Figure 2.2 in Chapter 2. If the sixteen narration segments and sixteen animation segments are your building blocks, how would you go about using them to create a short multimedia presentation?

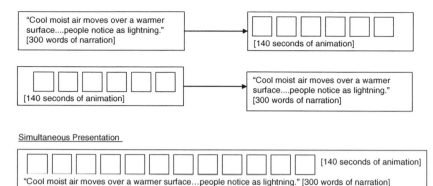

Figure 8.1. Successive and simultaneous presentations.

A straightforward approach is to present the entire narration followed by the entire animation (or vice versa). For example, when the learner clicks on a speaker icon the entire narration is presented, and when the learner clicks on a movie icon the entire animation is presented. In this way, the learner can first pay attention to the verbal description of lightning formation and then pay attention to a visual depiction of lightning formation (or vice versa). We refer to this as *successive presentation* because all the words are presented before all the pictures (or vice versa). In this case corresponding words and pictures are not contiguous in time, so there is a lack of what we call temporal contiguity.

An alternative approach is to present the narration and animation at the same time in close coordination, so that when the narration describes a particular action in words the animation visually depicts the same action at the same time. In this way, the learner sees and hears about the same step at the same time. We refer to this as *simultaneous presentation* because corresponding segments of words and pictures are presented at the same time. In this case the corresponding words and pictures are contiguous in time – creating what we call temporal contiguity. Figure 8.1 summarizes the successive and simultaneous presentation formats.

Which is better for your multimedia encyclopedia entry – successive or simultaneous presentation? In many cases decisions about how to use time in multimedia presentations are based on the best intuitions of the designers, on design principles that may not have a solid research base, or simply on the need to present a certain amount of information in an entertaining way. In this chapter, I take a more scientific approach by exploring some research that my colleagues and I have conducted over the years at Santa Barbara. The purpose of the research is to examine the cognitive consequences of learning from successive and simultaneous presentations, and thereby to contribute both to a theory of multimedia learning and to a research-based set of multimedia design principles.

As with research on spatial contiguity, our goal in examining temporal contiguity is to determine the conditions under which multimedia presentations are most likely to promote meaningful learning. In successive and simultaneous presentations the same material is presented – that is, the same animation and the same narration. Both are multimedia presentations because both contain words and pictures. The crucial difference between successive and simultaneous presentations is the way in which time is used in presenting the narration and animation. In the following two sections, I examine the case for successive multimedia presentations based on an information-delivery theory of multimedia learning and the case for simultaneous presentations based on a cognitive theory of multimedia learning.

The Case for Separating Words and Pictures

Common sense tells us that people will learn more from two exposures to the same material than from one exposure. The successive-presentation format allows for two separate exposures – first learners can devote their full attention to a verbal description of how lightning storms develop, and next they can devote their full attention to a visual depiction of the same events (or they can attend to the visual presentation followed by the verbal presentation). The simultaneous-presentation format allows for only one exposure because each of the sixteen major events is presented only once – with the verbal description and visual depiction happening at the same time. In terms of time, learners who receive the successive presentation get to spend twice as much time studying the material as compared to learners who receive the simultaneous presentation.

This commonsense analysis is based on the information-delivery view of multimedia learning in which learning involves placing presented information into one's memory for long-term storage. When you receive two deliveries – first a delivery via the word route and then a delivery via the picture route, or vice versa – you have a greater chance of placing more information into memory. When you receive one delivery – which comes via two separate routes – you have fewer opportunities to add information to your memory.

According to the information-delivery theory, students who receive successive presentations should learn more than students who receive simultaneous presentations. Thus, the theory predicts that students given successive presentations should outperform students given simultaneous presentations on tests of transfer.

The Case for Integrating Words and Pictures

The successive-presentation format seems to be an obvious choice for deciding where temporally to place the building blocks of animation and narration. What's wrong with the case for temporally separating words and pictures? As in Chapter 7, my main objection to separating words and pictures is that it is based on an incomplete conception of how people learn. According to the cognitive theory of multimedia learning, humans are not information storage machines who receive deliveries of information and store the deliveries in memory. Instead, humans are sense-makers who engage in active cognitive processes during learning such as selecting relevant words and pictures, organizing the selected material into verbal and visual mental models, and integrating the verbal and visual models.

Based on a cognitive theory of multimedia learning, I propose that students are more likely to be able to understand multimedia presentations when corresponding words and pictures are available in working memory at the same time. Simultaneous presentation increases the chances that a learner will be able to hold corresponding visual and verbal representations of the same event in working memory at the same time. This increases the chances that the learner will be able to mentally integrate the verbal and visual representations – a major cognitive process in meaningful learning.

Simultaneous presentations are designed to mesh with the human information-processing system – including the availability of separate visual and verbal channels as well as the extreme limits on the capacity of each channel. Narration can be processed in the verbal channel while the corresponding graphic is processed in the visual channel. That is, as students see cool (blue-colored) air moving over a warmer surface and becoming heated (red-colored) through their visual channel, they can also hear "Cool, moist air moves over a warmer surface and becomes heated" through their verbal channel. Although cognitive capacity is limited, there is enough cognitive capacity to hold each of these representations and to make connections between them.

By contrast, based on the cognitive theory of multimedia learning, I propose that students are less likely to be able understand multimedia presentations when corresponding words and pictures are greatly separated in time. In successive presentations, learners process the entire narration before seeing the entire animation (or vice versa). Given the severe limits on working memory, only a small part of the narration remains in verbal working memory when the animation begins (or only a small portion of the animation remains in visual working memory when the narration begins). Thus, the student may have difficulty in building connections between words and pictures.

Successive presentations seem to conflict with the way in which humans are designed to process information. Instead of taking advantage of our ability to process simultaneously within our visual and verbal channels, successive presentations first present material to be processed in one channel and then present material to be processed in the other one. Instead of being sensitive to human limitations in working memory capacity, successive presentations require that a learner be able to hold the entire narration in working memory until the narration is presented (or vice versa) – an impossible feat according to the cognitive theory of multimedia learning.

According to the cognitive theory of multimedia learning, the temporal arrangement of narration and animation in successive presentations fails to mesh with the way people's minds work, whereas the temporal arrangement of narration and animation in simultaneous presentations takes advantage of the way people's minds work. Even though successive and simultaneous presentations contain identical material – the same narration and the same animation – the cognitive theory of multimedia learning allows me to make quite different predictions: Students who receive simultaneous presentations are better able to understand the explanation than are students who receive successive presentations. This difference should be reflected in transfer test performance, with simultaneous treatments leading to better transfer than successive presentations.

Distinction Between Spatial Contiguity and Temporal Contiguity

As you can see, the cases for separating or integrating words and pictures in time (as discussed in this chapter) are similar to the cases for separating or integrating them in space (as discussed in Chapter 7). Spatial contiguity and temporal contiguity are two related forms of contiguity in the design of multimedia presentations. Spatial contiguity deals with placing corresponding words and pictures close to each other on the page, whereas temporal continuity deals with presenting corresponding words and pictures close to each other in time. Both are based on the same underlying cognitive mechanism, namely, that students are better able to build connections between words and pictures when they can mentally process them at the same time.

In spite of their similarities, spatial and temporal contiguity are not identical, so I have opted to discuss them in separate chapters and under separate names. Spatial contiguity is important for the layout of a page in a textbook or a frame on a computer screen. Spatial contiguity involves material that is processed, at least initially, by the eyes – printed text and graphics (such as illustrations or animations). In this situation, the temporal processing of the material is not controlled by the instructional designer – that is, the reader can choose to focus first on the text or first on the graphics. By contrast, temporal contiguity is important for the timing of computer-based presentations. Temporal contiguity involves material that is processed by the eyes – for example, animation – and material that is processed by the ears – for example, narration. In this situation, the temporal processing of the material is controlled by the instructional designer – that is, the instructional designer can choose to present first only words and next only graphics or vice versa.

Other researchers have used the term *split-attention effect* to refer to any situation in which the learner must process incoming information from diverse sources; in particular, they refer to the temporal contiguity effect as a "temporal example of split attention" (Mousavi, Low, & Sweller, 1995, p. 320). *Split attention* refers to the need to integrate material from disparate sources, which is a broader concept than temporal contiguity (Ayres & Sweller, 2005). I prefer to separate the various forms of split attention because they translate more directly into clear design principles; therefore, in this book I devote separate chapters to spatial contiguity effects, temporal contiguity effects, and modality effects, all of which could be considered forms of split attention.

RESEARCH ON THE TEMPORAL CONTIGUITY PRINCIPLE

Core Evidence Concerning the Temporal Contiguity Principle

Do students learn more deeply when corresponding narration and animation are presented simultaneously than when they are presented successively, as proposed by the cognitive theory of multimedia learning? Or do students learn better from a multimedia presentation when animation and narration are presented successively than when they are presented simultaneously, as proposed by the information-delivery theory of multimedia learning?

To answer these questions, I review the results of eight experimental comparisons of students who learned from successive presentations versus students who learned from simultaneous presentations (Mayer & Anderson, 1991, Experiments 1 and 2a; Mayer & Anderson, 1992, Experiments 1 and 2; Mayer, Moreno, Boire, & Vagge, 1999, Experiments 1 and 2; Mayer & Sims, 1994, Experiments 1 and 2). In each test, we compared the transfer performance of students who received successive presentations with the performance of those who received simultaneous presentations, including explanations of lightning formation (Mayer, Moreno, Boire, & Vagge, 1999, Experiment 1), how the human respiratory system works (Mayer & Sims, 1994, Experiment 2), how car brakes work (Mayer & Anderson, 1992, Experiment 2; Mayer, Moreno, Boire, & Vagge, 1999, Experiment 1; Mayer & Sims, 1994, Experiment 2), and how pumps work (Mayer & Anderson, 1991, Experiments 1 and 2a; Mayer & Anderson, 1992, Experiment 1). All experiments involved animation and narration presented in a computer-based environment, and learners took the same transfer tests as described in previous chapters. According to the information-delivery theory, the successive presentation should result in better learning than the simultaneous presentation, whereas the cognitive theory of multimedia learning yields the opposite prediction.

Table 8.2 shows the source, content, format, and effect size for eight experimental comparisons of the transfer test performance of the simultaneous and successive groups. The first set of two studies in Table 8.2 involves learning from a narrated animation explaining how a bicycle tire pump works (Mayer & Anderson, 1991). For some learners (simultaneous group), the words of the narration were synchronized with the events depicted in the animation, so that, for example, when the narrator said "the inlet valve opens" the animation showed the inlet valve opening. For other learners (successive group), the entire narration was presented either before or after the entire animation. On subsequent tests of problem-solving transfer, the simultaneous group outperformed the successive group. As shown in the remaining rows of Table 8.2, similar results were obtained with narrated animations concerning tire pumps and brakes (Mayer & Anderson, 1992), tire pumps and the human respiratory system (Mayer & Sims, 1994), and lightning and brakes (Mayer, Moreno, Boire, & Vagge, 1999). Importantly, the results reported by Mayer and

Table 8.2. Core Evidence Concerning the Temporal Contiguity Principle

Source	Content	Format	Effect Size
Mayer & Anderson (1991, Expt. 1)	Tire pump	Computer	0.92
Mayer & Anderson (1991, Expt. 2a)	Tire pump	Computer	1.14
Mayer & Anderson (1992, Expt. 1)	Tire pump	Computer	1.66
Mayer & Anderson (1992, Expt. 2)	Brakes	Computer	1.39
Mayer & Sims (1994, Expt. 1)	Tire pump	Computer	0.91
Mayer & Sims (1994, Expt. 2)	Lungs	Computer	1.22
Mayer, Moreno, Boire, & Vagge (1999, Expt. 1)	Lightning	Computer	2.22
Mayer, Moreno, Boire, & Vagge (1999, Expt. 2)	Brakes	Computer	1.40
Median			1.31

Sims hold for high-spatial learners but not for low-spatial learners, suggesting that low-spatial learners are less able to take advantage of improvements in temporal contiguity.

As you can see in Table 8.2, on eight out of eight tests of problem-solving transfer students who received corresponding segments of animation and narration simultaneously performed much better on generating solutions to problems than did students who received the same segments successively. In all eight cases the effect sizes were large, yielding a median effect size of 1.31. Thus, there is strong and consistent support for the *temporal contiguity principle*: People learn more deeply from a multimedia message when corresponding animation and narration are presented simultaneously rather than successively. Overall, the results summarized in Table 8.2 are evidence in support of the cognitive theory of multimedia learning and against the information-delivery theory.

Related Evidence Concerning the Temporal Contiguity Principle

In a recent review, Ginns (2006) identified thirteen experimental comparisons of the test performance of students learning with simultaneous versus successive multimedia lessons. Consistent with our findings as summarized in Table 8.2, there was strong evidence of

Table 8.3. Related Evidence Concerning the Temporal Contiguity Principle

Source	Content	Format	Effect Size
Baggett & Ehrenfeucht (1983, immediate)	Carnivorous plants	Movie	1.40
Baggett & Ehrenfeucht (1983, delayed)	Carnivorous plants	Movie	0.27
Baggett (1984, immediate)	Toy construction	Movie	0.48
Baggett (1984, delayed)	Toy construction	Movie	0.74
Moreno & Mayer (1999, Expt. 2)	Lightning	Computer	0.12
Mayer et al. (1999, Expt. 1)	Lightning	Computer	0.24
Mayer et al. (1999, Expt. 2)	Brakes	Computer	0.05
Michas & Berry (2000, Expt. 3)	Bandaging procedure	Computer	0.09

a temporal contiguity effect, yielding a median effect size of $d = .87$. Ginns (2006, p. 511) concluded, "the analyses indicate that, for complex learning materials in particular, increasing...temporal contiguity...can lead to substantial learning gains."

Table 8.3 lists the source, content, format, and effect size for several additional comparisons between groups that learned with simultaneous versus successive presentations of words and pictures. As summarized in the first four lines of Table 8.3, research on temporal contiguity has its roots in the classic studies by Baggett and her colleagues (Baggett, 1984; Baggett & Ehrenfeucht, 1983) in which students viewed films with voice overlay. For example, Baggett and Ehrenfeucht (1983) asked college students in the successive group to view an eleven-minute narrated movie on carnivorous plants, entitled "Plant Traps: Insect Catchers of the Bog Jungle." By contrast, students in the successive group saw the movie and then heard the narration or vice versa. On a test of memory for facts, the simultaneous group outperformed the successive group at a high level for an immediate test ($d = 1.40$) and at a lower level for a delayed test given a week after instruction ($d = .27$).

In a similar study, Baggett (1984) asked college students to view a film showing how to use an assembly kit called Fischer Technik 50, which is similar to Legos. For some students, the corresponding sound and images were presented simultaneously (as in our simultaneous group); for others, the sound track preceded the corresponding visual material by twenty-one seconds, or the sound track followed the visual material by twenty-one seconds (similar to our successive group).

After the multimedia presentation, students were tested on their memory for the names of the pieces in the assembly kit. In particular, for each test item, they were shown a piece and asked to write down its name. Students who received the simultaneous presentation performed better on the test than students in the twenty-one-second mismatch groups, yielding effect sizes of $d = .48$ on an immediate test and $d = .74$ on a delayed test that was given one week after instruction. Overall, across all four comparisons, this research is the first to demonstrate a temporal contiguity effect for instructional materials. However, the conclusion is limited by the lack of a transfer test as the dependent measure and by some difficulties in determining appropriate standard deviations for computing effect size. The research reported in this chapter extends Baggett's classic work by using tests that are intended to measure understanding rather than solely measuring retention and by comparing simultaneous presentations to successive presentations rather than to ones in which the sound and images are misaligned.

Boundary Conditions of the Temporal Contiguity Principle

The remaining studies in Table 8.3 suggest two possible boundary conditions for the temporal contiguity principle, including when the verbal and pictorial segments are short rather than long and when the lesson is learner-paced rather than system-paced. First, as summarized in the fifth through seventh lines of Table 8.3, my colleagues and I carried out three related comparisons (Mayer, Moreno, Boire, & Vagge, 1999, Experiments 1 & 2; Moreno & Mayer, 1999, Experiment 2), in which we compared the test performance of students who learned about lightning formation or car brakes from successive small-segments presentations and from a simultaneous presentation. In the successive small-segments presentations, some students listened to a short portion of the narration describing one major step and then viewed a short animation segment depicting the same step, and so on for each of many short segments, and other students viewed a animation segment followed by a corresponding narration segment, and so on for each of many short segments. The successive small-segments presentation is different from the successive presentation described for the previous experiments in Table 8.2; the successive small-segments presentation involves many alternations between a short narration followed (or preceded) by a short animation, whereas the successive presentation involves the entire narration followed (or preceded) by the entire animation. In sum, the successive presentation used in the

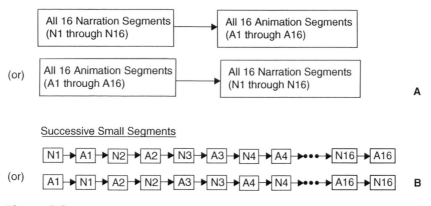

Figure 8.2. Successive presentation of narration and animation for (A) large segments (top frame) and (B) small segments (bottom frame). *Note*: The designations N1–N16 refer to the sixteen narration segments, and A1–A16 refer to the sixteen animation segments.

previous studies involved successive large segments (i.e., the entire animation followed by the entire narration or vice versa), whereas the successive presentation used in these follow-up studies involved successive small segments (e.g., ten seconds of narration followed by ten seconds of animation and so on, or vice versa). Figure 8.2 summarizes the procedure for the successive large-segments presentation used in the previous studies (top panel) and for the successive small-segments presentation used in these follow-up studies (bottom panel). The simultaneous presentation treatment was the same as in the previously described experiments – that is, the entire animation followed by the entire narration or vice versa.

We created the successive small-segments presentation to provide an additional way of testing the information-delivery and cognitive theories of multimedia learning. According to the information-delivery theory, as in the previous studies, the successive small-segments presentation should result in better test performance than the simultaneous presentation. In the successive small-segments version, students receive two exposures to the same material – one in verbal form followed (or preceded) by one in visual form. In addition, students in the successive small-segments group have twice as much time to study the material as compared to the students who receive the simultaneous presentation.

By contrast, consider what happens in the learner's information-processing system according to the cognitive theory of multimedia learning. In the successive small-segments group, students are able to hold a verbal description of a step in the explanation and a visual depiction of the same step at the same time in their working memory, thus allowing students to mentally integrate corresponding visual and verbal material. The capacity of working memory is not exceeded because the segments are short, thus enabling students to engage in meaningful learning. This situation contrasts with the successive presentations used in the previous experiments where the entire narration was presented before (or after) the entire animation. In that case, there was less chance that corresponding verbal and visual representations would be in working memory at the same time. In short, the successive small-segments presentation enables the same kind of active cognitive processing as simultaneous presentations, so the cognitive theory of multimedia learning predicts no difference between the groups.

As can be seen in rows five through seven of Table 8.3, there is not a strong temporal contiguity effect for transfer. Presenting animation and narration simultaneously resulted in essentially equivalent transfer performance as presenting animation and narration successively in small segments. The median effect size is below .20, which is considered negligible, thus confirming the prediction of no large differences between the groups. Thus, an important boundary condition is that the temporal contiguity principle does not hold when the segment sizes are small rather than large.

Lastly, the final line of Table 8.3 summarizes a study by Michas and Berry in which college students learned a bandaging procedure by watching a series of slides on a computer screen. In the successive group, students saw a series of seven line drawings followed by a series of seven text descriptions or vice versa, whereas in the simultaneous group they saw a series of seven slides – each containing a line drawing and corresponding text. However, in both conditions the learners were able to control the pace and order of the presentation by clicking on "next," "previous," and "go to start" buttons. In this study, there was no significant temporal contiguity effect ($d = .09$), perhaps because students could control the pace and order of the presentation and because the lesson was short. The authors noted that "after looking at the full set of text and line drawings, the majority of learners revisited the set of drawings more than the text" (Michas & Berry, 2000, p. 570). Overall, it appears that another important boundary condition for the temporal contiguity principle is that the principle applies most strongly when the lesson is fast-paced and the learner cannot control the pace or order of presentation.

IMPLICATIONS OF THE TEMPORAL CONTIGUITY PRINCIPLE

Implications for Multimedia Learning

The research reported in this chapter is largely inconsistent with the information-delivery theory of multimedia learning, and its commonsense notion that two deliveries of the same information must be better than one. Clearly, our results show that something is wrong with the seemingly obvious idea that learning occurs when students add presented information to their memory. In particular, the research on temporal contiguity fails to support the prediction that the successive group will outperform the simultaneous group.

By contrast, research on temporal contiguity provides consistent support for the cognitive theory of multimedia learning. Overall, when animation and narration are separated in time by more than a few seconds, students perform more poorly on problem-solving transfer than when animation and narration are presented simultaneously (or very near each other in time). We refer to this finding as the *temporal contiguity principle*: Separating corresponding words and pictures in time detracts from multimedia learning.

Why does simultaneous presentation aid students in their quest for making sense of a multimedia explanation? According to the cognitive theory of multimedia learning, simultaneous presentations mesh well with the way humans are designed to process incoming material – that is, simultaneous presentations are more consistent with the way the human mind works. In particular, simultaneous presentations take advantage of (a) the dual-channel capabilities of humans, by providing narration to the ears and animation to the eyes; (b) the limited capacity of each channel, by not requiring that learners hold a lot of material in either channel; and (c) the need for active cognitive processing, by encouraging learners to make connections between corresponding visual and verbal representations. In short, the cognitive advantage of simultaneous presentation is that corresponding words and pictures can more easily be held in working memory at the same time, thus encouraging learners to build connections between words and pictures.

Implications for Multimedia Instruction

The temporal contiguity effect yields an important design principle: Present corresponding words and pictures at the same time rather than far from each other in time. As you can see, the *temporal contiguity principle* complements the *spatial contiguity principle* (discussed in Chapter 7), which calls for presenting corresponding words and pictures near rather than far from each other on the page or screen. Together, these two contiguity principles form the basis of our premier recommendations for how to design understandable multimedia messages. If we want students to build cognitive connections between corresponding words and pictures, it is helpful to present them contiguously in time and space – that is, to present them at the same time or next to each other on the page or screen.

The temporal contiguity principle provides an important example of what is wrong with assuming that the instructional designer's job is to present information. Even though the simultaneous and successive presentations contain the same animation and narration, students do not appear to learn equally well from them. Apparently, students also benefit from some guidance concerning how to process the incoming material. Simultaneous presentations prime the learner to build connections between corresponding visual and verbal material, whereas successive presentations make this active cognitive processing much more difficult by creating extraneous processing. Thus, instructional design involves not just presenting information, but also presenting it in a way that encourages learners to engage in appropriate cognitive processing.

Limitations and Future Directions

Research on temporal contiguity yields two important boundary conditions: The principle may not apply as strongly to situations in which (1) the successive verbal and pictorial segments are short rather than long or in which (2) the lesson is learner-paced rather than system-paced. First, the temporal contiguity effect essentially disappeared when we broke the successive presentation into alternating bite-sized segments – such as segments containing 8 to 10 seconds of narration followed or preceded by 8 to 10 seconds of animation, and so on – rather than having 140 seconds of narration followed or preceded by 140 seconds of animation (Mayer et al., 1999; Moreno & Mayer, 1999). We chose this size because we thought it would not exceed the holding capacity of working memory, so that the learner could hold a sentence in working memory until the corresponding animation segment was presented or could hold a few visual images in memory until the corresponding sentence of narration was presented. Further research is needed to determine what constitutes an ideal segment size.

Second, the temporal contiguity effect did not materialize when students received a multimedia lesson on how to bandage a wound under learner control rather than under system control (Michas & Berry, 2000). Further research is needed in which the same simultaneous and successive lessons are presented under learner control and under system control. This boundary condition would be better justified if there is a strong temporal contiguity effect with system control – that is, a fast-paced presentation that is paced by the computer – but not with learner control – that is, a presentation where the learner can control when the next slide or segment is presented and can visit previous slides or segments.

It should be noted that both of these limitations on the spatial contiguity principle are consistent with the cognitive theory of multimedia learning, and therefore provide useful extensions of the theory. Instructional designers should not view the temporal contiguity principle as an immutable law that must apply to all situations, but rather should apply it in ways that are consistent with what we know about how people process words and pictures in their cognitive systems.

SUGGESTED READINGS

Asterisk (*) indicates that part of this chapter is based on this publication.

Ginns, P. (2006). Integrating information: A meta-analysis of the spatial contiguity and temporal contiguity effects. *Learning and Instruction, 16,* 511–525.

*Mayer, R. E., & Anderson, R. B. (1991). Animations need narrations: An experimental test of a dual-coding hypothesis. *Journal of Educational Psychology, 83,* 484–490.

*Mayer, R. E., & Anderson, R. B. (1992). The instructive animation: Helping students build connections between words and pictures in multimedia learning. *Journal of Educational Psychology, 84,* 444–452.

*Mayer, R. E., Moreno, R., Boire, M., & Vagge, S. (1999). Maximizing constructivist learning from multimedia communications by minimizing cognitive load. *Journal of Educational Psychology, 91,* 638–643.

*Mayer, R. E., & Sims, V. K. (1994). For whom is a picture worth a thousand words? Extensions of a dual-coding theory of multimedia learning. *Journal of Educational Psychology, 84,* 389–401.

*Moreno, R., & Mayer, R. E. (1999). Cognitive principles of multimedia learning: The role of modality and contiguity. *Journal of Educational Psychology, 91,* 358–368.

Section III

Principles for Managing Essential Processing in Multimedia Learning

Consider the following situation. You are interested in how the human digestive system works, so you go to an online encyclopedia and click on a movie icon labeled "How Digestion Works." You watch a series of eighteen slides, each appearing for about ten seconds and each containing a line drawing on the right and one or two sentences on the left. The lesson feels too fast-paced to you, because as soon as you finish your initial reading of one slide, the next one begins. As a result you don't have time to compare the sentences to the line drawing, or to draw causal connections from one slide to the next. On a subsequent retention test, you can remember parts of some of the sentences, and on a transfer test, you are not able to apply what was presented to solving new problems.

What is essential processing overload? This situation is an example of *essential processing overload* – that is, a situation in which the cognitive processing of the basic material in the lesson is so demanding that there is little or no remaining cognitive capacity to engage in deeper processing of the material (which I call *generative processing*). Essential processing overload is likely to happen when the essential material is complex, the learner is inexperienced, and the presentation is fast-paced. Box 3.1 summarizes two types of essential overload situations – one in which the material is so complex that the learner is unable to completely represent it in the time allowed, and one in which the complexity of the material is exacerbated by presenting words in printed form.

What is essential material? Essential material is the core information from the lesson that is needed to achieve the instructional goal. If the goal is to understand how digestion works, then the essential material consists of the words and graphics that describe the steps in the digestion process.

Box 3.1   What Is Essential Processing Overload?

Scenario 3: Essential processing (in both channels) > cognitive capacity

Description: Both channels are overloaded by essential processing demands.

Example: Fast-paced multimedia lesson with complex material and inexperienced learners

Principles: Segmenting and pre-training

Scenario 4: Essential processing (in visual channel) > cognitive capacity

Description: Visual channel is overloaded by essential processing demands.

Example: Printed words in a fast-paced multimedia lesson with complex material and inexperienced learners

Principle: Modality

What is essential processing? Essential processing is cognitive processing aimed at mentally representing the essential material in working memory. This form of processing is indicated by the *selecting* arrows in Figure 3.1 in Chapter 3. In the digestion example, essential processing involves paying attention to the key steps in the digestion process so that they are transferred to working memory, and eventually encoded in long-term memory.

How can we manage essential processing? In this section of the book, I address the problem of essential processing overload. In particular, as summarized in Box 3.2, we explore three principles for managing essential processing – segmenting (Chapter 9), pre-training (Chapter 10), and modality principles (Chapter 11). Segmenting involves breaking a whole presentation into coherent parts that can

---

Box 3.2   Three Ways to Manage Essential Processing

Principle	*Description*
Segmenting:	Present lesson in user-paced segments rather than as a continuous unit.
Pre-training:	Precede lesson with pre-training in the names and characteristics of key components.
Modality:	Present lesson using pictures and spoken words rather than pictures and printed words.

---

be digested sequentially. Pre-training involves helping learners get to know the names and characteristics of key concepts before receiving the whole presentation. Modality involves presenting the words as spoken text rather than as printed text. These techniques do not eliminate the need for essential processing, but they help manage essential processing in such a way that generative processing is also possible.

9

Segmenting Principle

Segmenting Principle: *People learn better when a multimedia message is presented in user-paced segments rather than as a continuous unit.*

Example: *A continuous version consists of a narrated animation on lightning formation that lasts about two and half minutes and describes sixteen steps. A segmented version consists of the same lesson, broken into sixteen segments – each containing one or two sentences and eight to ten seconds of corresponding animation – with a* CONTINUE *button in the lower-right corner. The next segment begins as soon as the learner clicks on* CONTINUE.

Theoretical Rationale: *In viewing a fast-paced narrated animation that explains the steps in a process, some learners may not fully comprehend one step in the process before the next one is presented, and thus, they may not have time to see the causal relation between one step and the next.*

Empirical Rationale: *In three out of three tests, people performed better on problem-solving transfer tests when a narrated animation was presented in bite-sized segments, each initiated by the learner, rather than as a continuous unit. The effect size was d = 0.98.*

Boundary Conditions: *The segmenting principle is most likely to apply when the material is complex, the presentation is fast-paced, and the learner is inexperienced with the material.*

▩ ▨ Chapter Outline

175

INTRODUCTION TO THE SEGMENTING PRINCIPLE

What Is Segmenting?

Consider a situation in which you view a fast-paced narrated animation on material that is not familiar to you. For example, the narrated animation lasts about two and a half minutes and describes the steps in the process of lightning formation (such as shown in Figure 2.2 in Chapter 2). You are not quite able to completely digest one step before the next one is presented, so you are not able to build a causal model of the system in which a change in one part causes a change in the next one. Therefore, when you are tested, you may be able to remember some isolated facts (on a retention test), but you have trouble using the material to solve new problems (on a transfer test).

In this situation your working memory is overloaded, that is, the cognitive processing needed to mentally represent the complexity of the essential material (in this case, a causal model of how lightning develops) exceeds your available cognitive capacity. What can be done to help learners in situations in which the required essential processing exceeds the learner's available cognitive capacity – in short, how can we manage essential processing?

Segmenting is an instructional design technique that is intended to help learners manage essential cognitive processing. In segmenting, we break a complex multimedia message into smaller parts that are presented sequentially with pacing under the learner's control. Thus, the two key features of segmenting are (a) breaking a lesson into parts that are presented sequentially, and (b) allowing the learning to control the pacing of movement from one part to the next.

For example, in the case of the lightning lesson, we can break the lesson into sixteen segments – each covering one or two sentences and eight to ten seconds of animation. Each segment describes one key event in the causal chain, as you can see in Table 9.1. At the end of each segment, a CONTINUE key appears in the lower right corner of the screen, as shown in Figure 9.1. When the learner clicks on the

Table 9.1. Breaking the Lightning Lesson into Sixteen Segments

1. Cool, moist air moves over a warmer surface and becomes heated.
2. Warmed moist air near the earth's surface rises rapidly.
3. As the air in this updraft cools, water vapor condenses into water droplets and forms a cloud.
4. The cloud's top extends above the freezing level, so the upper portion of the cloud is composed of tiny ice crystals.
5. Eventually, the water droplets and ice crystals become too large to be suspended by updrafts.
6. As raindrops and ice crystals fall through the cloud, they drag some of the air in the cloud downward, producing downdrafts.
7. When downdrafts strike the ground, they spread out in all directions, producing the gusts of cool wind people feel just before the start of the rain.
8. Within the cloud, the rising and falling air currents cause electrical charges to build.
9. The charge results from the collision of the cloud's rising water droplets against heavier, falling pieces of ice.
10. The negatively charged particles fall to the bottom of the cloud, and most of the positively charged particles rise to the top.
11. A stepped leader of negative charges moves downward in a series of steps. It nears the ground.
12. A positively charged leader travels up from objects such as trees and buildings.
13. The two leaders generally meet about 165 feet above the ground.
14. Negatively charged particles then rush from the cloud to the ground along the path created by the leaders. It is not very bright.
15. As the leader stroke nears the ground, it induces an opposite charge, so positively charged particles from the ground rush upward along the same path.
16. The upward motion of the current is the return stroke. It produces the bright light that people notice as a flash of lightning.

CONTINUE key, the next segment is presented, and so on. Thus, this example includes the two key features of segmenting – breaking the lesson into parts that are presented sequentially and allowing learners to control the time between the end of one segment and the start of the next one. In this way, the learner can intellectually digest one bite-sized segment before moving on to the next one.

Segmenting is similar to *modular presentation* – in which a worked example is presented in a sequence of meaningful clusters of steps – and *simplified whole task presentation* – in which a complex multimedia presentation is broken down into a sequence that starts with a less

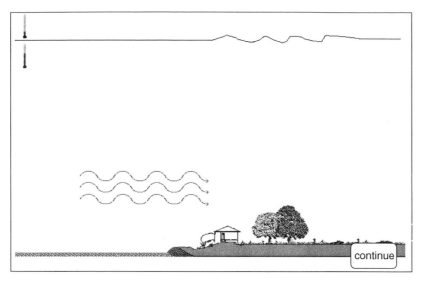

"Cool moist air moves over a warmer surface and becomes heated."

Figure 9.1. Frame from the segmented version of the lightning lesson.

complex version (Gerjets, Scheiter, & Catrambone, 2004; van Merrienboer & Kester, 2005; van Merrienboer, Kirschner, & Kester, 2003).

How Does Segmenting Work?

Consider what happens in the learner's information-processing system when the complexity of essential material in a multimedia lesson (such as a fast-paced narrated animation) exceeds the learner's cognitive capacity. For example, as shown in Figure 3.1 in Chapter 3, pictures enter through the eyes, and if attended to, they are represented as images in working memory; similarly, spoken words enter through the ears, and if attended to, they are represented as words in working memory. However, if the lesson is fast-paced, the learner may not have enough capacity to mentally organize the words into a verbal model and mentally organize the pictures into a pictorial model. Similarly, the learner may not have enough capacity to mentally integrate the verbal and pictorial models with each other and with other steps in the causal chain. In short, the learner may be able to capture some of the fragments of the lesson (indicated by the *selecting* arrows) but may be unable to engage in deep processing (indicated by the *organizing* and *integrating* arrows). Thus, the learner is less able to build a meaningful learning outcome that can be used to support problem-solving transfer.

By contrast, consider what happens when a fast-paced narrated animation is segmented into bite-sized segments that can be controlled by the learner. After viewing one segment, the learner is able to complete the deeper cognitive processes of organizing the essential material into coherent cognitive structures and integrating the cognitive structures with each other and with other steps in the causal chain. Then the learner can click on the CONTINUE button to go on to the next segment, and so on. In this way, the learner is better able to engage in deep cognitive processing of the essential material in the lesson. Thus, the learner is better able to build a meaningful learning outcome that can be used to support problem-solving transfer.

RESEARCH ON THE SEGMENTING PRINCIPLE

Based on this theoretical analysis, students who receive a segmented lesson should perform better on a problem-solving transfer test than students who receive a continuous lesson. This prediction was tested in a series of three experiments conducted in our lab (i.e., core evidence) as well as in related experiments (i.e., related evidence).

Core Evidence Concerning the Segmenting Principle

Do students learn more deeply when a narrated animation is presented in learner-controlled segments rather than as a continuous unit? Table 9.2 shows the source, content, format, and effect size for three experimental tests of the segmenting principle carried out in our lab, in which we compared the problem-solving transfer test performance of students who learned with continuous and segmented lessons. First, Mayer and Chandler (2001) compared the problem-solving transfer test performance of students who viewed a 140-second narrated animation on lightning formation as a continuous presentation (i.e., continuous group) to the test performance of students who viewed the same presentation broken into 16 segments (i.e., segmented group). Each segment explained one major step in the process of lightning formation; it contained one or two sentences of narration along with approximately eight to ten seconds of corresponding animation. After the animation segment was complete, a CONTINUE button appeared in the lower-right corner of the screen. When the learner clicked on the button, the next segment was

Table 9.2.   Core Evidence Concerning the Segmenting Principle

Source	Content	Format	Effect Size
Mayer & Chandler (2001, Expt. 2)	Lightning	Computer	1.13
Mayer, Dow, & Mayer (2003, Expt. 2a)	Electric motor	Computer	0.82
Mayer, Dow, & Mayer (2003, Expt. 2b)	Electric motor	Computer	0.98
Median			0.98

presented, so the learner had some control over the pace of the presentation. The procedure was repeated, so the learner saw the continuous presentation twice or the segmented presentation twice. The top line of Table 9.2 shows that the segmented group out-performed the continuous group, yielding an effect size of 1.13.

Second, Mayer, Dow, and Mayer (2003) compared the problem-solving transfer test performance of students who learned how an electric motor works from a continuous narrated animation presented by an on-screen agent named Dr. Phyz to the performance of students who learned from a segmented version of the lesson. In the continuous version, when the learner clicked on the START button, a narrated animation appeared in which Dr. Phyz explained the steps in the operation of an electric motor, including what goes on in the battery, wires, commutator, wire loop, and magnet when the motor is in the start position, rotated a quarter turn, rotated a half turn, rotated three-quarters turn, and rotated a full turn. In the segmented version, five questions appeared in the upper-right corner of the screen – "What happens when the motor is at the start position?," "What happens when the motor has rotated a quarter turn?," "What happens when the motor has rotated a half turn?," "What happens when the motor has rotated three-quarters turn?," and "What happens when the motor has rotated a full turn?" A frame from the segmented version is shown in Figure 9.2. When the learner clicked on a question, a corresponding portion from the continuous narrated animation was presented. By clicking on the five questions in order, the learner would see all the material from the continuous narrated animation. Thus, the segmented versions allowed the learners to digest a portion of the narrated animation before moving on to the next. In two experiments – Experiment 2a, with an immediate test, and Experiment 2b, with a delayed test given one week after instruction – the segmented

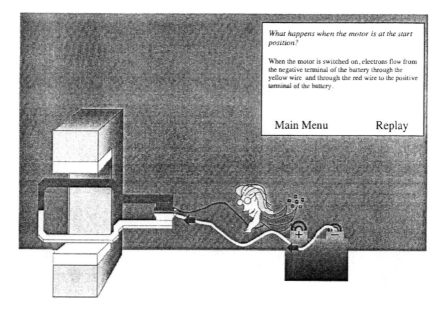

What happens when the motor is at the start position?

When the motor is switched on, electrons flow from the negative terminal of the battery through the yellow wire and through the red wire to the positive terminal of the battery.

Main Menu   Replay

Figure 9.2. Frame from the segmented version of the Dr. Phyz lesson.

group outperformed the continuous group on a problem-solving transfer test. The bottom two rows of Table 9.2 show that the effect sizes were $d = 0.82$ and 0.98, respectively.

Overall, the experimental tests summarized in Table 9.2 show large effects favoring the segmented group over the continuous group, with a median effect size of $d = 0.98$. These three experimental tests provide encouraging preliminary evidence for the *segmenting principle*: People learn more deeply when a multimedia message is presented in user-paced segments rather than as a continuous unit.

Related Evidence Concerning the Segmenting Principle

The essence of the segmenting principle is that when the essential material is too complex for the learner to grasp all at once, the material should be broken into smaller segments that the learner studies sequentially. In the previous section, I defined the segmenting principle with respect to a specific situation – a fast-paced narrated animation overloads the learner's working memory. In this section, let's examine research that involves related situations other than narrated animations – including comprehending functional relations

Table 9.3. Related Evidence Concerning the Segmenting Principle

Source	Content	Format	Effect Size
Mautone & Mayer (2007, Expt. 2)	Geography	Computer	0.60
Lee, Plass, & Homer (2006)	Chemistry	Computer	0.29
Ayres (2006, Expt. 1a)	Mathematics	Paper	0.78
Ayres (2006, Expt. 2a)	Mathematics	Paper	0.56
Gerjets, Scheiter, & Catrambone (2006, Expt. 1a)	Probability	Computer	0.86
Gerjets, Scheiter, & Catrambone (2006, Expt. 2a)	Probability	Computer	0.93

from a complex geography graph, comprehending functional relations from a complex chemistry simulation, learning to solve multistep math computation problems, and learning to solve multistep probability problems. This exemplary research related to segmenting is summarized in Table 9.3.

First, based on the first experiment in Table 9.3 (Mautone & Mayer, 2007), consider a situation in which a student has five minutes to write down a description of a complex scientific graph, such as the geography graph shown in Figure 9.3. The graph shows several functional relations, involving several different variables, such as, "The heavier the particle, the higher the velocity needed to transport it"; "The heavier the particle, the lower the velocity threshold at which it gets deposited"; and "The heavier the particle, the lower the velocity needed to erode it, up to a midpoint, at which point, the heavier it is, the greater the velocity required." Before this test, some students view the graph on a laptop computer screen for as long they like until they feel they understand what it says (control group), whereas other students view a series of slides (using PowerPoint on a laptop computer) that present the graph in successive layers (segmented group). For example, the slides in the segmented lesson begin with the x-axis, and in the next slide the y-axis is added; then sections of the curves for deposition, transportation, and erosion are added, starting on the left side beginning first with lines and then adding colored areas; and this is repeated for each progressive section of the curves going toward the right. Students controlled the pace by pressing an arrow key to move on to the next slide. On the

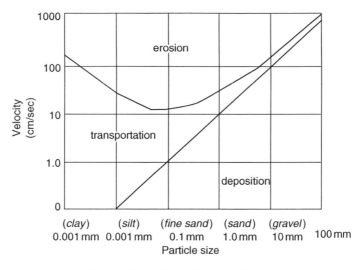

Figure 9.3. The Hjulstrom Curve.

subsequent test in which they had five minutes to write a description of the graph, students in the segmented group included more descriptions of the functional relations than did students in the control group, yielding an effect size of $d = 0.60$.

In a somewhat related experiment, summarized in the second row of the table, Lee, Plass, and Homer (2006) asked students to interact with a computer-based simulation on ideal gas laws in chemistry. In the control version, seventh grade students in Korea saw a single frame showing the relations among pressure, temperature, and volume. The student could enter values for some variables and then run the simulation to see the effects. In the segmented version, students could work on two screens in succession – one showing the relation between pressure and volume, and the other showing the relation between temperature and volume. The student could enter values for some variables and then run the simulation to see the effects by switching back and forth between the two screens. Students had fifteen minutes to enter variables and run the simulations, and then took a problem-solving transfer test. Overall, students in the segmented group performed better on the problem-solving transfer test than did the control group ($d = 0.29$). This effect was particularly strong for students with high prior knowledge ($d = 0.58$), presumably because they had the metacognitive skill to know how best to manage toggling between the two screens.

The third and fourth lines of the table summarize a study by Ayres (2006) in which eighth graders in Australia learned to solve bracket expansion problems, such as $-3(5x - 2) + 9(7 - 2x)$, either as a single unit or as four sequential computations. For example, a worked example for the control group is:

$$-3(5x - 2) + 9(7 - 2x)$$
$$= -3 * 5x - 3 * -2 + 9 * 7 + 9 * -2x$$
$$= -15x + 6 + 63 - 18x$$

By contrast, a worked example for the segmented group focused on one computation at a time, such as:

$$-3(5x - 2) + 9(7 - 2x)$$
$$\downarrow$$
$$= -3 * 5x$$
$$= -15x$$

On a subsequent test involving different bracket expansion problems (with no arrows or worked examples), the segmented group outperformed the control group ($d = .78$). In a follow-up experiment, the same pattern was obtained for lower-ability students ($d = .56$) but not for higher-ability students, reflecting an expertise reversal effect (Kalyuga, 2005).

Finally, the remaining lines in Table 9.3 are based on teaching students how to solve probability problems with worked-out examples by using a modular approach in which the problem is broken into a sequence of meaningful subgoals (segmenting group) or by using a molar approach in which the problem solution involves using an entire formula as a single unit (control group). For example, Gerjets, Scheiter, and Catrambone (2006) provided worked-out examples to teach college students to solve problems such as, "At the Olympics, seven sprinters participate in the 100-meter sprint. What is the probability of correctly guessing the winner of the gold, the silver, and the bronze medals?" In the molar version (control group), students learn to identify the problem type as "permutation-without-placement," select the formula $A = n!/(n-k)!$, insert values into the formula, and calculate the probability. In the modular version (segmented group), students learn to find the probability of the first event (1/7), find the probability of the second event (1/6), find the probability of the third event (1/5), and multiply them together to calculate the overall probability. On a subsequent test involving novel problems, the segmented group outperformed the control group ($d = .86$ in Experiment 1 and $d = .93$ in Experiment 2, for conditions that did not involve other manipulations as well). Similar results were reported by Catrambone (1994, 1995, 1998). In a review of experiments comparing modular and molar worked-out examples for teaching students how to solve probability problems, Gerjets, Scheiter, and Catrambone (2004, p. 33) concluded that "processing modular examples is associated with a lower degree of intrinsic cognitive load, and thus, improves learning."

This related research helps to broaden the applicability of the segmenting principle beyond narrated animations – to include a variety of complex multimedia learning tasks. In particular, segmenting can be expanded to include modularizing worked-out examples and breaking complex scientific graphs into layers.

Boundary Conditions of the Segmenting Principle

Based on the cognitive theory of multimedia learning, segmenting is most likely to have its strongest impact when the material is complex, the presentation is fast-paced, and the learners are inexperienced with the material. These are the conditions that are most likely to create a high level of essential processing, so steps to manage essential processing would be warranted. Consistent with this prediction, in each of the studies reported in the section on core evidence and related evidence that found a segmenting effect, the material was complex and the presentation was fast-paced. Also as predicted, in the experiment conducted by Ayres (2006) the effect of segmenting was strongest for low-experience learners. More research is needed to pinpoint the boundary conditions of the segmenting principle.

IMPLICATIONS OF THE SEGMENTING PRINCIPLE

Implications for Multimedia Learning

According to the cognitive theory of multimedia learning, essential processing is cognitive processing aimed at mentally representing the content in working memory (as indicated by the *selecting* arrow in Figure 3.1). When the to-be-learned material is complex for the learner, the learner must engage in a high level of essential processing. The need for a high level of essential processing can reduce the remaining capacity available for deeper cognitive processing required to support transfer performance (as indicated by the *organizing* and *integrating* arrows). Thus, techniques for managing essential processing during the learning of complex materials increase opportunities for deep processing and lead to improvements in the learner's problem-solving transfer performance. Research on segmenting provides support for this view of how multimedia learning works.

How can we measure the complexity of to-be-learned material? Sweller (1999) and others (Elen & Clark, 2006) have argued that complexity depends on the number of interacting elements – that is, the number of relations between elements – that must be processed at one time. However, complexity depends not only on the material in the lesson but also on the knowledge of the learner, because what constitutes an element depends in part on the learner's schemas for chunking the material in the lesson. Elen and Clark (2006, p. 2) note that complexity depends on "the interaction between the characteristics of tasks and the characteristics of individual learners." The calibration of the complexity of a lesson remains a fundamental theoretical challenge.

Implications for Multimedia Instruction

The practical implications of the segmenting principle are straightforward: When the essential material in a narrated animation is too complex – that is, when processing the essential material requires more capacity than is available to the learner – then break the narrated animation into meaningful segments that can be presented under the learner's control. Each segment should express a coherent step (or group of steps) in a process. When the to-be-learned material is a worked-out example, then break the list of steps into meaningful segments (or modules) that can be studied under the learner's control. Each segment (or module) should accomplish a clear subgoal. When the to-be-learned material is a complex graph showing functional relations among more than two variables, then break the graph into a set of less complex graphs that show just some of the variables at one time. A subgraph, for example, could show the functional relation between two variables. The overarching theme in applying the segmenting principle is to break complex material into more manageable parts that can be processed sequentially rather than all at once.

Limitations and Future Directions

If user control of pacing is useful, should designers incorporate slider bars or pause/continue buttons for all animations and video clips? Consider the implications for working memory with learners who are novices. When a learner has to decide when to use the slider bar or pause button, the decision-making process requires cognitive processing, which reduces the remaining capacity that can be used for making sense of the material. In short, giving the learner a great deal of control – through using the slider or pause button – also creates a great deal of extraneous cognitive processing. When using slider bars, the need for extraneous processing can be exacerbated because learners may have difficulty in moving back to the exact starting point of the segment. A related problem with incorporating slider bars and pause/continue buttons is that novice learners may lack the metacognitive skills to know where to pause, that is, learners may not be able to accurately evaluate whether they need to stop in order to digest a portion of the lesson. By contrast, in the user-paced segments examined in the three experiments summarized in Table 9.2, the segments corresponded to steps in the process, and the program automatically stopped at the end of each segment. In this way, the learner did not have to engage in the extraneous processing of determining how to segment the lesson. Research is needed to determine the relative effectiveness of continue buttons based on instructor-determined segments (as used in these experiments) versus pause/continue buttons and slider bars without instructor-determined segments.

Does this research suggest that segmenting should always be used? The answer is: no. The cognitive theory of multimedia learning suggests that segmenting may have its strongest effects when the material is complex rather than simple, when the learner has low prior knowledge rather than high prior knowledge, and when the lesson is fast-paced rather than slow-paced (or learner-paced). For example, concerning prior knowledge, research on the expertise reversal effect (Kalyuga, 2005) suggests that less-experienced learners may benefit more from continue buttons based on instructor-determined segments, whereas more experienced learners may benefit more from slider bars and pause/continue buttons, although this prediction needs to be subjected to empirical testing. For example, Ayres (2006) found evidence that segmenting of worked examples for math problems had a strong effect for lower-ability students but not for higher-ability students. Further research is needed to determine the role of the learner's prior knowledge in the segmenting effect. Similarly, research is needed to determine how the complexity of the material and the pace of presentation affect the segmenting principle.

Finally, another important issue concerns the optimal size of a segment. Research on working memory (Baddeley, 1999) suggests that learners are able to hold only a few pieces of information at a time – suggesting that the optimal size may be fairly small. Some of the research reported in this chapter also suggests that the segments should present a coherent conceptual unit of the material, such as a step in a process. Research is needed to determine what constitutes a bite-sized segment.

SUGGESTED READINGS

Asterisk (*) indicates that a portion of this chapter is based on this publication.

Ayres, P. (2006). Impact of reducing intrinsic cognitive load on learning in a mathematical domain. *Applied Cognitive Psychology, 20,* 287–298.

*Mayer, R. E., & Chandler, P. (2001). When learning is just a click away: Does simple user interaction foster deeper understanding of multimedia messages? *Journal of Educational Psychology, 93,* 390–397.

*Mayer, R. E., Dow, G., & Mayer, S. (2003). Multimedia learning in an interactive self-explaining environment: What works in the design of agent-based microworlds. *Journal of Educational Psychology, 95,* 806–813.

10

Pre-training Principle

Pre-training Principle: People learn more deeply from a multimedia message when they know the names and characteristics of the main concepts.

Example: A no pre-training version consists of a multimedia lesson such as a narrated animation explaining how a car's braking system works. A pre-training version consists of a multimedia lesson preceded by training on the names and characteristics of the key parts, such as a narrated animation on how a car's braking system works preceded by training that shows the location of the piston in the master cylinder, the brake tube, the wheel cylinders, and so on, as well as the states that each part can be in.

Theoretical Rationale: In viewing a fast-paced narrated animation that explains the steps in a process, learners have to mentally construct a causal model of the system (i.e., a model of how the system works) as well as component models for each key part in the system (i.e., a model of the key states that each part can be in). Pre-training can help manage these two demands for essential processing by distributing some processing to a pre-training episode that occurs before the main lesson.

Empirical Rationale: In five out of five tests, people performed better on problem-solving transfer tests when a multimedia lesson was preceded by pre-training in the names and characteristics of each key component. The median effect size was $d = 0.85$.

Boundary Conditions: The pre-training principle is most likely to be effective when the material is complex, the multimedia lesson is fast-paced, and the learner is unfamiliar with the material.

Chapter Outline

INTRODUCTION TO THE PRE-TRAINING PRINCIPLE
What Is Pre-training?
How Does Pre-training Work?

INTRODUCTION TO THE PRE-TRAINING PRINCIPLE

What Is Pre-training?

When the material in a multimedia lesson is complex for a learner and is presented at a fast pace, the learner may not have enough cognitive capacity to engage in the process of mentally representing the material – creating a situation we call *essential overload* (Mayer & Moreno, 2003). One way to manage essential processing is to equip the learner with knowledge that will make it easier to process the lesson. For example, suppose we present a narrated animation explaining how a car's braking system works. The script for the multimedia lesson and some selected frames are shown in Figure 10.1. As you can see, the goal of the lesson is to help the learner build a mental model of how a car's braking system works, such as the following step-by-step causal explanation: The brake pedal moves down, which CAUSES the piston to move forward in the master cylinder, which CAUSES brake fluid to become compressed in the tube, which CAUSES the wheel cylinders to move forward, which CAUSES the brake shoe to press against the brake drum, which CAUSES the wheel to slow down or stop. However, the learner must also know the names and character- istics of the key components in the system – for example, knowing that a *piston* is a "plunger-like" device that moves forward and back within a cylinder or that a *brake shoe* creates friction when it moves outward to press against the drum. For many learners, mentally representing this material is a cognitively demanding task.

Let's assume that the pace of presentation is so fast that by the time learners are able to figure out what is meant by concepts like *piston in master cylinder, fluid in tube*, or *brake shoe*, there is inadequate time left to build a causal step-by-step model of how the braking system works. To overcome this problem of essential overload, we can provide

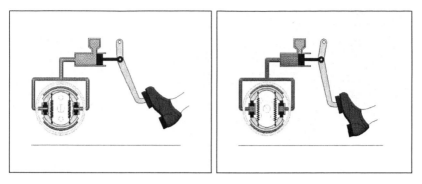

When the driver steps on the car's brake pedal, a piston moves
forward inside the master cylinder.
The piston forces brake fluid out of the master cylinder and through
the tubes to the wheel cylinders.
In the wheel cylinders, the increase in fluid pressure makes a
smaller set of pistons move.
These smaller pistons activate the brake shoes.
When the brake shoes press against the drum, both the drum and the
wheel stop or slow down.

Figure 10.1. Selected frames and script from narrated animation on how hydraulic brakes work.

pre-training to the learners concerning the names, locations, and characteristics of each component. For example, Figure 10.2 shows frames from a pre-training episode in which learners can click on any part in a diagram of the braking system – such as the piston in the master cylinder – and then be given the name of that part and shown the states the part can be in. After the learner has clicked on each part, the learner can be shown the narrated animation that explains how a braking system works. In this way, pre-training familiarizes the learner with the name and characteristics of each key component in the braking system.

How Does Pre-training Work?

When learners view a narrated animation, they must engage in two kinds of essential processing – understanding how the causal system works and understanding how each component works. When the learner already knows the name and characteristics of each part, the learner can engage in cognitive processes for building a causal model of the system, leading to better understanding. In this way, pre-training serves to off-load some of the essential processing onto the

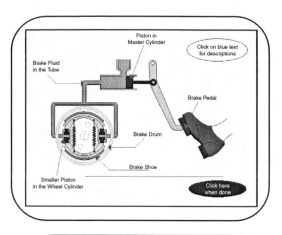

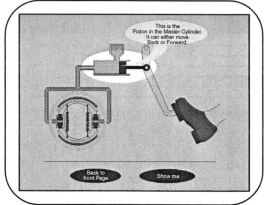

Figure 10.2.   Selected frames from pre-training on how hydraulic brakes work.

pre-training episode. Thus, pre-training provides prior knowledge that reduces the amount of processing needed to understand the narrated animation.

Mayer, Mathias, and Wetzell (2002) proposed a two-stage learning process in which learners first build component models for each major part in the system, and then build a causal model. Building component models consists of learning the name and behavior of each component, such as knowing that the piston in the master cylinder can move forward or backward, that the brake fluid in the tube can be compressed or not compressed, and so on. Building a causal model consists of learning the causal chain – for example, stepping on the car's brake pedal causes a piston to move forward in the master cylinder, which in turn causes brake fluid in the tube to compress, and so on.

Students who have appropriate prior knowledge already know the names and characteristics of the key components, so they can devote their cognitive resources to building a causal model – using essential and generative processing. However, students who lack appropriate prior knowledge could benefit from learning the names and characteristics of the components before a fast-paced multimedia explanation is presented. Thus, pre-training works by providing appropriate prior knowledge of key concepts in the lessons. By moving the learning of key terms to a pre-training episode, learners can engage more fully in cognitive processing of the causal explanation when the multimedia explanation is presented.

Prior knowledge is the single most important individual difference dimension in instructional design. If you could know just one thing about a learner, you would want to know the learner's prior knowledge in the domain. Novice learners – the target learners for this book – are defined as lacking domain-specific prior knowledge, and thus are prime candidates for pre-training. In this way the learner can manage essential processing by distributing it across two episodes – essential processing for building component models during pre-training, and essential processing for building mental models during the main lesson.

Research on the Pre-training Principle

Based on this explanation of the cognitive effects of pre-training, the cognitive theory of multimedia learning makes the following prediction: Students who receive pre-training in the names and characteristics of key concepts before receiving a multimedia lesson (pre-training group) should perform better on a problem-solving transfer test than students who receive the same information within the context of the lesson (no pre-training group). Furthermore, this theoretical account predicts that the positive effects of pre-training should be strongest for students who lack domain knowledge related to the lesson.

Core Evidence Concerning the Pre-training Principle

Do students understand a multimedia lesson better if we provide them with pre-training concerning the names and characteristics of the major elements in the lesson? Table 10.1 shows the source, content, format, and effect size for five experimental tests of the pre-training principle, in which we compared the problem-solving transfer test performance of students who learned with and without pre-training.

In the first set of studies (Mayer, Mathais, & Wetzell, 2002), students received a narrated animation explaining the workings of a car's braking system or a bicycle tire pump and then took problem-solving transfer tests. Before the brakes lesson, some students (pre-training group) received pre-training in which they learned the name and possible states of each component in the brake system – for example, the piston in the master cylinder could be forward or back, the fluid in the brake tube could be compressed or not compressed, and so on. Before the tire pump lesson, some students (pre-training group) received pre-training with a clear plastic model in which they were asked to pull up and push down on the handle several times. In this way they could see the behavior of individual components, such as the piston moving up and down in the cylinder, the inlet valve opening and closing, and the outlet valve opening and closing. On a subsequent test of problem-solving transfer, students in the pre-training group performed better than students in the no pre-training group across all three experiments. The first three rows of Table 10.1 show that the effect sizes were large.

In a second set of two studies (Mayer, Mautone, & Prothero, 2002), students learned about geology in a simulation game called the Profile Game. The goal of the game was to determine which geological feature was on a certain portion of the earth's surface, represented as a window on the computer screen. Students could use a mouse to draw lines and then were shown the depth or height at each point along the line. Some students (pre-training group) were shown illustrations of the major geological features – such as a ridge or a trench – before the lesson, whereas others (no pre-training group) were not. As you can see in the last two lines of Table 10.1, the pre-training group performed

Table 10.1. Core Evidence Concerning the Pre-training Principle

Source	Content	Format	Effect Size
Mayer, Mathias, & Wetzell (2002, Expt. 1)	Brakes	Computer	0.79
Mayer, Mathias, & Wetzell (2002, Expt. 2)	Brakes	Computer	0.92
Mayer, Mathias, & Wetzell (2002, Expt. 3)	Tire pump	Computer	1.00
Mayer, Mautone, & Prothero (2002, Expt. 2)	Geology game	Computer	0.57
Mayer, Mautone, & Prothero (2002, Expt. 3)	Geology game	Computer	0.85
Median			0.85

better on a subsequent test of problem-solving transfer than did the no pre-training group, yielding medium-to-large effect sizes.

Overall, Table 10.1 shows consistent effect sizes favoring the pre-training group, with a median effect size of .85, which is considered large. These findings are consistent with the *pre-training principle*: People learn more deeply from a multimedia message when they know the names and characteristics of the main concepts.

Related Evidence on the Pre-training Principle

The pre-training principle is based on the idea that information about the key terms – such as names, definitions, location, and characteristics – should be known to the learners before they receive the multimedia lesson. Table 10.2 summarizes exemplary experimental tests based on techniques that are related to pre-training. In the first set of studies (Pollack, Chandler, & Sweller, 2002), apprentices took a course in electrical engineering that included a two-phase multimedia lesson on conducting safety tests for electrical appliances. For some learners (pre-training group), the first phase focused on how each component worked and the second phase focused on how all the components worked together within the electrical system. For other learners (no pre-training group), both phases focused on how all the components worked together within the electrical system. On a subsequent problem-solving transfer test concerning how the elements worked together within the electrical system, learners in the pre-training group performed better than students in the no pre-training

Table 10.2. Related Evidence Concerning the Pre-training Principle

Source	Content	Format	Effect Size
Pollock, Chandler, & Sweller (2002, Expt. 1)	Electrical engineering	Paper	1.22
Pollock, Chandler, & Sweller (2002, Expt. 2)	Electrical engineering	Paper	1.15
Clarke, Ayres, & Sweller (2005, Expt. 1a)	Mathematics	Paper	1.87
Kester, Kirschner, & van Merrienboer (2004)	Statistics	Computer	0.75
Kester, Kirschner, & van Merrienboer (2006)	Electronics	Computer	0.72

group, yielding large effect sizes in both cases, as shown in the first two lines of Table 10.2. Importantly, these results were only for low-experience learners; high-experience learners did not show strong positive effects, indicating that high-experience learners were less likely to encounter essential overload.

The third line of Table 10.2 summarizes a study by Clark, Ayres, and Sweller (2005) in which high school students learned to use a spreadsheet to solve algebra problems involving functions. Some students (similar to our pre-training group) began by learning to use the key features of the spreadsheet – such as editing data, entering formulas, creating graphs, deriving slope functions, using drawing tools, and changing scales – before receiving the multimedia math lesson on functions. Other students (similar to our no pre-training group) learned from the multimedia math lesson at the same time that they learned how to use the corresponding features of the spreadsheet. As shown in Table 10.2, when students lacked spreadsheet skills, the pre-training group outperformed the no pre-training group on a subsequent math problem-solving test. However, as in the Pollock, Chandler, and Sweller (2002) studies, students who had high spread-sheet skills did not benefit from pre-training, again suggesting that they did not experience essential overload when learning in the no pre-training condition.

A similar pattern was found in a study by Kester, Kirshner, and van Merrienboer (2004) in which college students learned a statistical technique and took a problem-solving transfer test. Students who received pre-training concerning definitions of key terms in the formula (similar to our pre-training group) performed better on problem-solving transfer than students who received the same information within the context of learning the statistical technique (similar to our no pre-training group). Similar results were obtained in a study by Kester, Kirshner, and van Merrienboer (2006) in which high school students learned to solve electronics troubleshooting problems either by getting factual information before training (like our pre-training group) or during training (like our no pre-training group). These results are summarized in the fourth and fifth rows of Table 10.2, respectively. In summarizing this line of research, and related studies, van Merrienboer, Kester, and Paas (2006) noted that techniques aimed at reducing intrinsic cognitive load (or essential processing) need to be balanced with techniques for fostering germane load (or generative processing).

Boundary Conditions for the Pre-training Principle

As you can see, the pre-training effect was obtained mainly in situations where the learners were inexperienced, the material was complex, and the lesson was fast-paced. These boundary conditions are consistent with the cognitive theory of multimedia learning, in which the need to manage essential processing is most urgent when essential processing threatens to overload working memory capacity. In two experiments (Clarke, Ayres, & Sweller, 2005; Pollack, Chandler, & Sweller, 2002), the pre-training effect was obtained for low-experience learners but not for high-experience learners. Thus, there is preliminary evidence that the pre-training principle is most likely to apply when learners lack domain knowledge, although further research is warranted.

IMPLICATIONS OF THE PRE-TRAINING PRINCIPLE

Implications for Multimedia Learning

Students may be overwhelmed by a multimedia lesson containing an explanation of how something works (or how to use a strategy) that also includes many new terms. Students may need to use their limited cognitive resources to learn the names and characteristics of the new terms, thereby leaving less capacity for making sense of the to-be-learned explanation or strategy. In short, the cognitive theory of multimedia learning predicts that pre-training in the names and characteristics of key concepts will result in deeper learning of multimedia explanations or strategies for novice learners. We can interpret the consistent evidence for this prediction as support for the cognitive theory of multimedia learning. In short, ensuring that learners possess appropriate prior knowledge helps to solve the problem of essential overload.

IMPLICATIONS FOR MULTIMEDIA INSTRUCTION

If a learner must work on understanding the meaning of new terms in a lesson, the learner has less capacity available to make sense of the main theme of the lesson. Thus, the most important practical implication of the pre-training principle is as follows: When students would be overwhelmed by a multimedia lesson that uses many new terms to explain complex material, provide pre-training concerning the key terms before presenting the lesson. The basic implication for multimedia design is that students should know the names and characteristics of key concepts before they receive a multimedia lesson that contains them. If students do not already possess this knowledge of key concepts in an accessible form, then an appropriate instructional technique is to provide pre-training aimed at helping students develop appropriate prior knowledge of key concepts. In short, students should know the meanings of the words (and symbols) you are using to present a complex explanation or strategy, so that they can devote their full cognitive capacity to building a coherent cognitive representation during learning.

LIMITATIONS AND FUTURE DIRECTIONS

In this section, let's focus on three limitations of research on pre-training. First, the pre-training principle should not be taken as a blanket prescription to begin each lesson with a list of key terms and definitions for the learner to memorize. Students learn more deeply from a multimedia lesson when they already know the names and characteristics of key terms in the lesson. Research is needed to determine the best way to accomplish this goal – such as some sort of pre-lesson activity, putting the definitions in a margin, or allowing learners to click on new terms in hypertext to receive a definition. For example, Plass, Chun, Mayer, and Luetner (1998, 2003) asked English-speaking college students who were taking a German course to read a story in German, with clickable key terms. When students clicked on a term, they could see a verbal definition or a picture of the term.

Having access to the definitions and pictures helped improve comprehension for some students. Overall, more work is needed on how best to create effective pre-training experiences.

Second, the same pre-training experience is not appropriate for all learners. As you can see, you need to know what each student knows about the target domain in order to implement pre-training effectively. In our studies on the braking system, for example, through pilot testing we determined that most college students did not know how a piston works, although the piston is a key component in the braking system. Students who already know the key terms are not likely to be helped by pre-training, and in some cases may find that pre-training detracts from their learning. It is important to use pre-training appropriately – that is, to provide pre-training only on key concepts that the learner does not know. Research is needed on how to embed knowledge assessments within a lesson so that the appropriate level of pre-training can be provided for each individual learner.

Finally, when pre-training is not feasible, some of the same benefits (e.g., freeing up cognitive capacity for essential processing) can be gained through other techniques such as the segmenting principle, which was described in the previous chapter, and the modality principle, which is described in the next chapter. In addition, the spatial contiguity principle (described in Chapter 7) can be used to clarify key terms – for example, putting the name and description of the term next to its picture in an illustration or animation. Further research is needed on how best to ensure that students do not have to expend cognitive processing on trying to figure out what various key terms mean during a multimedia lesson.

SUGGESTED READINGS

Asterisk (*) indicates that a portion of this chapter is based on this publication.

*Mayer, R. E., Mathias, A., & Wetzell, K. (2002). Fostering understanding of multimedia messages through pre-training: Evidence for a two-stage theory of mental model construction. *Journal of Experimental Psychology: Applied, 8*, 147–154.

Pollock, E., Chandler, P., & Sweller, J. (2002). Assimilating complex information. *Learning and Instruction, 12*, 61–86.

11

Modality Principle

Modality Principle: *People learn more deeply from pictures and spoken words than from pictures and printed words.*

Example: *An animation-with-narration version consists of a narrated animation on how lightning storms develop, whereas an animation-with-on-screen-text version consists of the same animation with the words from the narration printed on the bottom of the screen as a caption.*

Theoretical Rationale: *In the animation-with-on-screen-text version, both the pictures and the words enter the cognitive system through the eyes, causing an overload in the visual system. In the animation-with-narration version, the words are off-loaded onto the verbal channel, thereby allowing the learner to more fully process the pictures in the visual channel.*

Empirical Rationale: *In seventeen out of seventeen tests, people performed better on problem-solving transfer tests when an animation or set of graphics was accompanied by narration rather than on-screen text. The median effect size was d = 1.02.*

Boundary Conditions: *The modality principle may be particularly applicable when the material is complex, the presentation is fast-paced, and the learners are familiar with the words. By contrast, printed words may be appropriate when the lesson includes technical words and symbols and when the learner is a non-native speaker or is hearing-impaired.*

▪ ▪ Chapter Outline

200

INTRODUCTION TO THE MODALITY PRINCIPLE

What Is Modality Off-Loading?

The previous two chapters explored two ways to manage essential cognitive processing when the learner experiences essential overload – that is, when the material is so complex that both channels are overloaded by essential processing. In that situation, which I call Scenario 3 (in the introduction to Section 3), two useful techniques for managing essential cognitive processing are *segmenting* and *pre-training*. In this chapter, I explore a slightly different situation involving essential overload – that is, when the words and pictures are both presented visually and are so complex that the visual channel is overloaded by essential processing. In this situation, which I call Scenario 4, a useful technique for managing essential cognitive processing is *modality off-loading* – presenting words as narration rather than as on-screen text.

For example, suppose learners are presented with an animation depicting the steps in lightning formation along with captions at the bottom of the screen describing the steps in words. Figure 11.1 shows selected frames from the lightning animation along with corresponding printed text that was presented at the bottom of the screen, which I call a captioned animation. This is an example of Scenario 4 if the learner does not have enough cognitive capacity to engage in all the necessary essential processing in the visual channel. In this case learners must read the words with their eyes and must view the animation with their eyes, so the visual channel can become overloaded.

What can be done to manage the essential processing that is required in this situation? One suggestion – initially proposed by

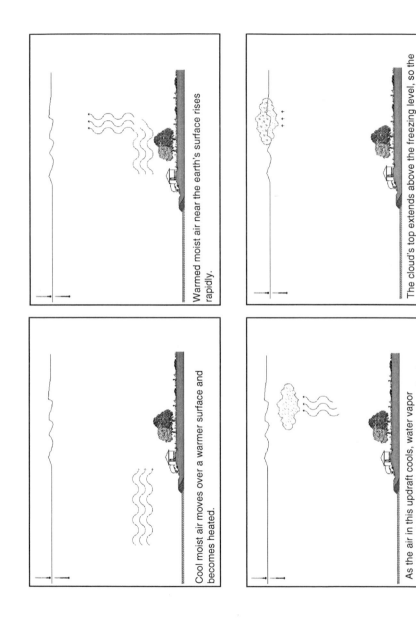

Figure 11.1. Selected frames and script from captioned animation on how lightning storms develop.

Cool moist air moves over a warmer surface and becomes heated.

Warmed moist air near the earth's surface rises rapidly.

As the air in this updraft cools, water vapor condenses into water droplets and forms a cloud.

The cloud's top extends above the freezing level, so the upper portion of the cloud is composed of tiny ice crystals.

Words as Narration

"As the air in this updraft cools, water vapor
condenses into water droplets and forms a cloud."

Words as On-Screen Text

As the air in this updraft cools, water vapor
condenses into water droplets and forms a cloud.

Figure 11.2. Example frames of animation on lightning with words as narration (top) or words as on-screen text (bottom).

Mousavi, Low, and Sweller (1995) – is to off-load some of the essential cognitive processing from the visual channel to the auditory channel. *Modality off-loading* occurs when the words in a multimedia lesson are presented as spoken text rather than as printed text. Thus, for the lightning animation, words can be presented as narration, as indicated in the top frame (A) in Figure 11.2, rather than as onscreen text, as indicated in the bottom frame (B). For each step in the process of lightning formation, the spoken words describing an event (e.g., "cool, moist air moves over a warmer surface and becomes heated") are presented at the same time that the animation depicts the event (e.g., wavy blue arrows move rightward over land and turn red). In short, modality off-loading occurs when printed words in a multimedia lesson (such as captions) are converted into spoken words (such as narration), changing the lesson from a captioned animation to a narrated animation.

Consider the cognitive consequences of the overload scenario that can be created by the multimedia lesson presented in Figure 11.1, which I call a captioned animation. When the presentation is fast-paced, this situation is likely to overwhelm the learner's visual channel because the learner can't look at the printed words and the animation at the same time. By contrast, when we off-load the words into spoken form, we create what can be called a narrated animation.

Does modality matter? Is learning the same when words are presented as speech (e.g., as in the top of Figure 11.2) as when words are presented as onscreen text (e.g., as in the bottom of Figure 11.2)? Is one modality better than the other? In the following sections, let's examine two competing theories based on the idea that modality does or does not matter.

Modality Does Not Matter: The Case for Expressing Words as On-Screen Text or Narration

The most straightforward approach is to assume that modality does not matter, so words can be presented either as on-screen text or as narration. The rationale for the claim that modality does not matter is the *information-delivery hypothesis* – the idea that multimedia learning involves presenting information to learners via as many routes as possible. In the case of narrated animations, two delivery paths are used – words are delivered to the learner, and pictures are delivered to the learner. In the case of captioned animations, two delivery paths are used – again both words and pictures are delivered to the learner. According to this view, learning should be the same for both multimedia presentations because the same information is presented to the learners.

The information-delivery hypothesis is represented in Figure 11.3. The top frame shows two delivery paths – one for pictures and one for words (which happen to be spoken). The bottom frame also shows two delivery paths – one for pictures and one for words (which happen to be printed). When identical information is presented in the same

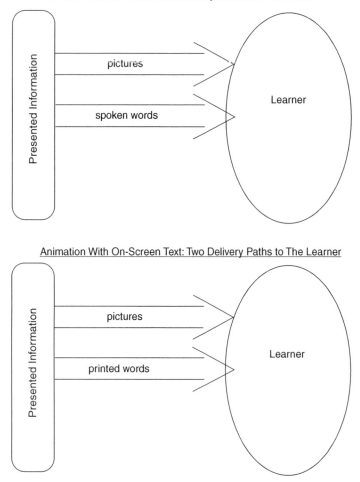

Figure 11.3. Why the information-delivery theory predicts no difference between narrated animation (top) and captioned animation (bottom).

temporal manner, the resulting learning outcome will be the same. The premise underlying the information-delivery hypothesis is that learners need to receive verbal and visual information (i.e., words and pictures); obviously, pictures are presented visually, but the modality of the words does not matter because they have the same informational value when expressed as speech as when expressed as printed text. Therefore, the information-delivery hypothesis predicts that learners who receive a multimedia lesson with words presented as on-screen text will perform the same on retention and transfer tests as learners who receive the identical lesson with words presented as narration.

Modality Matters: The Case for Expressing Words as Narration Rather Than as On-Screen Text

What's wrong with the information-delivery hypothesis? It is based on an outmoded conception of learning as information transmission in which learning involves taking presented information and placing it inside one's memory. According to this conception, learning occurs when information is presented by the instructor and received by the student. It follows that the main concern of a multimedia designer is to present information to the learner. Although this view seems to be consistent with common sense, it conflicts with our current under-standing of how the human mind works. In particular, it conflicts with what we know about dual-channel processing as described under the cognitive theory of multimedia learning in Chapter 3.

The case for the idea that modality matters is based on *the dual-channel hypothesis*: People have two separate information-processing channels – one for visual/pictorial processing and one for auditory/verbal processing. When words are presented as narration, the audi-tory/verbal channel can be used for processing words (i.e., the narration) and the visual/pictorial channel can be used for processing pictures (i.e., the animation). In this way the load is balanced between two channels, so neither one is overloaded. This situation is depicted in the top frame of Figure 11.4, in which pictures enter through the eyes (and are processed in the visual/pictorial channel), while spoken words enter through the ears (and are processed in the auditory/verbal channel).

By contrast, when words are presented as on-screen text the visual/pictorial channel is used – at least initially – for processing words (i.e., the on-screen text), and the visual/pictorial channel is used for pro-cessing pictures (i.e., the animation). At the same time, the auditory/verbal channel is not being used much at all. Each channel has limited capacity – each can process only a limited amount of material at one time – so one channel is overloaded with processing both words and pictures, while the other channel is relatively underused. This situa-tion is depicted in the bottom frame of Figure 11.4, in which both pictures and printed words must enter the learner's information processing through the eyes and initially be represented as images in

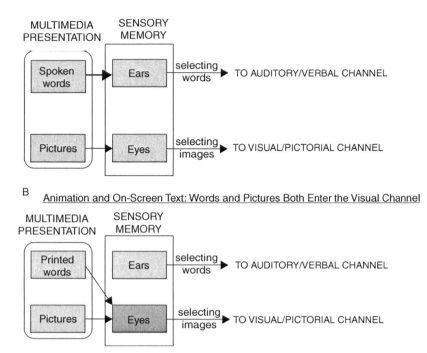

Figure 11.4. Why the cognitive theory of multimedia learning predicts differences between (A) narrated animation and (B) captioned animation.

working memory – thus, both compete for resources within the visual channel.

According to the cognitive theory of multimedia learning, the processes required for meaningful learning cannot be fully carried out when the visual channel is overloaded – that is, when pictures and printed words compete for limited cognitive resources in the visual channel – because both enter the learner's information processing through the eyes. By contrast, the most efficient way to present verbal material is through the verbal channel – that is, as spoken text only – because in this way it does not compete with pictures for cognitive resources in the visual channel. Instead, processing of words is off-loaded onto the verbal channel, which is otherwise underused. Based on this theory, I predict a *modality effect* in which presenting words as on-screen text rather than narration will result in poorer understanding as indicated by transfer tests.

Understanding the Modality Effect

Mousavi, Low, and Sweller (1995, p. 321) have used the term *modality effect* to refer to the idea that "effective cognitive capacity may be increased if both auditory and visual working memory can be used" to process incoming multimedia messages. In short, the "effective size of working memory can be increased by presenting information in a mixed (auditory and visual mode) rather than a single mode" (Mousavi, Low, & Sweller, 1995, p. 320). Mousavi, Low, and Sweller (1995) and Low and Sweller (2005) use the term *modality effect* in a broad sense to include situations in which presenting simultaneous visual and auditory material is superior to presenting the same material successively – a result that I call the *temporal contiguity effect*. In Mousavi, Low, and Sweller's (1995; Low & Sweller, 2005) view, modality effects are examples of *split attention* – a broader class of multimedia learning situations in which visual attention must be allocated to both pictorial and verbal material. By contrast, I use the term *modality effect* in a more restricted sense to refer only to situations in which presenting pictures and spoken text (e.g., animation and narration) is more effective than presenting pictures and printed text (e.g., animation and on-screen text).

A fundamental theoretical idea underlying the modality effect is dual-channel processing – the idea that there are separate channels for processing visually presented material and auditorily presented material. For example, Baddeley's (1992) model of working memory includes a distinction between a *visuo-spatial sketch pad* that is used for processing visual material and a *phonological loop* that is used for processing auditory material. Paivio's (1990) dual-coding theory makes a somewhat similar distinction. A second fundamental theoretical idea underlying the modality effect is limited capacity – the idea that each channel is limited in the amount of processing it can support at one time. Finally, a third fundamental theoretical idea is active learning – the idea that meaningful learning occurs when a learner selects, organizes, and integrates knowledge in each channel. These processes require cognitive capacity and therefore are restricted when one or both channels are overloaded.

RESEARCH ON THE MODALITY PRINCIPLE

Based on this explanation of the cognitive effects of modality principle, the cognitive theory of multimedia learning makes the following prediction: Students who receive a multimedia lesson will perform better on a problem-solving transfer test when the words are presented as spoken text rather than as printed text.

Core Evidence Concerning the Modality Principle

Do students understand a multimedia lesson better if the words are in spoken form rather than printed form? Table 11.1 shows the source, content, format, and effect size for seventeen experimental tests of the modality principle, in which we compared the problem-solving transfer test performance of students who learned with graphics and narration to the performance of students who learned with graphics and on-screen text. In our studies, the multimedia lesson was fast-paced and the words were intended to be familiar to the learner. In all cases, the words in the narration were identical to the words in the on-screen text.

First, let's see what happens when the multimedia lesson is based on a short, fast-paced animation. The first two lines of Table 11.1 summarize a study by Mayer and Moreno (1998) in which college students who received a narrated animation on lightning formation or a car braking system performed better on a subsequent transfer test than did students who learned with animation and on-screen text. This pattern was replicated in a study by Moreno and Mayer (1999), who used the lightning lesson, as summarized in the third and fourth lines of Table 11.1. Overall, the effect sizes are large across all four comparisons involving short, fast-paced animations.

Next, let's see what happens when the multimedia lesson is presented within a game or interactive simulation. The fifth line of Table 11.1 summarizes a study in which nonstudent adults learned about the fuel system of an aircraft by playing a game involving virtual reality (O'Neil et al., 2000). The adults performed better on a subsequent transfer test if they had received commentary about the parts of the fuel system they were seeing in the form of spoken words rather than printed words. The next nine lines of Table 11.1 (lines six through fourteen) are based on an environmental science game that was presented either on a desktop computer or in virtual reality (Moreno et al., 2001; Moreno & Mayer, 2002). As part of the game, the on-screen tutor – Herman the Bug – explained how plant growth works through a series of fast-paced animations. In each of nine comparisons, students performed better on a subsequent transfer test if the animations were accompanied by spoken text rather than printed text. In another interactive simulation, an on-screen tutor – Dr. Phyz – explained

Table 11.1. Core Evidence Concerning the Modality Principle

Source	Content	Format	Effect Size
Mayer & Moreno (1998, Expt. 1)	Lightning	Computer	1.49
Mayer & Moreno (1998, Expt. 2)	Brakes	Computer	0.78
Moreno & Mayer (1999b, Expt. 1)	Lightning	Computer	1.02
Moreno & Mayer (1999b, Expt. 2)	Lightning	Computer	1.09
O'Neil et al. (2000, Expt. 1)	Aircraft simulation	Virtual reality	1.00
Moreno et al. (2001, Expt. 4a)	Environmental science game	Computer	0.60
Moreno et al. (2001, Expt. 4b)	Environmental science game	Computer	1.58
Moreno et al. (2001, Expt. 5a)	Environmental science game	Computer	1.41
Moreno et al. (2001, Expt. 5b)	Environmental science game	Computer	1.71
Moreno & Mayer (2002, Expt. 1a)	Environmental science game	Computer	0.93
Moreno & Mayer (2002, Expt. 1b)	Environmental science game	Virtual reality	0.62
Moreno & Mayer (2002, Expt. 1c)	Environmental science game	Virtual reality	2.79
Moreno & Mayer (2002, Expt. 2a)	Environmental science game	Computer	0.74
Moreno & Mayer (2002, Expt. 2b)	Environmental science game	Virtual reality	2.24
Mayer, Dow, & Mayer (2003, Expt. 1)	Electric motor	Computer	0.79
Harskamp et al. (2007, Expt. 1)	Biology	Computer	0.86
Harskamp et al. (2007, Expt. 2a)	Biology	Computer	1.02
Median			1.02

aspects of an electric motor to students through fast-paced animations. As shown in row fifteen, students performed better on a transfer test if they had received narration with animation rather than on-screen text with animation. Overall, the effect sizes were large.

Finally, the last two rows of Table 11.1 summarize the results of a study examining whether the modality effect would apply to regular science lessons presented in school settings (Harskamp, Mayer, Suhre, & Jansma, 2007). In two experiments, high school students who received multimedia science lessons using illustrations and narration performed better on subsequent transfer tests than did students who received illustrations with on-screen text. The effect sizes were large in this field study, indicating that the modality effect is not limited to lab environments. However, in the second experiment, faster learners showed the modality effect (as shown in Table 11.1), whereas slower learners did not.

Overall, across a wide variety of learning situations, there was strong and consistent support for the modality principle, with a median effect size of 1.02. In all seventeen comparisons reported in Table 11.1, people scored better on transfer tests after learning with graphics and narration rather than graphics and printed text. These findings strongly support the modality principle: People learn more deeply from multimedia messages when the words are presented as spoken text rather than as printed text.

Related Evidence Concerning the Modality Principle

Although research in our lab has produced consistent support for the modality principle (as shown in Table 11.1), it is worthwhile to ask whether other researchers have found similar results. Table 11.2 summarizes exemplary research concerning the modality principle, comparing the problem-solving transfer performance of students who learned with graphics and narration to the performance of students who learned with graphics and on-screen text.

All of the studies reported in Table 11.1 involved computer-based environments; by contrast, the first nine rows in Table 11.2 summarize similar results involving paper-based environments, comparing diagrams containing printed text to diagrams paired with tape-recorded speech (Leahy, Chandler, & Sweller, 2003; Mousavi, Low, & Sweller, 1995; Tindall-Ford, Chandler, & Sweller, 1997). In the first set of studies to establish the modality effect with instructional materials, Mousavi, Low, and Sweller (1995) found medium-to-large effects in five experimental tests involving geometry problems (summarized in rows one through five). In rows six through nine, similar results were reported for lessons on electrical circuits (Tindall-Ford, Chandler, & Sweller, 1997) and on graph reading (Leahy, Chandler, & Sweller, 2003), except when the materials consisted mainly of a list of isolated elements, as indicated in the eighth row. Thus, an important boundary condition for the modality effect is that the modality effect applies most strongly when the materials require building a mental model rather than simply memorizing isolated elements (Ginns, 2005; Tindall-Ford, Chandler, & Sweller, 1997).

The next three rows of Table 11.2 summarize three experiments conducted by Jueng, Chandler, and Sweller (1997) in which elementary school students learned to solve geometry problems by viewing a computer-based presentation containing worked problems along with printed commentary or spoken commentary. Students performed better on a subsequent transfer test if they had learned with the spoken commentary rather than printed commentary; however, this modality effect occurred only if the elements of a diagram were highlighted as the commentary described them. Apparently, an important limitation of spoken text is that learners may need to engage in visual search to determine the corresponding part of the graphic, thus creating extraneous processing. This study shows that graphics-with-narration is most likely to be more effective than graphics-with-on-screen-text in situations where the need for visual search is minimized – such as when the graphic is simple or the relevant portion is highlighted as the corresponding commentary is spoken. This line of research is noteworthy because it pinpoints an important boundary condition for the modality principle – that is, the modality principle may not apply to situations in which learners experience difficulty in identifying which part of the graphic the words are talking about.

The next set of studies (Kalyuga, Chandler, & Sweller, 1999, 2000) examined how workers at a manufacturing company learned electronics troubleshooting or machinery operation from a computer-based presentation containing diagrams with printed or spoken commentary. In two experiments (summarized in rows thirteen and fourteen), workers scored better on a problem-solving transfer test if they had learned with spoken rather than printed commentary. This line of research is particularly useful because it demonstrates that the modality effect can apply to a real-world training environment.

The fifteenth row of Table 11.2 summarizes a study by Craig, Gholson, and Driscoll (2002) in which college students learned about lightning formation from an on-screen pedagogical agent who explained an animation with either spoken words or printed words. Consistent with previous research on the lightning lesson by Mayer and Moreno (1998) and by Moreno and Mayer (1999b), students

Table 11.2. Related Evidence Concerning the Modality Principle

Source	Content	Format	Effect Size
Mousavi, Low, & Sweller (1995, Expt. 1)	Geometry	Paper	0.93
Mousavi, Low, & Sweller (1995, Expt. 2)	Geometry	Paper	0.88
Mousavi, Low, & Sweller (1995, Expt. 3)	Geometry	Paper	0.65
Mousavi, Low, & Sweller (1995, Expt. 4)	Geometry	Paper	0.68
Mousavi, Low, & Sweller (1995, Expt. 5)	Geometry	Paper	0.63
Tindall-Ford, Chandler, & Sweller (1997, Expt. 1)	Electrical circuits	Paper	1.68
Tindall-Ford, Chandler, & Sweller (1997, Expt. 2)	Electrical circuits	Paper	1.07
Tindall-Ford, Chandler, & Sweller (1997, Expt. 3)	Electrical circuits	Paper	0.23
Leahy, Chandler, & Sweller (2003, Expt. 1)	Graph reading	Paper	0.76
Jeung, Chandler, & Sweller (1997, Expt. 1)	Math problems	Computer	0.87
Jeung, Chandler, & Sweller (1997, Expt. 2)	Math problems	Computer	0.33
Jeung, Chandler, & Sweller (1997, Expt. 3)	Math problems	Computer	1.01
Kalyuga, Chandler, & Sweller (1999, Expt. 1)	Electrical engineering	Computer	0.85
Kalyuga, Chandler, & Sweller (2000, Expt. 1)	Electrical engineering	Computer	0.79
Craig, Gholson, & Driscoll (2002, Expt. 2)	Lightning	Computer	0.97
Atkinson (2002, Expt. 1a)	Math problems	Computer	0.89
Atkinson (2002, Expt. 1b)	Math problems	Computer	0.72
Atkinson (2002, Expt. 2)	Math problems	Computer	0.69
Tabbers, Martens, & van Merrienboer (2004)	Instructional design	Computer	−0.47

performed better on a transfer test if they had received animation with narration rather than animation with on-screen text. The sixteenth through eighteenth rows summarize experiments by Atkinson (2002) in which students learned to solve math problems better from a pedagogical agent who explained on-screen worked-out examples using spoken text rather than printed text. This line of research demonstrates that the modality effect extends to situations involving on-screen pedagogical agents.

Finally, the last row in Table 11.2 summarizes a study in which Tabbers, Martens, and van Merrienboer (2004) asked college students to study a computer-based lesson on instructional design consisting of a series of diagrams with spoken commentary or printed commentary. In contrast to all of the foregoing thirty-five experiments, students in the graphics-with-spoken-text group performed worse on a transfer test than did students in the graphics-with-printed-text group, yielding an effect size of $d = -0.47$. This study suggests a potentially important boundary condition for the modality effect – the effect is less likely to occur when the pace of the lesson is slow and under learner control rather than fast and under system control. These boundary conditions are consistent with the cognitive theory of multimedia learning, which predicts that the modality effect should be strongest when the lesson is fast-paced and under system control. The use of many jargon terms may also favor using printed text over spoken text.

Overall, the modality principle has been the focus of dozens of published experiments, beginning with a classic set of studies by Mousavi, Low, and Sweller (1995). Importantly, there is also evidence that graphics-with-onscreen-text creates greater cognitive load during learning than does graphics-with-narration (Brunken, Plass, & Leutner, 2004; Brunken, Steinbacher, Plass, & Leutner, 2004).

Consistent with the preponderance of evidence summarized in Tables 11.1 and 11.2, three recent reviews have also found strong support for the modality principle (Ginns, 2005; Low & Sweller, 2005; Moreno, 2006). For example, Low and Sweller (2005, p. 147) reviewed "evidence documenting the importance of presentation mode, specifically the modality effect that occurs when information presented in a mixed mode (partly visual and partly auditory) is more effective than when the same information is presented in a single mode (either visual or auditory alone)." In a meta-analysis of 39 between-subjects comparisons, Ginns (2005) found an overall weighted mean effect size of $d = .72$ favoring graphics-with-spoken-text over graphics-with-printed-text. Unlike the studies summarized in Tables 11.1 and 11.2, Ginns's review included studies that were not published in peer-reviewed research journals as well as studies using dependent measures other than problem-solving transfer. Finally, Moreno (2006) reviewed experiments involving forty-six comparisons of learning with graphics and narration versus learning with graphics and on-screen text, involving a variety of dependent measures as well as a variety of learning venues. In all cases there was a modality effect, with the majority of effect sizes in the large range. Overall, the modality principle is supported by the largest evidence base of any of the principles described in this book.

Boundary Conditions of the Modality Principle

In a recent review of the modality principle in multimedia learning, Low and Sweller (2005, p. 147) concluded that "under certain, well-defined conditions, presenting some information in the visual mode and other information in the auditory mode can expand effective working memory capacity and so reduce the effects of excessive cognitive load." Based on the cognitive theory of multimedia learning, what are the boundary conditions that determine when the modality principle is likely to hold or not hold? The cognitive theory of multimedia learning predicts that the positive effects of using spoken text should be strongest when the material is complex, the presentation is fast-paced, and the learners are familiar with the words.

First, concerning complexity, Tindale-Ford, Chandler, and Sweller (1997) offer some preliminary evidence that the modality principle is weaker for material that is low in complexity rather than high in complexity. When the material is complex, printed text and graphics may overload the visual channel, so that the modality principle is helpful; however, when the material is simple there may not be a need to free up cognitive capacity. Similarly, Ginns's (2005) meta-analysis of the modality effect shows that the modality effect is stronger for high- rather than low-complexity material.

Additionally, in some cases the modality principle is stronger when the relevant portions of the graphic are highlighted (Jeung, Chandler, & Sweller, 1997). For example, Jueng, Chandler, and Sweller (1997) found that spoken text was more effective than printed text when the corresponding part of the graphic was highlighted (by flashing) but not when it was not highlighted. Again, the audio script is fleeting, so when the graphic is hard to process the learner may not be able to identify the appropriate part of the graphic before the next segment of the script is presented. Jeung, Chandler, and Sweller (1997, p. 329) noted an important boundary condition for the modality effect: "if visual search was clearly high, then audio-visual instruction was only beneficial if visual indicators in the form of electronic flashing were incorporated into the instructional format . . . [but] visual indicators were not necessary in areas of low visual search." In short, when the graphic is difficult to process, the benefits of narration (caused by freeing up capacity in the visual channel) can be offset by the costs of increased extraneous processing (caused by the need to scan the graphic).

By contrast, printed text lasts longer, so the learner has a better chance to make a connection between the words and the corresponding part of the graphics. The benefits of printed text may be increased when it is placed next to the corresponding part of the graphic – as called for by the spatial contiguity principle (as described in Chapter 7). Research is needed to determine whether the modality effect is diminished or even reversed when pictures are difficult to process for the learner.

Second, concerning pacing, Tabbers, Martens, and van Merrienboer (2004) provide preliminary evidence that the modality principle does not apply when the lesson is slow-paced or under learner control. To understand this finding, consider what happens in the learner's cognitive system when a learner has adequate time to process captioned graphics – such as being able to pause an animation or being able to control the pace of slides. In this case, the learner can take all the time that is needed to read the text and to view the corresponding parts of the graphic. The learner can create his or her own segmenting technique (as discussed in Chapter 9) by reading a description of one event and then looking at the corresponding part of the graphic, reading the description of the next event and then looking at the corresponding part of the graphic, and so on. In this case, the learner is able to engage in all of the cognitive processes necessary for meaningful learning as depicted in Figure 3.1 in Chapter 3 – namely, selecting relevant words and images, organizing relevant words and images, and integrating verbal and pictorial representations with each other and with prior knowledge. Under these conditions of slow pacing, the advantages of narration may be diminished, lost, or even reversed.

This analysis helps to explain the only study in the published peer-reviewed literature in which using graphics with printed words resulted in poorer transfer performance than using graphics with spoken words (Tabbers et al., 2004). Tabbers and colleagues (2004, p. 80) interpret these results as "contrary to what both cognitive load theory and Mayer's theory of multimedia learning would predict," but it would be more appropriate to say that the results suggest a boundary condition for the modality principle that is consistent with the predictions of both theories. Similarly, Ginns's (2005) meta-analysis of the modality effect shows that the modality effect is stronger for system-paced rather than learner-paced learning.

Third, concerning learner familiarity, students tend to benefit more from the modality principle when they are familiar with the words than when the words are unfamiliar (Harskamp, Mayer, Suhre, & Jansma, 2007). The higher-skilled learners may be better able to process the spoken words without needing to refer back to them.

These boundary conditions for the modality principle suggest an important admonition concerning principles of instructional design. Design principles – such as the modality principle – are not immutable laws that must apply in all situations. Rather, the principles should be used in ways that are consistent with a research-based theory of how people learn from words and pictures, such as the cognitive theory of multimedia learning.

IMPLICATIONS OF THE MODALITY PRINCIPLE

Implications for Multimedia Learning

In seventeen separate tests, we began with a concise narrated graphic that provided a scientific explanation and found that learning was hurt when we substituted on-screen text for the narration. We refer to this finding as a *modality principle:* Substituting on-screen text for narration detracts from multimedia learning.

On the surface, the results seem to conflict with common sense. The on-screen text and the narration contained the same words, so both treatment groups received identical information – the same words and the same pictures. The only difference was that one group received the words as text and one group received the words as narration. Clearly, there is something wrong with the commonsense view that student learning will be equivalent when students are presented with the same information. This prediction is based on what we call the information-delivery theory – the idea that the amount of learning depends on the amount of information that is delivered to the learner. In order to understand the modality effect it is necessary to move beyond common sense, that is, beyond the information-delivery theory, to consider a cognitive theory of how people process multimedia material.

These results are most consistent with a cognitive theory of multimedia learning that posits dual information processing channels. When a concise narrated animation is presented, the pictures (i.e., animation) are processed in the visual channel, while the words (i.e., narration) are processed in the auditory channel. However, when we present the words as on-screen text rather than as narration, both the words and pictures must be processed – at least initially – through the visual channel. The visual system is more likely to become overloaded for the animation-and-text presentation than for the animation-and-narration presentation – resulting in less learning and understanding.

Although on-screen text proved to be detrimental in this research, it does not follow that all instances of printed text should be avoided. Our research on the spatial contiguity effect in Chapter 7, for example, found that students learn better when illustrations and corresponding printed text appear near rather than far from each other on a page or screen. In these cases, students seem to have engaged in meaningful learning from printed words and illustrations.

What is the relationship between the spatial continuity effect and the modality effect? In the spatial contiguity effect, text and pictures can result in meaningful learning, whereas in the modality effect, presenting text and pictures results in poorer learning. First, the spatial contiguity effect compares placing text near the corresponding part of the illustration (or animation) to placing text far from it. According to the cognitive theory of multimedia learning, placing text near the picture it describes increases the chances that the learner will be able to make mental connections between corresponding words and pictures. Second, the modality effect compares animation and narration with animation and text – when the text is placed far from the corresponding part of the animation. Consistent with the spatial contiguity effect, the animation-and-text group performs poorly on transfer. In both the spatial contiguity principle and the modality principle, the key to meaningful learning lies in fostering meaningful cognitive processing – such as making mental connections between corresponding words and pictures. In both studies, learning is hurt when printed words are placed far from the pictures they describe.

Implications for Multimedia Instruction

The modality principle suggests an important design principle: When making a multimedia presentation consisting of animation and words, present the words as narration rather than as on-screen text. It is important to note that this design principle has been demonstrated mainly in situations in which the animated narration contains complex material and runs at a fast pace without learner control of the presentation.

There may be situations in which printed text can foster meaningful learning, especially when it is used in a way that is consistent with the spatial contiguity principle. Printed words may also be appropriate when the learners are non-native speakers or hearing-impaired or when the lesson contains hard-to-pronounce words and symbols. Therefore, the modality effect should not be used to justify a blanket prescription to never present printed text and graphics together. Instead, multimedia design decisions should be based on an under-standing of how people process information – such as the cognitive theory of multimedia learning – rather than on a set of blindly fol-lowed rules. Presenting words in printed form may be harmful in some situations – such as in the studies described in this chapter – but not in other situations – as was demonstrated for the spatial contiguity effect in Chapter 3.

In answer to the question, "Does modality matter?," research on the modality principle consistently demonstrates that the answer is yes – at least in the kinds of situations we examined in this chapter. Words-as-text and words-as-narration may be processed differently by learn-ers even when the words are identical. Based on the research reviewed in this chapter, the best way to present words and pictures in a computer-based environment seems to be as a concise narrated graphic.

Limitations and Future Directions

Research on the modality principle suggests boundary conditions involving the complexity of the material, the pacing of presentation, and the learner's familiarity with the words. Further research is needed to pinpoint the boundary conditions of the modality principle, and to determine the implications for a cognitive theory of multimedia learning. Social cues inherent in the narrator's voice are also worthy of further study, such as the preliminary research on the voice principle summarized in Chapter 13.

SUGGESTED READINGS

Asterisk (*) indicates that part of this chapter is based on this publication.

Ginns, P. (2005). Meta-analysis of the modality effect. *Learning and Instruction*, 15, 313–331.

Low, R., & Sweller, J. (2005). The modality principle in multimedia learning. In R. E. Mayer (Ed.), *The Cambridge handbook of multimedia learning* (pp. 147–158). New York: Cambridge University Press.

*Mayer, R. E., & Moreno, R. (1998). A split-attention effect in multimedia learning: Evidence for dual processing systems in working memory. *Journal of Educational Psychology*, 90, 312–320.

*Moreno, R., & Mayer, R. E. (1999). Cognitive principles of multimedia learning: The role of modality and contiguity. *Journal of Educational Psychology, 91,* 358–368.

Mousavi, S., Low, R., & Sweller, J. (1995). Reducing cognitive load by mixing auditory and visual presentation modes. *Journal of Educational Psychology, 87,* 319–334.

Section IV

Principles for Fostering Generative Processing in Multimedia Learning

Consider the following situation. You play an online science game in which you travel to a distant planet that has high winds and rain, and your job is to design a plant that would survive there – including choosing appropriate roots, stem, and leaves. You get feedback from an on-screen character named Herman the Bug, who also explains how plants grow. Herman is not very friendly and seems to be just listing fact after fact, so you do not put much effort into trying to understand what he says. On a subsequent retention test, you can remember parts of some of his sentences, and on a transfer test, you are not able to apply what was presented to solving new problems.

What is generative processing underutilization? This is a situation in which you have cognitive capacity available but you do not choose to use it for making sense of the material – a situation that can be called *generative processing underutilization*. Learners may fail to engage in generative processing because they are not motivated to make sense of the material. When the on-screen tutor is not very friendly or presents boring material, learners may not be inclined to work hard to understand what he is saying. Box 4.1 summarizes the problem of generative processing underutilization – in which the speaker appears to be unfriendly or does not use graphics to help concretize the material. In short, generative processing underutilization is likely to occur when learners have cognitive capacity available but are not motivated enough to use it for generative processing during learning.

What is generative processing? Generative processing is cognitive processing aimed at making sense of the material and includes organizing the incoming material into coherent structures and integrating these structures with each other and with prior knowledge. This form of processing is indicated by the *organizing and integrating* arrows in Figure 3.1 in Chapter 3. In the science game example, generative

---

Box 4.1.   What Is Generative Processing Underutilization?

Scenario 5: Cognitive capacity > essential processing + generative processing

Description: Learners do not engage in generative processing even though cognitive capacity is available.

Example: Speaker is unfriendly or uses no graphics.

Principles: Multimedia, personalization, voice, image

---

processing involves building a mental model of how plants grow, including a causal chain that links the characteristics of the roots, stems, and leaves with climatic factors.

How can we foster generative processing? In this section of the book, I address the problem of generative processing underutilization. In particular, as summarized in Box 4.2, I explore three principles for fostering generative processing that have worked in our research – multimedia (Chapter 12), personalization (Chapter 13), and voice principles (Chapter 13) – and one principle that has not worked in our research – the image principle (Chapter 13). Multimedia techniques involve presenting material using words and pictures rather than with words alone. Personalization involves putting the words of a multi-media message in conversational style rather than formal style. Voice techniques involve having the narrator or tutor speak with a human voice rather than a machine voice. Image techniques involve having an image of the narrator or tutor on the screen during learning. These techniques are intended to encourage the learner to work harder to process the material more deeply. Our research evidence is consistent with all of these techniques except using an image of the speaker.

Box 4.2.   Four Ways to Foster Generative Processing

Technique	*Description*
Multimedia:	Present words and pictures rather than words alone.
Personalization:	Present speech in conversational style rather than formal style.
Voice:	Present speech with human voice rather than machine voice.
Image:	Present speaker's image on the screen during learning [not supported].

12

Multimedia Principle

Multimedia Principle: *People learn better from words and pictures than from words alone.*

Example: *A multimedia lesson consists of an animation depicting the steps in lightning formation along with concurrent narration describing the steps in lightning formation, whereas a singe-medium lesson consists of narration alone. A multimedia lesson consists of illustrations depicting the steps in lightning formation along with printed text describing the steps, whereas a single-medium lesson consists of text alone.*

Theoretical Rationale: *When words and pictures are both presented, learners have an opportunity to construct verbal and visual mental models and to build connections between them. When words alone are presented, learners have an opportunity to build a verbal mental model but are less likely to build a visual mental model and make connections between the verbal and visual mental models.*

Empirical Rationale: *In eleven out of eleven tests, learners who received text and illustrations or narration and animation (multiple-representation group) performed better on transfer tests than did learners who received text alone or narration alone (single-representation group). The median effect size is d = 1.39.*

Boundary Conditions: *The multimedia principle may apply more strongly to low-knowledge learners than to high-knowledge learners, presumably because low-knowledge learners need guidance in building connections between pictorial and verbal representations.*

▨ ▨ Chapter Outline

INTRODUCTION TO THE MULTIMEDIA PRINCIPLE
    Does Multimedia Work?
    Are Pictures Different from Words?

223

INTRODUCTION

Does Multimedia Work?

How can we encourage learners to engage in generative processing
during learning? One straightforward approach is to present corresponding words and pictures together so that the learner is encouraged
to build connections between them. When learners engage in this
mental act of integrating verbal and pictorial representations, they are
engaging in the essence of generative processing. Multimedia presentations are intended to foster generative processing because they
help the learner hold corresponding verbal and pictorial representations in working memory at the same time.

An important question concerns whether multimedia works: Do
students learn better when a lesson is presented in two formats than
when it is presented solely in one? In this book, I focus on a
straightforward version of this question: Do students learn better
when a lesson is presented in words and pictures than when it is
presented solely in words? In short, does adding pictures to a verbal
lesson help students learn better?

In order to answer this question it is useful to define what is meant
by "lesson," "words," "pictures," and "learn better." A lesson is a
presentation that is intended to foster learning by a student; in our
studies, the lessons are brief explanations of how some physical,
mechanical, or biological system works. By "words," I mean printed or
spoken text; in our studies, the words are often short passages or

narrations adapted from encyclopedias or science textbooks. By "pictures," I mean any form of static or dynamic graphic, including photos, graphs, charts, illustrations, video, and animation; in our studies, the pictures are illustrations (consisting of two or more frames of line drawings) or animations. I use the term "learn better" to refer to improvements in understanding of the presented material; in our studies, understanding is measured by transfer tests in which the student is asked to generate creative solutions to novel problems related to the lesson. As you can see, by "learn better" I do not mean the same as "learn more." Instead of focusing on the quantitative question of "how much is learned," I am most interested in the qualitative question of "what is learned." In particular, by focusing on transfer, I can examine whether multimedia presentations improve student understanding.

Asking whether multimedia works is an important question. If the answer is no, that is, if multimedia presentations do not result in better learning than single-medium presentations, then it is not necessary to conduct more in-depth studies concerning most of the other principles examined in this book. If the answer is yes, that is, if multimedia presentations result in better learning that single-medium presentations, then it is worthwhile to conduct in-depth studies aimed at pinpointing effective features of multimedia presentations. In particular, we would want to retain complementary chapters that focus on the conditions under which multimedia presentations foster meaningful learning.

Are Pictures Different from Words?

Consider the following description of how a bicycle tire pump works:

> As the rod is pulled out, air passes through the piston and fills the area between the piston and the outlet valve. As the rod is pushed in, the inlet valve closes and the piston forces air through the outlet valve.

These sentences provide a very brief and concise summary of the cause-and-effect chain involved in the operation of a tire pump: Pulling out the rod causes air to pass through the piston and fill the area between the piston and the outlet valve; pushing in the rod causes the inlet valve to close and the piston to force air through the outlet valve.

Now, examine Figure 12.1, which shows a pictorial version of this cause-and-effect chain, consisting of two line drawings. In the first

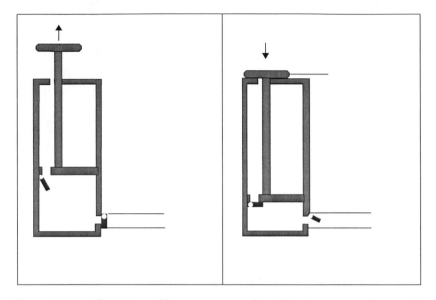

Figure 12.1. Illustration of how a pump works, without corresponding words.

frame, the rod is up and air is passing through the piston into the area between the piston and the outlet valve. In the second frame, the rod is pushed in, the inlet valve is closed, the piston has moved down, and air is moving out through the outlet valve.

Do you think that the words convey the same basic information as the picture? Do you learn the same thing from reading the two sentences as from viewing the two frames of the illustration? In short, are the two modes of presentation – words and pictures – informationally equivalent? According to the information-delivery view, the answer is yes, because words and pictures are simply two different vehicles for presenting the same information. According to the cognitive theory of multimedia learning, the answer is no, because words and pictures prime two qualitatively different knowledge representation systems in learners – a verbal channel and a visual channel. I explore these two views in the following two sections.

The Case for Presenting Words Only: Words and Pictures Are Informationally Equivalent

The information-delivery view is that different presentation formats – such as words and pictures – are vehicles for presenting the same information. A basic premise of this view is that information is an objective commodity that can be transported from the outside world to inside the human mind. This delivery can be made by words or by pictures, but the result is the same – information is stored in that great warehouse that we call long-term memory. Thus, the words presented in the previously presented box convey information on how a tire pump works; the picture in Figure 12.1 conveys the same information and therefore adds nothing new.

According to a strict interpretation of this view, multimedia presentations are not needed because the same information is delivered twice. Consider what happens when pumps are explained in both words and pictures. The presented words allow the learner to add the information to his or her memory, so a cause-and-effect chain is added to memory. The pictures allow the learner to add the same information to memory, but the information is redundant because it has already been delivered using words. Thus, the pictures are not needed because they add no new information beyond what has already been delivered by words.

The argument for words-only presentation is straightforward. Words are the most common way of presenting information because verbal messages are efficient and easy to create. If the learner receives the verbal message – the word-based delivery of information – then a pictorial message that delivers the same information is a waste of effort. Once a learner has received information in one format, it is useless to deliver the same information again in a different format.

In the information-delivery view, the teacher's role is to deliver information, and the learner's role is to store it in memory. As long as the information is delivered the instructor's job is done, so the instructor need only present a complete verbal explanation. Thus a book author need not include illustrations that repeat the information in the text; a computer-based instructional designer need not include animations that repeat the information in on-screen text or narration.

According to this strict interpretation of the information-delivery view, students who receive presentations in words should perform as well on transfer tests as students who receive presentations in words and pictures – as long as the delivery of words is fully received by the learner. This is the prediction I make for the information-delivery view in this chapter.

The Case for Adding Pictures to Words: Words and Pictures Are Qualitatively Different

The cognitive theory of multimedia learning (as described in Chapter 3) is based on the idea that humans possess two qualitatively different channels for processing material – one for visually based representations and one for verbally based representations. A premise underlying this view is that pictorial mental representations and verbal mental representations are qualitatively different; by their natures, visual and verbal representations cannot be informationally equivalent.

This premise can be summarized by saying that words and pictures are two qualitatively different systems for representing knowledge. On the one hand, language is one of the most important cognitive tools ever invented by humans. By using words we can describe material in an interpreted or abstracted manner that requires some mental effort to translate. On the other hand, pictures are probably the original mode of knowledge representation in humans. By using pictures we can depict material in a form that is more intuitive and closer to our visual sensory experience. Although the same material can be described in words and depicted in pictures, the resulting verbal and pictorial representations are not informationally equivalent. Although the verbal and pictorial representations may complement one another, they cannot be substituted for one another.

The instructor's job is not only to present material but also to help guide the learner's cognitive processing of the presented material. In particular, learners are expected to build verbal and pictorial representations and to build connections between them. Carefully designed multimedia messages can foster these processes in learners.

According to the cognitive theory of multimedia learning, multimedia presentations have the potential to result in deeper learning and understanding than presentations that are presented solely in one format. In short, multimedia presentations have the potential to foster generative processing. They foster generative processing by making it easier for learners to build connections between words and pictures – that is, they encourage learners to build connections between verbal and pictorial representations. For example, Figure 12.2 shows what happens when we combine words and corresponding pictures to produce a multimedia message. The cognitive theory of multimedia learning predicts that students will learn more deeply from a multimedia message such as the one in Figure 12.2 than from a presentation in only one format – such as a message presenting only the words or only the drawings. Thus, students who learn with words and pictures should perform better on transfer tests than students who learn only with words.

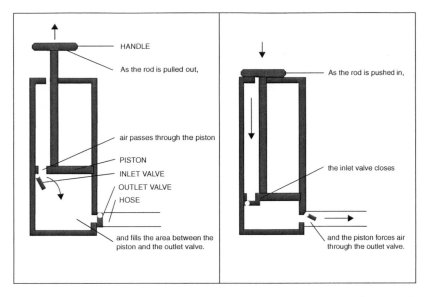

Figure 12.2. Illustration of how a pump works, with corresponding words.

The rationale for this prediction is that a multimedia presentation guides the learner to build both a verbal mental model of the pump system and a pictorial mental model of the pump system and to build connections between the two. The multimedia presentation allows learners to hold corresponding verbal and pictorial representations in working memory at the same time, thus increasing the chances that learners will be able to build mental connections between them. According to the cognitive theory of multimedia learning, the act of building connections between verbal and pictorial mental models is an important step in conceptual understanding; therefore, students who receive well-constructed multimedia messages should perform better on transfer tests – which are designed to measure under-standing – than students who receive messages presented only in words.

Distinction Between Multimedia Effects and Media Effects

It is useful to make a distinction between multimedia effects and media effects. The research question for multimedia effects concerns whether students learn more deeply when material is presented using two presentation forms – such as words and pictures – rather than one – such as words alone. In short, we can ask, "Are words and pictures more effective than words alone?" The research question for media effects concerns whether students learn more deeply when material is presented via one medium – such as computer-based animation and narration – rather than another medium – such as book-based illustrations and text. In short, we can ask, "Are computers more effective than textbooks?"

Media scholars have come to the conclusion that it is not productive to continue with traditional media research in which one medium is compared to another (Clark, 1983, 2001; Clark & Salomon, 1986; Salomon, 1994; Wetzel et al., 1994). Media research can be criticized on empirical, methodological, conceptual, and theoretical grounds. First, media research has a somewhat disappointing history, with inconclusive empirical results (Clark, 2001; Clark & Salomon, 1986; Mayer, 1997). Although our goal was not to examine media effects in our research, I decided to reanalyze our studies to look at every possible comparison between learning from computers and learning from textbooks. Consistent with prior research on media effects, I found no substantive differences on test performance between students who received an explanation presented via animation and narration and students who received an explanation of the same system using illustrations and text (Mayer, 1997). More recently, we found no evidence that animation was more effective than static diagrams in multimedia lessons (Mayer, Hegarty, Mayer, & Campbell, 2005).

Second, as demonstrated in our own comparisons, there are serious methodological confounds in comparing learning from two media. In our comparisons, for example, the tone of voice of the speaker and the way words were stressed in the narration for the computer-based presentation are different from the way that printed text was formatted into paragraphs and laid out on the page for the book-based presentation. Similarly, in some versions of the computer-based presentation students could repeat the presentation, whereas in the text-based presentation students had a certain time limit to study the text and illustrations. In short, it is not possible to determine whether differences in what students learn from text-based and computer-based presentations are caused by the medium or by the content and study conditions that are inseparable from the medium.

On the conceptual side, a third problem with media research is that learning depends on the quality of the instructional message rather than on the medium per se. It is possible to design a textbook so that students have great difficulty in understanding the material, and it is possible to design a textbook so that students can understand the presented material more easily. Similarly, it is possible to design a computer-based presentation in ways that hinder or promote meaningful learning. Importantly, our research has shown that the same factors that improve student understanding in a book-based environment also promote student understanding in computer-based environment – such as adding pictures to words (this chapter), placing text close to the corresponding graphic (Chapter 7), and eliminating extraneous material (Chapter 4). In both media, ineffective instructional messages can be converted into effective ones by applying the same instructional design principles (Fleming & Levie, 1993; Mayer, Hegarty, Mayer, & Campbell, 2005).

The fourth problem with media research concerns the theory that underlies it. Research on media effects is based on an information-delivery view of learning in which media are delivery systems for carrying information from teacher to learner. By asking, "Which medium is more effective in delivering information?" media researchers adopt the information-delivery view of learning. This theory conflicts with the cognitive theory of multimedia learning and with several key ideas in cognitive science – including the ideas of dual-channel processing, limited capacity, and active processing that I described in Chapter 3. The cognitive theory of multimedia learning is based on a knowledge-construction view in which learners actively build mental representations in an attempt to make sense out of their experiences. Instead of asking which medium makes the best deliveries, we might ask which instructional techniques help guide the learner's cognitive processing of the presented material.

In summary, the consensus among educational psychologists is that questions about which medium is best are somewhat unproductive questions. The rationale is empirical (in general, media effects are small), methodological (it is not possible to separate the effects of the medium from the effects of the instructional method), conceptual (learning outcomes depend on the quality of the instructional method rather than on the medium per se), and theoretical (learning involves knowledge construction rather than information delivery). For example, Clark (1994, 2001) has shown how media effects can never be separated from method effects; Jonassen, Campbell, and Davidson (1994) have argued for research that focuses on how instructional treatments affect cognitive processing in the learner rather than on the effects of media per se; and Kozma (1994) has called for research on the ways that instructional methods within a medium interact with cognitive and social processes in learners. In short, Kozma (1994, p. 13) reflects the consensus "to shift the focus of our research from media as conveyors of methods to media and methods as facilitators of knowledge construction and meaning making on the part of learners." In the remainder of this chapter – and, indeed, throughout this book – we focus on how to design multimedia presentations that foster understanding in learners rather than on which medium is best.

Research on the Multimedia Principle

Are two presentational formats better than one? Is it better to present words and pictures rather than words alone? We addressed this question in eleven separate tests in which we compared the transfer performance of students who received text with illustrations on pumps, brakes, generators, or lightning to the performance of students who received text alone (Mayer, 1989a, Experiments 1 and 2; Mayer et al., 1996, Experiment 2; Mayer & Gallini, 1990, Experiments 1, 2, and 3); or we compared the transfer performance of students who received a narrated animation on pumps, brakes, or lightning to the performance of students who received narration alone (Mayer & Anderson, 1991, Experiment 2a; Mayer & Anderson, 1992, Experiments 1 and 2; Moreno & Mayer, 2002b); or we compared the problem-solving performance of students who learned a mathematical procedure in a computer game that involved animation and words to the performance of students who received words alone (Moreno & Mayer, 1999a, Experiment 1).

Figure 12.2 provides an example of the kind of material we presented to students who received both words and pictures (which I call the multiple-representation group); by contrast, the text in Figure 12.2 constitutes an example of what would be presented to students who received words alone (which I call the single-representation group). The transfer test involved writing answers to problem-solving questions, generally with a 2.5-minute time limit for each question; the transfer score is based on the number of creative solutions generated across all of the problem-solving transfer questions. According to the cognitive theory of multimedia learning, the multiple-representation group should outperform the single-representation group, whereas there should be no difference between the multiple- and single-representation groups according to the information-delivery theory.

Core Evidence Concerning the Multimedia Principle

Does encouraging learners to mentally integrate words and pictures foster generative processing, which in turn is reflected in improvements in transfer performance? Table 12.1 shows the standardized differences in transfer scores for students who received words and pictures (multiple-representations group) and for students who received words only (single-representation group) for each of eleven experimental comparisons we conducted.

The first six lines in Table 12.1 summarize comparisons between learning from a booklet containing printed text and illustrations (multiple-representation group) and learning from a booklet containing printed text alone (single-representation group). The booklets explained how brakes work (Mayer, 1989a, Experiments 1 and 2; Mayer & Gallini, 1990, Experiment 1), how pumps work (Mayer & Gallini, 1990, Experiment 2), how generators work (Mayer & Gallini, 1990, Experiment 3), and how lightning works (Mayer et al., 1996, Experiment 2). The illustrations consisted of two (or more) frames depicting the states of the system in simple line drawings, such as the braking system before and after the driver steps on the car's brake pedal. After reading the booklet, learners took a transfer test in which they wrote answers to questions. In all six paper-based experiments, learners who received printed text with illustrations performed better in solving transfer problems than did learners who received the identical printed text alone. All of the effect sizes are large.

The next three lines in Table 12.1 summarize comparisons in computer-based environments in which learners received animation with concurrent narration (multiple-representation group) or narration alone (single-representation group). The lessons explained how pumps work (Mayer & Anderson, 1991, Experiment 2a; Mayer & Anderson, 1992, Experiment 1) or how brakes work (Mayer & Anderson, 1992, Experiment 2). In all three comparisons, learners performed better on transfer tests after receiving narrated animations rather than narration alone, yielding large effect sizes.

The tenth line of Table 12.1 summarizes a study (Moreno & Mayer, 2002b) in which students viewed an animation on lightning formation followed by a narration on lightning formation (multiple-representation group) or received only a narration on lightning formation (single-representation group). As you can see, learners who received animation and narration outperformed learners who received narration alone. The effect size is smaller than that obtained in the previous comparisons where animation and narration were presented concurrently. A plausible

Table 12.1. Core Evidence Concerning the Multimedia Principle

Source	Content	Format	Effect Size
Mayer (1989a, Expt. 1)	Brakes	Paper	1.50
Mayer (1989a, Expt. 2)	Brakes	Paper	1.71
Mayer & Gallini (1990, Expt. 1)	Brakes	Paper	1.19
Mayer & Gallini (1990, Expt. 2)	Pumps	Paper	1.00
Mayer & Gallini (1990, Expt. 3)	Generators	Paper	1.35
Mayer et al. (1996, Expt. 2)	Lightning	Paper	1.39
Mayer & Anderson (1991, Expt. 2a)	Pumps	Computer	2.43
Mayer & Anderson (1992, Expt. 1)	Pumps	Computer	1.90
Mayer & Anderson (1992, Expt. 2)	Brakes	Computer	1.67
Moreno & Mayer (2002b, Expt. 1)	Lightning	Computer	0.45
Moreno & Mayer (1999a, Expt. 1)	Arithmetic	Game	0.47
Median			1.39

explanation is that sequential presentation of animation and narration is less effective than concurrent presentation (as described in Chapter 6 on the temporal contiguity principle).

Finally, the eleventh line of Table 12.1 summarizes a study in which elementary school children learn to add and subtract signed numbers in a computer-based simulation game (Moreno & Mayer, 1999a). Some learners see problems presented in symbolic form (e.g., $3 - 2 = $ _____) and must type in an answer for which they receive feedback (single-representation group). Other learners see problems in symbolic form and are shown a number line with a bunny positioned at the 0 point and a clickable on-screen joystick that can be used to move the bunny along the number line (multiple-representation group). These students were asked to move the bunny in correspondence to each step in the computation (e.g., move the bunny to the 3 point, turn the bunny to the left, and jump backward two steps), and to type in the correct answer. They received feedback in terms of an animation showing the bunny's movements on the number line and the correct numerical answer. High-skill students (i.e., those scoring high on a computation pretest) benefited more from the multiple-representation treatment than from the single-representation, yielding a medium effect size.

In each of the eleven comparisons conducted in our lab, the multiple-representation group performed better than the single-representation group on a transfer test. In short, students who learned with words and pictures generated considerably more creative answers to problems than did students who learned with words alone. This pattern of results supports the *multimedia principle* because adding pictures to words resulted in improvements in students' understanding of the explanation. As you can see, the effect sizes are generally large, with a median of 1.39.

Overall, these results are inconsistent with the information-delivery theory, which predicted no differences between the two groups; and these results are consistent with the cognitive theory of multimedia learning, which predicted that adding pictures to words would greatly enhance the understandability of an explanation.

Related Research Concerning the Multimedia Principle

Table 12.2 summarizes some related research concerning the multimedia principle. The first two lines summarize the results of an experiment conducted by Moreno and Valdez (2005) in which college students learned from sixteen frames that described how lightning storms develop using either pictures with concurrent words (multiple-representation group) or words alone (single-representation group). In the first comparison there was no learner interactivity, and in the second comparison there was some simple learner interactivity. In both cases, adding pictures to words increased students' performance on a transfer test in which students had to solve problems based on the lesson.

The next three lines in Table 12.2 summarize experiments in which students learned about teaching principles from a lecture followed by a video showing a case example (multiple-representation group) or from a lecture followed by an equivalent text booklet describing a case example (single-representation group). In all three cases (Moreno & Valdez, 2007; Moreno & Ortegano-Layne, 2008), the multiple-representation group outperformed the single-representation group on a transfer test. Overall, most of the effect sizes were in the large range.

In addition, classic research on memory for prose shows that people learn better from printed text and supporting illustrations than from printed text alone (Levie & Lentz, 1982; Levin, Anglin, & Carney, 1987). Similar findings favoring learning from words and pictures rather than from words alone have been reported with learning foreign language vocabulary (Plass & Jones, 2005), that is, students learned the meanings of new words better from text definitions and graphics than from text definitions alone (Al-Seghayer, 2001; Chun & Plass, 1996; Jones & Plass, 2002; Plass et al., 1998). In addition, Reiber

Table 12.2.   Related Evidence Concerning the Multimedia Principle

Source	Content	Format	Effect Size
Moreno & Valdez (2005, Expt. 1a)	Lightning	Computer	0.52
Moreno & Valdez (2005, Expt. 1b)	Lightning	Computer	0.95
Moreno & Valdez (2007, Expt. 1)	Learning principles	Lecture	0.91
Moreno & Valdez (2007, Expt. 2)	Learning principles	Lecture	0.91
Moreno & Ortegano-Layne (2008, Expt. 1)	Learning principles	Lecture	1.95

(2005) found that in some situations graphics could improve learning in computer-based games and simulations. In a recent review of research on the multimedia principle, Fletcher and Tobias (2005, p. 128) concluded: "The multimedia principle, which suggests that learning and understanding are enhanced by adding pictures to text rather than by presenting text alone, appears to be well supported by findings from empirical research."

Graphics play an important role in both book-based and computer-based instruction, but often are not used in a way that fosters learning. For example, in an analysis of how space is used in sixth grade science textbooks, I found that about half of the page space was devoted to illustrations and about half was devoted to words (Mayer, 1993). Based on a taxonomy developed by Levin (Levin & Mayer, 1993), I categorized each illustration as belonging to one of the following categories:

decorative – illustrations that are intended to interest or entertain the reader but that do not enhance the message of the passage, such as a picture of a group of children playing in a park for a lesson on physics principles;

representational – illustrations that portray a single element, such as a picture of the space shuttle with a heading, "The Space Shuttle";

organizational – illustrations that depict relations along elements, such as a map or chart showing the main parts of the heart; and

explanative – illustrations that explain how a system works, such as the frames explaining how pumps work in Figure 12.2.

The results were that the overwhelming majority of illustrations served no important instructional purpose: 23 percent were decorational and

62 percent were representational. By contrast, only a small minority of the illustrations enhanced the instructional message: 5 percent were organizational, and 10 percent were explanative. From this kind of analysis, we can conclude that the potential power of graphics is not being met.

Similarly, in an analysis of fifth grade mathematics textbooks, my colleagues and I found that about 30 percent of the space was used for illustrations, but again the majority of the illustrations were irrelevant to the goal of the lesson (Mayer, Sims, & Tajika, 1995). For example, in a section on positive and negative numbers, one book had a full-color picture of a golfer teeing off. The text went on to talk about being above and below par in a golf game. As with our analysis of science textbooks, this analysis of mathematics textbooks shows that the authors are not maximizing the potential power of graphics to enhance human learning.

Research on *graphic advance organizers* offers an important line of research that complements research on the multimedia effect. A graphic advance organizer is material – usually involving a combination of graphics and text – that is presented before a text passage and that is intended to foster understanding of the text. Because the graphic advance organizer is intended to foster understanding, I have referred to graphic advance organizers as models for understanding (Mayer, 1989b). In particular, the organizer is intended to prime relevant prior knowledge in the learner – including both visual and verbal knowledge structures – which the learner can integrate with the incoming text.

In one study, for example, students were given a short passage about how radar works and later took retention and transfer tests (Mayer, 1983). For the retention test, students were asked to write down all they could remember from the passage; for the transfer test, students were asked to write answers for problems that required creative solutions, such as inventing a way to increase the area under surveillance for radar. Some students were asked to study a graphic advance organizer for sixty seconds before listening to the passage. The graphic advance organizer was a sheet of paper containing five labeled line drawings showing a pulse traveling from an antenna (transmission), a pulse bouncing off an aircraft (reflection), a pulse returning to the receiver (reception), measuring the difference between "time out" and "time back" on a clock (measurement), and converting time to a measure of distance (conversion). The drawings were intended to prime the learner's prior knowledge with bouncing balls. Students who received the graphic advance organizer generated

80 percent more useful solutions on the transfer test than did students who did not receive the graphic advance organizer. Similar results were obtained on more than a dozen additional tests involving lessons on topics such as Ohm's Law, the nitrogen cycle, and how a camera works (Mayer, 1989b).

Overall, research on illustrations in text yields two important results relevant to the multimedia effect: (a) textbook authors who add illustrations to their text often fail to take full advantage of the potential power of graphics as an aid to understanding, and (b) adding a carefully designed graphic advance organizer to a text passage can greatly enhance student understanding. Thus, this pioneering line of research on illustrations in text is consistent with what we have found in this chapter concerning the multimedia effect – adding certain kinds of pictures to words can help students to understand the instructional message.

Boundary Conditions for the Multimedia Principle

There is preliminary evidence that the multimedia principle may be stronger for learners with low prior knowledge rather than high prior knowledge. For example, Mayer and Gallini (1990) asked students to read a booklet that explained how brakes work, how pumps work, or how electrical generators work and then take a transfer test. For students who reported low prior mechanical knowledge, there was a strong multimedia effect in which students performed better on the transfer test if their booklet contained both text and diagrams rather than text alone. By contrast, for students who reported high prior mechanical knowledge, there was not a strong multimedia effect – that is, students performed almost as well when they learned from printed text as when they learned from printed text with diagrams.

Somewhat similar results were reported in a series of experiments by Kalyuga, Chandler, and Sweller (1998, 2000) involving learning to solve engineering problems. Low-prior-knowledge learners performed better on transfer tests when they learned from text and diagrams rather than text alone or from audio narration and diagrams rather than diagrams alone, but the reverse pattern was obtained for high-prior-knowledge learners. Kalyuga (2005) refers to this pattern as the *expertise reversal effect* – instructional manipulations that are effective for low-knowledge learners can be harmful for high-knowledge learners. Apparently, the high-prior-knowledge learners were able to generate a verbal explanation from the diagrams on their own, whereas the low-prior-knowledge learners needed more guidance in building connections between pictorial and verbal representations.

Another boundary condition concerns the quality of graphics. Schnotz and Bannert (2003) taught students about time zones in a hypermedia environment consisting of words alone (single-representation group) or words and graphics (multiple-representation group). Performance on problem-solving tests was not consistently better in the multiple-representation group, leading Schnotz and Bannert to conclude that the benefits of adding graphics depend on the quality and pedagogic value of the graphics.

IMPLICATIONS OF THE MULTIMEDIA PRINCIPLE

Implications for Multimedia Learning

The research summarized in this chapter has shown that multimedia works – that is, at least in the case of scientific explanations, adding illustrations to text or adding animation to narration helps student to better understand the presented explanation. We refer to this result as the *multimedia principle*: Presenting an explanation with words and pictures results in better learning than presenting words alone.

The results clearly contradict the commonsense notion that the main goal of instructional messages is to present information. I call this idea the information-delivery theory because it is based on the premise that instructional messages are vehicles for delivering information to the learner. According to this view, if information is presented in the form of words, then presenting the same information in pictures adds nothing to student learning. The results overwhelmingly contradict the prediction that students given words only will perform as well as students given words and pictures, and thus cast doubt on a strict interpretation of the information-delivery theory.

The results are consistent with the cognitive theory of multimedia learning that was presented in Chapter 3. In particular, the results coincide with the idea that humans process pictures and words using qualitatively different mental representations. A central premise in the cognitive theory of multimedia learning is that meaningful learning occurs when learners build systematic connections between word-based representations and picture-based representations (as indicated by the *integrating* arrow in Figure 3.1). This cognitive processing (which constitutes generative processing) is primed by the multiple-representation treatment – in which words and corresponding pictures are presented to learners.

By contrast, presenting information as words alone may encourage learners to build a word-based representation but does not prime learners to build a picture-based representation or to build systematic connections between word-based and picture-based representations. Some learners may be able to do this – by forming their own mental images based on the presented words – but the opportunities for meaningful learning are greater for the multiple-representation group. In short, our results support the thesis that a deeper kind of learning occurs when learners are able to integrate pictorial and verbal representations of the same message. This deeper processing can be called generative processing. Rather than adding information to memory, learners are actively constructing pictorial and verbal mental models and trying to understand how they are related to one another.

Implications for Multimedia Instruction

The multimedia principle is perhaps the most fundamental principle of multimedia design: Present words and pictures rather than words alone. The implications for instruction are clear. When you see a book that has page after page of text without any supporting graphics, the author has lost an opportunity to foster learning. When you attend a presentation in which the lecturer talks and talks without presenting any supporting graphics, the presenter has lost an opportunity to foster learning. In short, when instruction is based solely on words, the instructor is not doing all he or she can to foster learning.

Over the past 100 years, educators have tended to rely on words to present explanations to learners, and educational researchers have discovered many useful methods for presenting verbal material. However, the research presented in this chapter demonstrates that educators should consider ways to incorporate graphics into their lessons. In short, the main implication for instruction is that a words-only lesson can be improved by adding appropriate graphics.

Limitations and Future Directions

The multimedia principle demonstrates that student learning can be enhanced when pictures are added to words, that is, when material is presented in two forms rather than one. However, not all multimedia messages are equally effective. The central task in this book is to pinpoint the conditions under which multimedia presentations are effective. In short, we want to know how to design multimedia messages to maximize student understanding of the presented material.

The multimedia principle is somewhat vague and needs to be clarified. We live in an age when it is possible to create or select a wide array of graphics ranging from illustrations to photos to animations to video – but not all graphics are effective for all kinds of learners on all kinds of tasks. What kind of pictures should be added, how should they be added, for whom should they be added, and when should they be added? These are the kinds of clarifying issues that I address throughout this book. Thus, although the multimedia principle is a good starting place, it must be used in conjunction with other clarifying principles described in the other chapters. A summary of what we have learned about what makes an effective graphic is presented in the final chapter of this book (Chapter 14).

SUGGESTED READINGS

Asterisk (*) indicates that part of the chapter is based on this publication.

*Mayer, R. E. (1989). Systematic thinking fostered by illustrations in scientific text. *Journal of Educational Psychology, 81*, 240–246.

*Mayer, R. E., & Anderson, R. B. (1991). Animations need narrations: An experimental test of a dual-coding hypothesis. *Journal of Educational Psychology, 83*, 484–490.

*Mayer, R. E., & Anderson, R. B. (1992). The instructive animation: Helping students build connections between words and pictures in multimedia learning. *Journal of Educational Psychology, 84*, 444–452.

*Mayer, R. E., Bove, W., Bryman, A., Mars, R., & Tapangco, L. (1996). When less is more: Meaningful learning from visual and verbal summaries of science textbook lessons. *Journal of Educational Psychology, 88*, 64–73.

*Mayer, R. E., & Gallini, J. K. (1990). When is an illustration worth ten thousand words? *Journal of Educational Psychology, 82*, 715–726.

13

Personalization, Voice, and Image Principles

Personalization Principle: People learn better from multimedia presentations when words are in conversational style rather than formal style.

Example: In a narrated animation on how the human lungs work, personalization involves using "you" and "your" in the narration script – for example, saying "your nose" rather than "the nose" and "your throat" rather than "the throat."

Theoretical Rationale: When learners feel that the author is talking to them, they are more likely to see the author as a conversational partner and therefore will try harder to make sense of what the author is saying.

Empirical Rationale: In eleven out of eleven tests, learners who received the words of a multimedia lesson in conversational style performed better on transfer tests than learners who received the words in formal style, yielding a median effect size of $d = 1.11$.

Boundary Conditions: The personalization principle may be most effective when it is not overdone and when the learners are beginners.

Preliminary Research on the Voice Principle: People learn better when narration is spoken in a human voice rather than in a machine voice. The voice principle was supported in three out of three experiments, with a median effect size of $d = 0.78$.

Preliminary Research on the Image Principle: People do not necessarily learn better when the speaker's image is added to the screen. In five experiments, the median effect size favoring adding the speaker's image to the screen was $d = .22$, which is in the small-to-negligible range.

▪ ▪ Chapter Outline

242

The Case for Personalization

INTRODUCTION TO THE PERSONALIZATION PRINCIPLE

Learning Alone as a Social Event

Consider these learning situations: Sarah sits at her desk reading her biology textbook. Ken goes online to search for information about digital photography and finds a narrated animation on the topic. Dave plays a video game designed to improve his skill in solving problems involving electrical circuits. In each case, it appears that the learner is alone. Yet reading a book, viewing a multimedia presentation, or playing an interactive educational game can be seen as a social event. How so? In each case, there is an implied conversation between the instructor and the learner – based on the author's words in the textbook, the instructor's voice in the narrated animation, and the tone of the tutor's feedback in the simulation game. In this chapter, we explore the idea that multimedia learning can be viewed as a conversation between the learner and the instructor. If multimedia learning is a social event, then social cues may affect how hard learners try to make sense of the presented material.

Mayer, Fennel, Farmer, and Campbell (2004) have argued that there are two paths for fostering meaningful learning in multimedia learning environments: (a) designing multimedia instructional messages in ways that reduce the learner's cognitive load, thus freeing the learner to engage in active cognitive processing (as described in previous sections of the book), and (b) designing multimedia messages in ways that increase the learner's motivational commitment to active cognitive processing (as described in this section). Although cognitive considerations have received the most attention in research on multimedia learning (Mayer, 2005; Mayer & Moreno, 2003; Paas, Renkl, & Sweller, 2003; Sweller, 1999), progress in designing computer-based learning environments also can be made by attending to social considerations that affect the learner's motivation to engage in cognitive processing (Lepper, Woolverton, Mumme, & Gurtner, 1993; Mayer, Fennel, Farmer, & Campbell, 2004; Reeves & Nass, 1996).

How can we modify multimedia instructional messages so that they activate appropriate social responses in learners? In other words, what can we do to a multimedia instructional message to increase the learner's feeling of social presence, that is, to make the learner feel a stronger personal relationship with the instructor? In this chapter, I focus on a potentially important social cue – personalizing the script of the multimedia lesson.

Personalization involves taking the words in a multimedia lesson and converting them from formal style to conversational style. Two major techniques for creating conversational style are (a) to use "you" and "I" rather than relying solely on third-person constructions, and (b) to add sentences in which the instructor makes direct comments to the learner. For example, suppose a learner clicks on "lightning" in a multimedia encyclopedia and a 140-second narrated animation appears explaining the steps in lightning formation. The words are in formal style, such as shown in Table 13.1. Then, to help personalize the script, (a) in eight locations you change some words, such as "the" to "your" or "people" to "you," and (b) in six locations you add a sentence that speaks directly to the learner, such as, "Brr! I'm feeling cold just thinking about it." In Table 13.1, the added material is indicated by the brackets, and the deleted words are in italics. In converting the lightning script from formal to conversational style, however, the instructional content remains the same – that is, the explanation of the steps in lightning formation is not altered.

As another example, suppose you are a learner playing a science simulation game concerning how to design plants to survive in an alien environment. An on-screen agent named Herman the Bug

Table 13.1. Nonpersonalized and Personalized Versions of the Script for the Lightning Lesson (with Personalized Additions Indicated in Brackets and Deletions Indicated by Italics)

[Let me tell you what happens when lightning forms. Suppose you are standing outside, feeling the warm rays of the sun heating up the earth's surface around you.] Cool, moist air moves over a warmer surface and becomes heated. The warmed moist air near the earth's surface rises rapidly. As the air in this updraft cools, water vapor condenses into water droplets and forms a cloud. [Congratulations! You have just witnessed the birth of your own cloud.]

[As you watch, you tilt your head skyward. Your] *The* cloud's top extends above the freezing level, so the upper portion of [your] *the* cloud is composed of tiny ice crystals. [Brr! I'm feeling cold just thinking about it!] Eventually, the water droplets and ice crystals become too large to be suspended by updrafts. As raindrops and ice crystals fall through [your] *the* cloud, they drag some of the air in [your] *the* cloud downward, producing downdrafts. When downdrafts strike the ground, they spread out in all directions, producing the gusts of cool wind [you] *people* feel just before the start of the rain. [If you could look inside your cloud, you would see a neat pattern:] *Within the cloud* the rising and falling air currents cause electrical charges to build. The charge results from the collision of [your] *the* cloud's rising water droplets against heavier, falling pieces of ice. The negatively charged particles fall to the bottom of the cloud, and most of the positively charged particles rise to the top.

[Now that your cloud is charged up, I can tell you the rest of the story:] A stepped leader of negative charges moves downward in a series of steps. It nears the ground. A positively charged leader travels up from objects [around you] such as trees and buildings. The two leaders generally meet about 165 feet above the ground. Negatively charged particles then rush from [your] *the* cloud to the ground along the path created by the leaders. It is not very bright. As the leader stroke nears the ground, it induces an opposite charge, so positively charged particles from the ground rush upward along the same path. The upward motion of the current is the return stroke. It produces the bright light that [you] *people* notice as a flash of lightning.

interacts with you, giving you suggestions, feedback, and basic explanations of how plants grow. In the nonpersonalized version of the program, Herman speaks in a formal style, without using "I" or "you" and without making direct comments to you. Portions of this nonpersonalized script are shown in Table 13.2. In order to personalize the script, we can reword sentences to use conversational style, such as exemplified in the personalized portions of the script shown in Table 13.2. As with the lightning script, the personalized and non-personalized versions contain the same instructional content.

Table 13.2. Portion of Text of Nonpersonalized and Personalized Versions for an Environmental Science Simulation Game

Nonpersonalized Version of the Game's Introduction

This program is about what type of plant survives on different planets. For each planet, a plant will be designed. The goal is to learn what type of roots, stem, and leaves allow plants to survive in each environment. Some hints are provided throughout the program.

Personalized Version of the Game's Introduction

You are about to start on a journey where you will be visiting different planets. For each planet, you will need to design a plant. Your mission is to learn what type of roots, stem, and leaves will allow your plant to survive in each environment. I will be guiding you through by giving out some hints.

Nonpersonalized Introduction to First Environment

The goal is to design a plant that will survive, maybe even flourish, in an environment of heavy rain. It is perfect for any root and stem, but the leaves need to be flexible so they won't be damaged by the heavy rain.

Personalized Introduction to First Environment

Your only goal here is to design a plant that will survive, maybe even flourish, in this environment of heavy rain. It is perfect for any of the roots and stems, but your leaves need to be flexible so they won't be damaged by the heavy rain.

Nonpersonalized Explanation Concerning Rainy Environments

In very rainy environments, plant leaves have to be flexible so they are not damaged by the rainfall. What really matters for the rain is the choice between thick and thin leaves.

Personalized Explanation Concerning Rainy Environments

This is a very rainy environment and the leaves of your plant have to be flexible so they're not damaged by the rainfall. What really matters for the rain is your choice between thick leaves and thin leaves.

Finally, consider a sixty-second narrated animation explaining how the respiratory system works. The nonpersonalized version of the script is shown in Table 13.3. To personalize the script, we can simply change "the" to "your" in twelve places, as shown by the brackets in Table 13.3. Although the changes are modest, the goal is to create a conversational style without altering the instructional content of the lesson.

What are the consequences of adding personalization to a multi-media lesson? In the following two sections, we explore the case against personalization and the case for personalization.

Table 13.3. Nonpersonalized and Personalized Versions of the Lungs Script (with Personalized Additions Indicated in Brackets and Deletions Indicated by Italics)

There are three phases in respiration: inhaling, exchanging, and exhaling. During inhaling, *the* [your] diaphragm moves down, creating more space for *the* [your] lungs; air enters through *the* [your] nose or mouth, moves down through *the* [your] throat and bronchial tubes to tiny air sacs in *the* [your] lungs. During exchange, oxygen moves from *the* [your] air sacs to the bloodstream running nearby, and carbon dioxide moves from the bloodstream to *the* [your] air sacs. During exhaling, *the* [your] diaphragm moves up, creating less room for *the* [your] lungs; air travels through *the* [your] bronchial tubes and throat to *the* [your] nose and mouth, where it leaves *the* [your] body.

The Case Against Personalization

Social cues such as personalization add no new information to the lesson and therefore should not improve learning. This analysis is based on the information-delivery view of learning in which learners add information to their memories based on what the instructor presents. When personalization is too obvious, it may even distract the learner from the key information in the lesson, thereby hurting learning. Thus, personalization may act as a sort of seductive detail (as described in Chapter 4) that takes the learner's attention away from the essential information in the lesson. Overall, according to the information-delivery view, personalization adds no new information and may even distract the learner, so it should not have any positive effect on transfer test performance.

The Case for Personalization

Social cues such as personalization may encourage learners to try harder to understand a multimedia lesson – that is, personalization may encourage learners to engage in each of the cognitive processes summarized in Figure 3.1 in Chapter 3. How do social cues affect multimedia learning? The top portion of Figure 13.1 lays out a framework in which social cues in a multimedia instructional message – such as the conversational style – prime the activation of a social response in the learner – such as the commitment to try to make sense out of what the speaker is saying. This social response causes increases in active cognitive processing by the learner – as the learner works harder to select, organize, and integrate incoming information – which

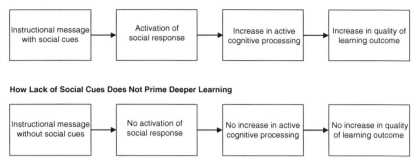

Figure 13.1. Social agency theory.

in turn leads to a learning outcome that is better able to support problem-solving transfer performance. The bottom portion of Figure 13.1 summarizes the scenario in which multimedia instructional messages lack social cues – in which a social response is not activated, the learner does not work harder to process the incoming information, and the learning outcome is not improved.

Concerning the arrow from the first box to the second box, Reeves and Nass (1996) and Nass and Brave (2005) have shown that people are easily induced into accepting computers as social partners. This line of research suggests that subtle cues such as a speaker's voice or conversational style can encourage learners to respond socially to an online tutor. Concerning the arrow from the second box to the third box, Grice (1975) has shown that in human-to-human communication, people assume the speaker is trying to make sense by being informative, accurate, relevant, and concise. Based on what Grice calls the *cooperation principle,* the listener works hard to understand the speaker because the listener and speaker have an implicit agreement to cooperate. Concerning the arrow from the third box to the fourth box, the cognitive theory of multimedia learning proposes that increases in active processing, such as the five processes shown in Figure 3.1 in Chapter 3, lead to higher-quality learning outcomes that better support problem-solving transfer. We use the term *social agency theory* to refer to the theoretical framework summarized in Figure 13.1, that is, the idea that social cues in multimedia instructional messages can prime a social response in learners that leads to deeper cognitive processing and better learning outcomes. Social agency theory can be seen as an enhancement or addition to the cognitive theory of multimedia learning. According to the social agency view, adding personalization cues to a multimedia script should foster generative processing, which in turn will result in improvements on transfer test performance.

RESEARCH ON THE PERSONALIZATION PRINCIPLE

Core Evidence Concerning the Personalization Principle

Do students learn more deeply when the words in a multimedia lesson are changed from formal style to conversational style? Table 13.4 summarizes comparisons between a group that received instruction with the words presented in conversational style (personalized group) and a group that received the words presented in formal style (non-personalized group). The left side of the table lists the experiment that is the source of the data, the middle portion of the table lists the content and format of the lesson, and the right side of the table lists the effect size.

In one set of studies, Moreno and Mayer (2000b, Experiments 1 and 2) compared the learning outcomes of students who viewed a 140-second narrated animation on lightning formation in which the speaker used conversational style (personalized group) or an animation in which the speaker used formal style (nonpersonalized group). In the version with conversational style, the speaker used first person ("I") and second person ("you") and made comments directly to the learner; in the version with formal style, the speaker did not use "I" or "you" and did not directly comment to the learner. However, both versions contained the same description of the steps in lightning formation – the core of the lesson. For example, Table 13.1 presents the words used in the personalized and nonpersonalized versions. A subsequent transfer test involved writing answers to problem-solving questions such as how to reduce the intensity of lightning storms. The top line of Table 13.4 shows that the personalized group performed better than the nonpersonalized group on a problem-solving transfer test in which the learner had to use what was learned to solve new problems about lightning. Similarly, the same pattern was found when the words were presented as on-screen text in personalized or nonpersonalized style (as shown in the second line of Table 13.4). In both comparisons the effect size was large, which is defined as greater than .8.

In a second set of studies, we (Moreno & Mayer, 2000b, Experiments 3, 4, and 5; Moreno & Mayer, 2004, Experiments 1a and 1b) compared

Table 13.4. Core Evidence Concerning the Personalization Principle

Source	Content	Format	Effect Size
Moreno & Mayer (2000b, Expt. 1)	Lightning (narration)	Computer	1.05
Moreno & Mayer (2000b, Expt. 2)	Lightning (text)	Computer	1.61
Moreno & Mayer (2000b, Expt. 3)	Botany (narration)	Game	1.92
Moreno & Mayer (2000b, Expt. 4)	Botany (text)	Game	1.49
Moreno & Mayer (2000b, Expt. 5)	Botany (narration)	Game	1.11
Moreno & Mayer (2004, Expt. 1a)	Botany (narration)	Game	1.58
Moreno & Mayer (2004, Expt. 1b)	Botany (narration)	Virtual reality	1.93
Mayer et al. (2004, Expt. 1)	Lungs (narration)	Computer	0.52
Mayer et al. (2004, Expt. 2)	Lungs (narration)	Computer	1.00
Mayer et al. (2004, Expt. 3)	Lungs (narration)	Computer	0.79
Wang et al. (2008)	Engineering (text)	Game	0.71
Median			1.11

the learning outcomes of students who learned from an environmental science simulation game in which they interacted with an on-screen agent named Herman-the-Bug. In the personalized version, Herman spoke (or produced on-screen text) that was in conversational style, and in the nonpersonalized version Herman spoke (or produced on-screen text) that was in formal style. Table 13.2 lists some of the script for the personalized and nonpersonalized versions. The instructional content of both versions was identical, that is, both provided the same descriptions of how plants grow. As shown in lines three through seven of Table 13.4, the personalized group produced much better transfer test performance than the nonpersonalized group, yielding large effect sizes in all cases. Even when the lesson was presented in virtual reality (Moreno and Mayer, 2004, Experiment 1b), using a head-mounted display rather than on a desktop computer, the personalization effect was strong (as shown in the seventh line of Table 13.4).

In a third set of studies, we (Mayer, Fennell, Farmer, & Campbell, 2004, Experiments 1, 2, and 3) examined a much more modest form of personalization in a sixty-second narrated animation explaining how the human respiratory system works. As shown in Table 13.3, in the nonpersonalized version the article "the" was used, whereas in the personalized version "the" was changed to "your" in twelve places in the narration script. On a transfer test, learners were asked to write answers to problems such as how to redesign the lungs to get oxygen into the bloodstream faster. Even this seemingly minor change created medium to large effect sizes favoring the personalization group across three separate experiments, as shown in lines eight through ten of Table 13.4.

Finally, in a twist on the personalization principle, we compared the transfer test performance of students who learned to solve industrial engineering problems using a computer game called Virtual Factory (Wang, Johnson, Mayer, Rizzo, Shaw, & Collins, 2008) with an on-screen tutor who used direct wording (e.g., "Save the factory now") to the performance of students who learned with a tutor who used polite wording (e.g., "Do you want to save the factory now?" or "Why don't we save the factory now?") when giving suggestions or feedback. The content of the suggestions or feedback was identical for the direct and polite tutors, but the conversational style was more personal with the polite tutor. The polite tutor used politeness strategies developed by Brown and Levinson (1978) in which the goal is to save positive face – allowing the learner to feel appreciated and respected by the conversational partner – and to save negative face – allowing the learner to feel that his or her freedom of action is unimpeded by the other party in the conversation. After interacting with the Virtual Factory program for about an hour to solve several practice problems, learners were given a transfer test based on the underlying industrial engineering principles for designing assembly lines. Learners who had the polite tutor performed substantially better on the transfer test than learners who had the direct tutor, as shown in the eleventh line of Table 13.4.

Overall, there is strong and consistent evidence for the *personalization principle*: People learn more deeply when words are presented in conversational style rather than formal style. The personalization principle was supported in eleven out of eleven tests, yielding a median effect size of 1.11.

Related Evidence Concerning the Personalization Principle

In the interest of scholarship, many textbooks are written in an *anonymous-author style* – that is, the writing is in the third person with no indication of the author's personal characteristics, interests, or opinions. Here is an example of anonymous-author style in a history chapter on Julius Caesar: "Caesar's rivals, afraid of losing their influence, stabbed him to death in 44 B.C." By contrast, Paxton (2002) suggests that textbooks should be written in a *visible-author style*, in which the author is self-revealing about his or her opinions and experiences, and writes in the first and second person. For example, in a history chapter on Julius Caesar, the visible-author style could include: "You don't have to trust me on this: Caesar's own point of view is spelled out in his book, *The Gallic Wars*, one of the best-known works of Latin literature." Paxton (2002) found that students who read an introductory text written in visible-author style displayed deeper learning on subsequent material than did students who read an introductory text written in anonymous-author style. Similar results were reported by Paxton (1997) with history texts, by Nolen (1995) with statistics texts, and by Inglese, Mayer, and Rigotti (2007) with online interview videos in political philosophy. Overall, these results appear to complement the personalization principle, in which using conversational style encourages learners to learn more deeply.

Boundary Conditions for the Personalization Principle

The personalization effect may be strongest when the personalization strategy is not overdone and when the learner is not familiar with the tutor. First, in pilot studies conducted in conjunction with a multimedia lesson on how the lungs work (Mayer, Fennell, Farmer, & Campbell, 2004), a "super-personalized" treatment was tested in which the speaker added several conversational sentences throughout the lesson, such as, "Now I am going to tell you all about your lungs." These sentences were friendly, used the first and second person, but did not add any pedagogically useful information. Thus, they can be seen as extraneous material, somewhat like the seductive details described in Chapter 4. In our pilot testing, we found that the "super-personalized" treatment did not improve test performance above the nonpersonalized treatment, although the pilot work is not reported in the paper. Thus, there is preliminary unpublished research suggesting that personalization works best when it does not intrude on the pedagogical content of the lesson. Additional research is needed to determine the boundary conditions under which too much personalization violates the coherence principle (as described in Chapter 4).

Second, Mayer, Johnson, Shaw, and Sandhu (2006) asked students to rate the various printed comments from online tutors on the basis of negative politeness ("how much the tutor allows me freedom to make my own decisions") and positive politeness ("how much the tutor is working with me"). Statements such as "Click the ENTER button" were rated as low in politeness, whereas statements such as "Do you want to click the ENTER button?" or "Let's click the ENTER button" were rated as high in politeness. The differences in politeness ratings were stronger for students with low rather than high computing experience, suggesting that the effects of conversational style may diminish as learners gain more experience with an online tutor. Additional research is needed to determine the boundary conditions of the personalization principle, particularly whether it applies better early in training rather than later and for students who are less experienced working with online tutors rather than more experienced.

McLaren, Lim, Gagnon, Yaron, and Koedinger (2006) asked college students in a chemistry course to interact with an online tutor to learn how to solve sixteen chemistry problems. Students who learned from a polite tutor – using strategies as described by Wang and colleagues (2008) – did not perform better on a subsequent transfer test as compared to students who learned from a direct tutor. McLaren and colleagues (2006) speculated that the personalization effect was not obtained because the majority of the participants were not native speakers of English and therefore perhaps not able to appreciate the subtle differences in conversational style, or because most learners were experienced. Again, additional research is needed to pinpoint for whom personalization is most effective.

IMPLICATIONS OF THE PERSONALIZATION PRINCIPLE

Implications for Multimedia Learning

The research results summarized in Table 13.4 provide support for social agency theory as summarized in Figure 13.1. Social cues such as the conversational style of the speaker can have substantial effects on how well learners understand the material in a multimedia presentation. Table 13.4 shows that there is strong and consistent evidence for the personalization principle in which conversational style serves as a social cue. This work shows that the cognitive theory of multimedia learning described in Chapter 3 can be improved by incorporating how social cues can encourage learners to work hard to engage in appropriate cognitive processing during learning.

Implications for Multimedia Instruction

The research reviewed in this chapter shows that instructional designers should be sensitive to social considerations as well as cognitive considerations when they create multimedia instructional messages. Based on the personalization principle, multimedia instructional messages should be presented in conversational style rather than formal style. However, too much emphasis on extraneous conversational tactics might create a seductive detail that distracts the learner (Harp & Mayer, 1998). This recommendation applies to the design of paper-based materials, computer-based presentations, and simulation games involving on-screen animated pedagogical agents – computer-based characters that help students learn, as described by Moreno (2005) and by Cassell, Sullivan, Prevost, and Churchill (2000).

Limitations and Future Directions

Although the research summarized in Table 13.4 provides somewhat consistent support for the personalization principle, the existing research base is limited in terms of the task environment, dependent measures, and independent variables. First, concerning the task environment, many of the reported studies involve short narrated animations presented to college students in laboratory settings with immediate tests. Further studies are needed that are conducted within a more realistic, ecologically valid environment, while still maintaining rigorous experimental control.

Second, concerning dependent measures, all of the effects reported in Table 13.4 are based on measures of problem-solving transfer because I am particularly interested in how to promote understanding. Studies that focus only on measures of retention do not adequately inform the issue of learner understanding, so future research should continue to use measures of transfer. In addition, social agency theory is based on the idea that social cues prime social responses in learners, such as responding to the computer as a social partner. For example, in some studies, the authors included surveys in which the learners rated their affect for the instructor (e.g., Mayer, Fennell, Farmer, & Campbell, 2004). Although such measures represent a useful first step that should be continued, more systematic and direct measures of social responses are needed. The current research base lacks direct evidence concerning whether or not social cues activate social responses in learners, so direct measures of social response should be included in future research.

Third, concerning the independent variables, I am concerned with the fidelity and consistency of the treatments across studies as well as possible confounding variables. For example, there are no firm guidelines for how to add personalization to a script, or for how much personalization to add. Research is needed to calibrate how much personalization and what kind of personalization are most effective and under what conditions.

Finally, although social cues are intended to prime deeper processing in learning, a potential confounding factor is the role of cognitive load. Adding certain kinds of personalization – such as extraneous sentences – may create extraneous cognitive load (Sweller, 1999) by serving as a seductive detail that distracts the learner (Harp & Mayer, 1998). Possible increases in cognitive load may offset or reduce the advantages of some social cues. Future research should investigate this possibility by incorporating measures of cognitive load (Brunken, Plass, & Leutner, 2003; DeLeeuw & Mayer, 2008; Paas, Tuovinen, Tabbers, & van Gerven, 2003).

In the following two sections, I explore two additional principles that may be seen as extensions of the personalization principle: the voice principle and the image principle. Both are in their preliminary stages, but I include them with the hope that future research will clarify their robustness.

A PRELIMINARY LOOK AT THE VOICE PRINCIPLE

In addition to the personalization principle, we have also begun to examine an additional cue in multimedia lessons – the role of the speaker's voice. Our goal is to determine how to use aspects of the instructor's voice to foster a sense of social partnership in a human-computer interaction. The voice principle is that people learn more deeply when the words in a multimedia message are spoken by a friendly human voice rather than by a machine voice.

Voice Cues

How can we create voice cues that are intended to affect the learner's social response to a multimedia instructional message? In particular, we focus on how to alter the voice in the narration of a multimedia message. For example, suppose that the words in the nonpersonalized lightning script shown in Table 13.1 were spoken by a native English speaker with a standard accent and a friendly tone. A friendly human voice, speaking with a standard accent, conveys a sense of social

Table 13.5. Core Evidence Concerning the Voice Principle

Source	Content	Format	Effect Size
Mayer, Sobko, & Mautone (2003, Expt. 2)	Lightning	Computer	0.79
Atkinson, Mayer, & Merrill (2005, Expt. 1)	Mathematics word problems	Computer	0.69
Atkinson, Mayer, & Merrill (2005, Expt. 2)	Mathematics word problems	Computer	0.78
Median			0.78

presence – that is, it conveys the idea that someone is speaking directly to you. By contrast, we could run the same script through a speech synthesizer such as *Bruce (high quality)* provided in the voice folder of Macintosh G4 computers (Mayer, Sobko, & Mautone, 2003). A machine-synthesized voice – although perceptually discernable – may not convey as much sense of social presence – that is, it may not strongly convey the idea that someone is speaking directly to you. Thus, voice cues may affect the degree to which a learner feels a social response to the instructional message.

Core Evidence Concerning the Voice Principle

Does it hurt student understanding of a multimedia lesson to change the speaker's voice from a human voice with a standard accent to a machine voice? Table 13.5 lists three tests of the voice principle. In the first study (Mayer, Sobko, & Mautone, 2003, Experiment 2), students received a 140-second narrated animation on lightning formation in nonpersonalized style in which the words were spoken by a machine-synthesized voice or by a human voice with a standard accent. Although the machine-synthesized voice was clearly discernable, it resulted in much worse performance on a subsequent problem-solving transfer test as compared to the standard-accented human voice.

In the second set of studies (Atkinson, Mayer, and Merrill, 2005, Experiments 1 and 2), students studied worked examples of arithmetic word problems that were explained by an on-screen cartoon-like character named Peedy who spoke either in a machine voice or in a human voice. On a subsequent test of problem-solving transfer to dissimilar problems, students in the machine-voice group performed worse than those in the human-voice group across two separate experiments.

Overall, Table 13.5 shows consistent, medium-to-large effect sizes favoring the friendly human voice over the machine voice, yielding a median effect size of $d = 0.78$. These findings are consistent with the *voice principle*: People learn more deeply when narration in a multimedia lesson is spoken by a friendly human voice rather than by a machine voice. However, you should consider the voice principle to be preliminary until it is tested in additional experiments.

Related Evidence Concerning the Voice Principle

The voice principle may also apply to certain foreign accents or voices with certain emotional tones. Mayer, Sobko, and Mautone (2003, Experiment 1) gave students a 140-second narrated animation on lightning formation in nonpersonalized style in which the words were spoken with a Russian accent (in which the speaker also seemed somewhat bored) or a standard accent. On a subsequent transfer test, students who received the standard-accented voice performed better on a subsequent transfer test than did students who received the Russian-accented voice, with an effect size of $d = .90$. This work constitutes preliminary evidence that a human voice with certain nonstandard accents – such as a Russian accent that sounds as if the speaker is bored – may also diminish the learner's social response to the message.

Nass and Brave (2005) also provide evidence that people are sensitive to the social aspects of online voices, including the speaker's gender, ethnicity, race, and emotional state. Although most of their research does not focus on learning and instruction, they point to the value of studying "the social aspects of human-technology interactions" and note that "nothing is more social than speech" (p. ix). The rationale for examining the voice principle is summarized by Nass and Brave: "As a result of human evolution, humans are automatic experts at extracting the social aspects of speech" (p. 3). In short, humans are "wired for speech" (p. 1).

Overall, there is a need for more research on the role of the speaker's voice in multimedia messages, and in particular there is a need for research on which aspects of the instructor's voice prime which cognitive processes in which kinds of learners.

Boundary Conditions of the Voice Principle

Nass and Brave (2005) present evidence that people may be more influenced by online spoken messages when they perceive the speaker's voice to be coming from someone like them in terms of gender, race, ethnicity, or emotional state. Thus, research is needed to determine how the effects of voice cues in multimedia instructional messages may be different for different kinds of learners and, in particular, to determine whether people learn better when they perceive that the instructor's voice comes from someone like them.

A PRELIMINARY LOOK AT THE IMAGE PRINCIPLE

Given the promising evidence concerning the potential role of voice cues in fostering social partnership between learner and instructor, we were tempted to consider another possible social cue – having the instructor's image on the screen. Although voice may be a powerful social cue, we feared that adding the instructor's image could cause the learner to engage in extraneous processing – attending to the instructor's face or body rather than to the instructional content in the graphic. Placing the instructor's image on the screen can create split attention in the learner – that is, when the learner is looking at the instructor (which may be instructionally irrelevant), he or she is not able to look at the relevant material in the graphic. When the instructor's image carries little or no pedagogically relevant information, then wasting precious cognitive resources on attending to it may outweigh any potential social benefits. The image principle is that people do not necessarily learn more deeply from a multimedia presentation when the speaker's image is on the screen rather than not on the screen.

Image Cues

A seemingly straightforward way to increase the learner's sense of social presence is to add an on-screen character who delivers the script. An animated pedagogical agent is an on-screen character who appears to interact with the learner. In a narrated animation of lightning formation, we could add an on-screen character in the form of a man who points to the events in the narration as he describes them (Craig, Gholson, & Driscoll, 2002). In an environmental science game, we could add an on-screen cartoon-like character named Herman-the-Bug who gestures as he speaks the words in the script in Table 13.2 (Moreno, Mayer, Spires, & Lester, 2001). Alternatively, in a lesson that explains worked examples of how to solve arithmetic word problems, we can add an on-screen character – Peedy the parrot – who points to steps in the solution as he describes them (Atkinson, 2002), or in a simulation game explaining the operation of electric motors we can add an on-screen character named Dr. Phyz who flies around the relevant portions of the screen as he gives his explanation (Mayer, Dow, & Mayer, 2003). In each case, the animated pedagogical agent uses exactly the same words as are used in the lesson that did not have an on-screen agent.

Core Evidence Concerning the Image Principle

Does adding an image of the speaker on the screen – such as a cartoon-like character or even as a video of a talking head – help students learn more deeply from a multimedia lesson? Table 13.6 summarizes the results of five separate tests of the image principle carried out in our lab.

The first set of four studies in Table 13.6 involves learning about environmental science in a simulation game, with the help of an on-screen animated pedagogical agent named Herman-the-Bug (Moreno, Mayer, Spires, & Lester, 2001). In the first experiment (shown in the first line of Table 13.6), students who had Herman's image on the screen as he spoke performed worse on a subsequent problem-solving transfer test than did students who only heard his voice. In a second experiment (shown in the second line of Table 13.6), students who had Herman's image on the screen as his comments appeared as on-screen text performed slightly better than students who saw only the on-screen text. In two follow-up studies (shown in lines 3 and 4 of Table 13.6), students who saw a window with video of a human talking head performed slightly better on a subsequent transfer test than did students who only heard the human voice.

Finally, the bottom line in Table 13.6 is based on an interactive lesson on how electric motors work (Mayer, Dow, & Mayer, 2003). When the learner clicked on a question, a narrated animation appeared on the screen. For some learners, the explanation was accompanied by an on-screen character named Dr. Phyz, whereas for others Dr. Phyz did not appear on the screen. Students in the image-present group performed slightly better than those in the no-image-present group.

Overall, the studies conducted in our lab did not produce strong and consistent support for adding the speaker's image to the screen. The median effect size is on the borderline between negligible and small – at $d = .22$. In all of these studies, the on-screen agent or talking head provided little or no pedagogically relevant information – such as pointing to relevant locations on the screen. Based on these findings,

Table 13.6. Core Evidence Concerning the Image Principle

Source	Content	Format	Effect Size
Moreno et al. (2001, Expt. 4a)	Environmental science game (cartoon image, voice)	Computer	−.50
Moreno et al. (2001, Expt. 4b)	Environmental science game (cartoon image, text)	Computer	.22
Moreno et al. (2001, Expt. 5a)	Environmental science game (video image, voice)	Computer	.22
Moreno et al. (2001, Expt. 5b)	Environmental science game (video image, voice)	Computer	.35
Mayer, Dow, & Mayer (2003, Expt. 4)	Electric motor (cartoon image, voice)	Computer	.19
Median			.22

the current state of the image principle is: People do not necessarily learn more deeply from a multimedia lesson when the speaker's image is added to the screen.

Related Evidence Concerning the Image Principle

Table 13.7 summarizes some related research concerning the image principle. The first study in Table 13.7 involves a narrated animation explaining how lightning forms (Craig, Gholson, and Driscoll, 2002). Some students received a narrated animation that included a cartoon-like character who pointed to relevant aspects of the animation as he spoke, whereas others received the narrated animation without an on-screen character. The image-present group performed slightly better than the no-image-present group on a subsequent problem-solving transfer test.

The next set of studies in Table 13.7 (shown in lines 2 through 4) involves a lesson in which students learn to solve mathematics problems from worked examples (Atkinson, 2002). Some students received an on-screen cartoon-like character, named Peedy, who spoke to them (or generated on-screen text) as he pointed to relevant parts of the example, whereas others received the identical words without an on-screen character. Across three comparisons, respectively, the image-present group performed slightly worse, slightly better, and moderately better than the no-image-present group.

Overall, these studies do not provide strong, consistent support for the notion that people learn better when the agent's image is on the

Table 13.7. Related Evidence Concerning the Image Principle

Source	Content	Format	Effect Size
Craig, Gholson, & Driscoll (2002, Expt. 1)	Lightning (cartoon image, voice)	Computer	.26
Atkinson (2002, Expt. 1a)	Mathematics word problems (cartoon image, voice)	Computer	.26
Atkinson (2002, Expt. 1b)	Mathematics word problems (cartoon image, text)	Computer	−.22
Atkinson (2002, Expt. 2)	Mathematics word problems (cartoon image, voice)	Computer	.58

screen, although there may be some benefit to having the agent point to relevant features of the graphic.

Boundary Conditions of the Image Principle

Although the research reported in this section does not encourage including the instructor's image on the screen, there may be situations in which including the instructor's image might be effective in promoting learning. For example, when an on-screen agent points to a relevant portion of the graphic, this may serve to direct the learner's visual attention – thereby reducing extraneous cognitive processing. In short, the pointing behavior of on-screen agents may serve as a form of signaling, as discussed in Chapter 5. More research is needed to determine the conditions under which the presence of on-screen agents on the screen can foster learning – perhaps through pointing to relevant parts of the screen that the learner might otherwise have difficulty finding.

SUGGESTED READINGS

Asterisk (*) indicates that part of this chapter is based on this publication.

*Atkinson, R. K., Mayer, R. E., & Merrill, M. M. (2005). Fostering social agency in multimedia learning: Examining the impact of an animated agent's voice. *Contemporary Educational Psychology, 30*, 117–139.

*Mayer, R. E., Fennell, S., Farmer, L., & Campbell, J. (2004). A personalization effect in multimedia learning: Students learn better when words are in conversational style rather than formal style. *Journal of Educational Psychology, 96*, 389–395.

*Mayer, R. E., Sobko, K., & Mautone, P. D. (2003). Social cues in multimedia learning: Role of speaker's voice. *Journal of Educational Psychology, 95,* 419–425.

*Moreno, R., & Mayer, R. E. (2000). Engaging students in active learning: The case for personalized multimedia messages. *Journal of Educational Psychology, 92,* 724–733.

*Moreno, R., & Mayer, R. E. (2004). Personalized messages that promote science learning in virtual environments. *Journal of Educational Psychology, 96,* 165–173.

*Wang, N., Johnson, W. L., Mayer, R. E., Rizzo, P., Shaw, E., & Collins, H. (2008). The politeness effect: Pedagogical agents and learning outcomes. *International Journal of Human Computer Studies, 66,* 98–112.

Section V

Conclusion

The final chapter summarizes principles of multimedia instruction that are based on evidence and grounded in theory. The chapter also describes two boundary conditions that can determine when a principle is likely or unlikely to apply – the applicability of some principles depends (a) on the prior knowledge of the learner and (b) on the complexity and pacing of the material in the lesson.

14

Principles of Multimedia Design

This chapter summarizes twelve principles of multimedia design, including five principles for reducing extraneous processing – coherence, signaling, redundancy, spatial contiguity, and temporal contiguity principles; three principles for managing essential processing – segmenting, pre-training, and modality principles; and four principles for fostering generative processing – multimedia, personalization, voice, and image principles. In addition, this chapter introduces two possible boundary conditions for some of the principles – the individual differences condition and the complexity and pacing condition. Next, this chapter addresses six questions about multimedia design: Does multimedia work? When does multimedia work? For whom does multimedia work? On what kinds of material does multimedia work? How does multimedia work? What makes an effective multimedia presentation? Finally, the chapter closes with comments concerning the contributions and challenges of multimedia research.

▓ ▒ Chapter Outline

TWELVE PRINCIPLES OF MULTIMEDIA DESIGN

My goal in writing this book is twofold: On the theoretical side, my goal is to improve our understanding of how people learn from words and pictures (that is, to contribute to the science of multimedia learning); and on the practical side, my goal is to improve the design of multimedia presentations (that is, to contribute to the science of multimedia instruction). Concerning contributions to theory, I began with the cognitive theory of multimedia learning – as described in Chapter 3 – that made specific predictions concerning twelve kinds of design effects. My colleagues and I tested the predicted design effects in a large series of experimental comparisons, all involving measures of transfer. Overall, the results are generally consistent with the predictions of the cognitive theory of multimedia learning – lending support to our conception of how people integrate pictorial and verbal presentations.

In particular, we have been able to arrange our twelve principles according to the theoretical function they serve – reducing extraneous processing, managing essential processing, and fostering generative processing. This triarchic framework has proven to be a useful way to arrange and understanding our principles. In addition, the cognitive theory of multimedia learning suggests various boundary conditions under which our principles tend to apply, including when learners are low in prior knowledge and when the material is complex and fast-paced for the learner.

Concerning contributions to practice, the results offer a set of twelve basic principles for the design of multimedia presentations. Tables 14.1, 14.2, and 14.3 define each of the twelve principles of multimedia design that I have presented in this book. The principles are presented as prescriptions for how to design a multimedia presentation, but I do not intend the principles to stand alone as a to-be-memorized list of rules. Rather, I intend for each principle to be implemented in light of the cognitive theory of multimedia learning that I presented in Chapter 3. In short, the principles should be used in ways that are consistent with what we know about how people learn from words and pictures.

The evidence concerning each of the twelve design principles is based on transfer effects in which we compare the transfer test performance of two groups. One group learns from a multimedia presentation that is based on the design principle, and the other learns from a multimedia presentation that is not based on the design principle. On a typical problem-solving transfer test the learner is asked to

Table 14.1. Principles for Reducing Extraneous Processing

Principle	ES	Tests
1. *Coherence Principle:* People learn better when extraneous words, pictures, and sounds are excluded rather than included.	0.97	14 of 14
2. *Signaling Principle:* People learn better when cues that highlight the organization of the essential material are added.	0.52	5 of 6
3. *Redundancy Principle:* People learn better from graphics and narration than from graphics, narration, and on-screen text.	0.72	5 of 5
4. *Spatial Contiguity Principle:* People learn better when corresponding words and pictures are presented near rather than far from each other on the page or screen.	1.19	5 of 5
5. *Temporal Contiguity Principle:* People learn better when corresponding words and pictures are presented simultaneously rather than successively.	1.31	8 of 8

write as many solutions as possible to new problems. To standardize the comparison, I convert the difference in scores into an effect size using Cohen's *d*, as described in Chapter 2. In short, I examine the effect on transfer of implementing the design principle, and I search for large and consistent effect sizes. The right sides of Tables 14.1, 14.2, and 14.3 summarize the empirical evidence based on transfer tests that my colleagues and I have collected concerning each of the twelve principles: The column labeled "ES" lists the effect size based on Cohen's *d*, and the column labeled "Tests" lists how many experimental comparisons favored the treatment group out of the total number of experimental comparisons conducted.

Principles for Reducing Extraneous Processing

Table 14.1 lists five principles that are intended to reduce extraneous processing during learning – coherence, signaling, redundancy, spatial contiguity, and temporal contiguity principles. As you can see, there is generally strong and consistent support for the principles, with three principles yielding median effect sizes that are high (i.e., above .8), and two principles yielding median effect sizes in the medium-to-large range (i.e., between .5 and .8).

Table 14.2. Principles for Managing Essential Processing

Principle	ES	Tests
6. *Segmenting Principle:* People learn better when a multimedia lesson is presented in user-paced segments rather than as a continuous unit.	0.98	3 of 3
7. *Pre-training Principle:* People learn better from a multimedia lesson when they know the names and characteristics of the main concepts.	0.85	5 of 5
8. *Modality Principle:* People learn better from graphics and narration than from animation and on-screen text.	1.02	17 of 17

Table 14.3. Principles for Fostering Generative Processing

Principle	ES	Tests
9. *Multimedia Principle:* People learn better from words and pictures than from words alone.	1.39	11 of 11
10. *Personalization Principle:* People learn better from multimedia lessons when words are in conversational style rather than formal style.	1.11	11 of 11
11. *Voice Principle:* People learn better when the narration in multimedia lessons is spoken in a friendly human voice rather than a machine voice.	0.78	3 of 3
12. *Image Principle:* People do not necessarily learn better from a multimedia lesson when the speaker's image is added to the screen.	0.22	5 of 5

Principles for Managing Essential Processing

Table 14.2 lists three principles that are intended to manage essential processing during learning – segmenting, pre-training, and modality principles. As you can see, there is strong and consistent support for each principle, with median effect sizes above .8 for each principle. However, the segmenting principle is based on only three experimental tests, so more evidence is warranted.

Principles for Fostering Generative Processing

Table 14.3 lists four principles aimed at fostering generative processing during learning – multimedia, personalization, voice, and image principles. The multimedia principle and the personalization principle

Table 14.4. Boundary Conditions for Design Principles

Individual Differences Condition: Design effects are stronger for low-knowledge learners than for high-knowledge learners.

Complexity and Pacing Conditions: Design effects are stronger for multimedia lessons with high-complexity content rather than low-complexity content, and fast-paced presentations rather than slow-paced presentations.

receive strong and consistent support, with median effect sizes well above .8. Although the median effect size for the voice principle is close to .8, it is based on only three experimental comparisons, so more evidence is warranted. Finally, the image principle can be considered an "un-principle" because the evidence does not support a design change in which the instructor's image is placed on the screen.

BOUNDARY CONDITIONS FOR DESIGN PRINCIPLES

Each principle is subject to boundary conditions, including the individual characteristics of the learners and the complexity and pace of the presentation, as summarized in Table 14.4. First, according to the *individual-differences condition*, some design effects are stronger for low-experience learners than for high-experience learners.

Table 14.5. Meteorology Questionnaire

Please place a check mark next to the items that apply to you:
___ I regularly read the weather maps in a newspaper.
___ I know what a cold front is.
___ I can distinguish between cumulous and nimbus clouds.
___ I know what low pressure is.
___ I can explain what makes wind blow.
___ I know what this symbol means: [symbol for cold front]
___ I know what this symbol means: [symbol for warm front]

Please place a check mark indicating your knowledge of meteorology (weather):
___ very much

___ average

___ very little

Table 14.6. Car Mechanics Questionnaire

Please place a check mark next to the things you have done:
___ I have a driver's license.
___ I have put air into a car's tire.
___ I have changed a tire on a car.
___ I have changed the oil in a car.
___ I have installed spark plugs in a car.
___ I have replaced the brake shoes in a car.

Please place a check mark indicating your knowledge of car mechanics and repair:
___ very much

___
___ average

___
___ very little

For example, please complete the questionnaire in Table 14.5. For the top part, place a check mark next to each item that applies to you; for the bottom part, place a check mark indicating your knowledge of meteorology.

The purpose of this little questionnaire is to obtain a quick and simple assessment of your knowledge of meteorology. To score the questionnaire, give yourself one point for each item you checked on the list given at the top, and add one to five more points based on your level of knowledge (with one point for "very little" up to five points for "very much"). If your total score was six or less, you would be considered a low-knowledge learner in our research on the lightning lesson; if your total score was seven or more, you would be considered a high-knowledge learner with respect to the lightning lesson.

Table 14.6 presents a similar knowledge questionnaire that we used to assess students' knowledge of car mechanics (for use with the brakes lesson), and Table 14.7 presents a questionnaire to assess knowledge of household repair (for use with the pump lesson). These questionnaires were scored in much the same way as the meteorology questionnaire. As you can see, our goal is to obtain a rough measurement of how much knowledge and familiarity a person has had with a specific topic – such as weather (for the lightning lesson), car mechanics (for the brakes lesson), and household repair (for the pump lesson). Thus, when I talk about the learner's existing knowledge, I mean the learner's knowledge and familiarity with specific situations

Table 14.7. Household Repair Questionnaire

Please place a check mark next to the things you have done:
___ I own a screwdriver.
___ I own a power saw.
___ I have replaced the heads on a lawn sprinkler system.
___ I have replaced the washer in a sink faucet.
___ I have replaced the flush mechanism in a toilet.
___ I have replaced or installed plumbing pipes or fixtures.

Please place a check mark indicating your knowledge of how to fix household appliances and machines:
___ very much

___ average

___ very little

that are related to the lesson's theme. This can be called *domain-specific knowledge* because it is knowledge about a specific set of situations.

Figure 14.1 summarizes the percent correct on the transfer test for low- and high-knowledge learners who learned from well-designed instructional messages and poorly designed instructional messages. In three of the studies, the well-designed message included text and illustrations, whereas the poorly designed message contained text only (Mayer & Gallini, 1990, Experiments 1, 2, and 3). In these studies, a multimedia effect would be reflected in better transfer test performance for presentations containing multiple representations (i.e., words and pictures) than for presentations containing a single representation (i.e., words alone). In one of the studies, the well-designed message included text that was integrated with illustrations, and the poorly designed message had text that was separated from the illustrations (Mayer et al., 1995, Experiment 2). In this study, a spatial contiguity effect would be reflected in better transfer performance for integrated rather than separated presentations. As you can see in each of the four cases presented in Figure 14.1, there is a strong multimedia or contiguity effect for low-knowledge learners but not for high-knowledge learners. I computed an effect size difference for the transfer results by subtracting the effect size for the high-knowledge learners from the effect size for the low-knowledge learners, yielding a median effect size of $d = .8$. In short, our research provides preliminary evidence for what I (Mayer, 2001) have called the *individual differences principle* – the idea that certain of the twelve design principles

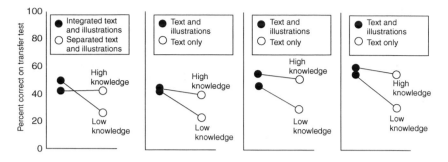

Figure 14.1. Individual differences condition: strong effects for low-knowledge but not for high-knowledge learners.

reviewed in this book may help low-experience learners but not help high-experience learners.

There is converging evidence that high-quality multimedia design is more important for low- rather than high-experience learners. In one set of studies (Kalyuga, Chandler, & Sweller, 1998), learners with low and high levels of expertise learned about the operation of a bell and light circuit. Low-expertise learners learned better when diagrams and text were physically integrated than when they were separated or when only the diagram was presented; however, the reverse pattern was produced for high-expertise learners, who learned best from the diagram alone. In another set of studies (Kalyuga, Chandler, & Sweller, 2000), low- and high-experience workers learned to operate a drilling machine based on a diagram with auditory narration or from a diagram alone. Low-experience learners performed best with the diagram and narration, whereas high-experience learners performed best when learning from the diagram alone. It appears that integrating words and pictures is most helpful for learners who lack much experience in a domain. In a recent review, Kalyuga (2005) presented additional evidence for what he calls the *expertise reversal effect* – the idea that instructional methods that are helpful for low-knowledge learners may not help or may even hinder high-knowledge learners.

The individual differences effects that we and others have obtained are also consistent with the cognitive theory of multimedia learning. High-knowledge learners may be able to create and use images on their own, so they do not need well-designed multimedia presentations. By contrast, low-knowledge learners may need to have images supplied to them, and therefore are more likely to benefit from multimedia presentations.

The second boundary condition listed in Table 14.4 is that some of the design principles reviewed in this book may apply more strongly when the material is complex or the pacing of the lesson is fast for the learner. Although we have not systematically varied this factor in our own research, related research from other researchers suggests that more attention should be paid to this potentially important boundary condition, particularly with respect to the signaling, spatial contiguity, and modality principles.

As the field of research on multimedia learning matures, new research can be expected to clarify the boundary conditions under which the principles apply. Sometimes researchers may frame such results as a "failure to replicate," but a more productive approach is to search for boundary conditions based on cognitive theory, such as the cognitive theory of multimedia learning. The theoretical rationale is that complex and fast-paced lessons are more likely to overload the learner's cognitive system, so techniques that reduce extraneous processing and manage essential processing are especially useful.

SIX QUESTIONS ABOUT MULTIMEDIA

The material summarized in Tables 14.1, 14.2, 14.3, and 14.4 provides some answers to six questions about multimedia: Does multimedia work? When does multimedia work? For whom does multimedia work? For what kinds of materials does multimedia work? How does multimedia work? What makes an effective multimedia presentation?

Does Multimedia Work?

A preliminary question concerns whether or not multimedia works. In order to answer this question, we must begin by defining what is meant by multimedia and what is meant by saying that it works. Our definition of multimedia is simple – multimedia presentations consist of coordinated verbal and pictorial messages. We can compare a multimedia presentation to one that consists solely of a verbal message. In short, we can restate the question as: "Is it better to learn from words and pictures than from words alone?"

We measure whether or not multimedia works by determining whether it promotes transfer – being able to use the material in the presentation to solve new problems. In short, we restate the question as: "Do students who learn from words and pictures perform better on transfer tests than students who learn from words alone?"

The multimedia principle – listed in Table 14.3 – addresses this question. As you can see in the first line of Table 14.3, students perform better on transfer tests when they learn from words and pictures than when they learn from words alone. These results provide clear and consistent evidence that multimedia works – that is, it is better to present a multimedia explanation using both words and pictures than using words alone.

When Does Multimedia Work?

The question of whether or not multimedia works is a bit too superficial, because not all multimedia messages are equally effective. A deeper question concerns identifying effective features of multimedia presentations, which can be stated as: "When does multimedia work?" The bulk of the research presented in this book addresses this crucial question.

Overall, our research allows us to identify ten features that lead to effective multimedia presentations: (a) coherence – when extraneous words, sounds, and pictures are minimized, (b) signaling – when the essential material is highlighted, (c) redundancy – when words are presented as speech rather than as speech and text in multimedia presentations, (d) spatial contiguity – when corresponding words and pictures are presented near rather than far from each other on the page or screen, (e) temporal contiguity – when corresponding words and pictures are presented simultaneously rather than successively in time, (f) segmenting – when a fast-paced, complex multimedia lesson is presented in user-paced segments rather than as a continuous presentation, (g) pre-training – when the learner knows the names and characteristics of the key concepts, (h) modality – when words are presented as speech rather than as printed text in multimedia presentations, (i) personalization – when the words are presented in conversational style rather than in formal style, and (j) voice – when the words are spoken by a friendly human voice rather than by a machine voice. These principles are summarized in Tables 14.1, 14.2, and 14.3. Although my colleagues and I have not been able to find much evidence for the image principle in our research, there may be conditions under which including the instructor's image is helpful, so more research is needed.

For Whom Does Multimedia Work?

There is a growing research literature examining the question of who learns best from well-designed multimedia lessons (Kalyuga,

2005). The first boundary condition listed in Table 14.4 states that well-designed multimedia presentations work best for learners who are low rather than high in prior knowledge about the subject matter, which I have called the *individual differences principle* (Mayer, 2001) and which Kalyuga (2005) has called the *expertise reversal effect*. Although the results from our lab are preliminary, they show how the design principles need to be qualified with respect to different kinds of learners. Additional research is needed to pinpoint the role of individual differences in multimedia learning.

For What Kinds of Material Does Multimedia Work?

Another possible boundary condition for design principles concerns the complexity and pacing of the material, as indicated in the second boundary condition in Table 14.4. In short, there is some reason to propose that well-designed multimedia presentations work best when the material is complex and presented at a rapid pace for the learner. In addition, there may be differences in the effectiveness of the design principles depending on the type of material – such as whether the goal is to help people learn facts, concepts, procedures, strategies, or beliefs. Again, additional research is needed to pinpoint the role of the nature of the material in multimedia learning.

How Does Multimedia Work?

Our results are most consistent with a cognitive theory of multimedia learning that is based on three assumptions – that people have separate visual and auditory channels, that the channels are limited in capacity, and that meaningful learning involves actively selecting, organizing, and integrating incoming visual and auditory information. Each of the design effects summarized in Tables 14.1, 14.2, and 14.3 is consistent with the cognitive theory of multimedia learning.

First, the cognitive theory of multimedia learning helps to explain the coherence principle. When extraneous material is presented, working memory may become cluttered with irrelevant words and/or irrelevant images, making it more difficult to hold corresponding relevant words and images in working memory at the same time. By contrast, when only relevant material is presented, working memory is more likely to hold corresponding relevant words and images at the same time. This situation facilitates a key step in meaningful learning, namely, integrating corresponding words and images.

The same theoretical analysis applies to the signaling principle and the redundancy principle. Concerning signaling, when the learner's attention is directed toward essential material and away from extraneous material, the learner is more likely to hold corresponding relevant words and images in working memory at the same time, thus enabling the process of integrating. Concerning redundancy, when redundant text is removed, the need to engage in extraneous processing is eliminated.

Next, the cognitive theory of multimedia learning helps to explain the spatial contiguity effect. When corresponding words and pictures are separated from one another on the page, the learner is less likely to be able to hold corresponding verbal and visual representations in working memory at the same time. By contrast, when corresponding words and pictures are presented next to one another on the page, the learner is more likely to be able to hold corresponding verbal and pictorial representations in working memory at the same time. Thus, the process of integrating relevant words and images is more likely to occur when words and pictures are integrated rather than separated.

Similarly, the cognitive theory of multimedia learning helps to explain the temporal contiguity principle. When corresponding words and pictures are separated from one another in time, the learner is less likely to be able to hold corresponding verbal and pictorial representations in working memory at the same time. By contrast, when corresponding words and pictures are presented simultaneously, the learner is more likely to be able to hold corresponding verbal and pictorial representations in working memory at the same time. Again, the process of integrating relevant words and images is facilitated by simultaneous rather than successive presentation.

The cognitive theory of multimedia learning is also consistent with the pre-training principle and the segmenting principle, because these techniques are intended to manage essential processing during learning. Pre-training reduces the amount of essential processing needed when a fast-paced lesson is presented because the learner already knows about the key concepts. Segmenting gives learners enough time to fully process each segment in a lesson before moving on to the next.

The cognitive theory of multimedia learning can also account for the modality principle. When words are presented as text, they must compete for visual attention with the animation in the visual channel, creating what can be called *split attention*. In short, visual attention is split between the animation and the text, resulting in less relevant material being selected for further processing. By contrast, when words are presented as speech, they can be processed in the auditory channel, thus freeing the visual channel for processing of the animation. This situation is most likely to promote key steps in meaningful learning, including integrating corresponding words and pictures.

The cognitive theory of multimedia learning helps to explain the multimedia principle. When only words are presented, the most likely cognitive processes are selecting words, organizing words, and integrating words with prior knowledge. When both words and pictures are presented, learners can also engage in selecting images, organizing images, and integrating words and images. The process of integrating relevant words and images is a key step in meaningful learning, and is facilitated by presenting an explanation using words and pictures rather than using words alone.

The personalization and voice principles are consistent with the idea that social cues prime a conversational stance in the learner, in which the learner sees the instructor as a conversational partner. When in a conversation, people try harder to make sense of the presented material. In short, they are more likely to engage in generative processing. By contrast, the image principle is consistent with the idea that the agent's image on screen can serve as extraneous material that distracts the learner.

In no case did we find support for the information-delivery theory, in which visual and verbal modes of presentation are viewed as two delivery channels. The information-delivery metaphor does not seem to be a productive one for the design of effective multimedia messages. Instead, I view multimedia learners as active sense-makers who actively process the incoming words and pictures through visual and auditory channels that are highly limited in capacity. In order to understand multimedia design it is helpful to begin with a research-based theory of how people learn from words and pictures.

What Makes an Effective Multimedia Presentation?

Our work allows us to suggest the characteristics of an effective multimedia presentation. To begin, let's focus only on computer-based multimedia presentations that seek to explain how something works using animation and narration. First, the presentation should consist of both words and pictures – for example, narration and animation rather than narration alone. In short, the presentation should be multimedia. Second, corresponding portions of the animation and narration should be presented simultaneously. In short, the presentation should be integrated. Third, only the core cause-and-effect explanation should be presented, without extraneous words, sounds, or pictures. In short, the presentation should be concise. Fourth, the words should be presented as speech (i.e., narration) rather than as text (i.e., on-screen text) or as speech and text. In short, the presentation should be channeled – with words directed toward the auditory channel and pictures directed toward the visual channel. Thus, the most effective computer-based multimedia presentation is a *concise narrated animation* (CNA), which I define as a concise narration describing the cause-and-effect system coordinated with a concise animation depicting the cause-and-effect system. Concise narrated animations are the building blocks of effective computer-based multimedia messages.

Similarly, let's examine the characteristics of effective book-based multimedia presentations, consisting of text and illustrations. First, the presentation should consist of both words and pictures, that is, text and illustrations rather than text alone. In short, the presentation should be multimedia. Second, corresponding portions of the text and illustrations should be presented next to each other on the page. In short, the presentation should be integrated. Third, the core cause-and-effect explanation should be presented without extraneous text and illustrations. The illustration should consist of a series of frames depicting various states of the system, and each frame should include text describing the state of the system in words. Thus, the most effective book-based multimedia presentation is a *concise annotated illustration* (CAI), which I define as a concise series of frames each with concise coordinated text. In short, concise annotated illustrations are the building blocks of effective book-based multimedia presentations.

Finally, the words in both kinds of multimedia lessons should be presented in a conversational style rather than a formal style. When words are spoken, the speaker should have a friendly human voice rather than a machine voice.

THE CONTRIBUTIONS AND CHALLENGES OF RESEARCH IN MULTIMEDIA LEARNING

Suppose you want to create a multimedia presentation to be delivered online. What would be your criteria for building the presentation? Certainly, an important criterion is content – you want to make sure it presents the information that you intend to convey. Another criterion is aesthetics – you want to make sure the presentation looks good. Finally, another criterion is sophistication – you want to make sure the presentation takes advantage of the latest technological developments.

Yet, if you designed a technologically sophisticated, aesthetically pleasing, information-rich presentation, you would have failed to take into account an important human criterion: Is the presentation designed to be compatible with the way people learn from words and pictures? This book is concerned with this human criterion, and with the premise that multimedia design can be based on scientific research and theory. In short, an important consideration for multimedia design is how to help people learn from the presentation.

Can multimedia design be based on scientific research? In many cases, recommendations for multimedia design are based on intuitions rather than scientific research. Clearly, the intuitions of thoughtful scholars have a place. Perhaps the best-known and most acclaimed work in this area is Edward Tufte's work on the design of data graphics, which he calls "principles of information design" (Tufte, 1990, p. 10). Tufte (1983, 1990) provides many useful suggestions for how to design data graphics such as charts, tables, diagrams, and graphs. For example, like the contiguity principle proposed in this book, Tutfe (1990) states that "words and pictures belong together."

The goal of this book is to offer a scientific approach to the development of design principles. The advantage of this approach is that it allows us to determine whether or not the principles work, but a disadvantage is that it causes us to narrow our focus. In this book, I summarize a systematic program of research aimed at understanding how people learn from words and pictures that explain how something works. Much of the work is limited to short, causal explanations, to learning by college students, and to a few fundamental principles. Yet even this modest examination required approximately twenty years of concentrated study by a team of educational and cognitive psychologists. This project demonstrates that it is possible to formulate testable questions about multimedia learning, that it is possible to conduct scientifically rigorous research to answer the questions, and that it is possible to develop a cognitive theory of multimedia learning to guide the research. In short, an important outcome of this project is a demonstration of how it is possible to create design principles based on empirical research and cognitive theory.

Progress is being made in the field of multimedia learning. For example, *The Cambridge Handbook of Multimedia Learning* (Mayer, 2005) gives you access to the growing research base on evidence-based principles of multimedia instruction, and *e-Learning and the Science of*

Instruction (Clark & Mayer, 2008) shows you how research evidence can be used to design multimedia instruction in practical situations.

What needs to be done? Research in multimedia learning is still in its early stages. The major challenge is to create a useful base of empirical research and cognitive theory. The ultimate goal should be to systematize design principles based on empirical research and a comprehensive theory. Although multimedia explanations are an important type of multimedia message, there are many other uses of multimedia that require study. The field of study needs to include a range of multimedia learning situations, a range of learners, and a range of design principles. Because the goal of multimedia learning is usually meaningful learning, it is worthwhile to use measures of learning that are sensitive to learner understanding – like the transfer measures used throughout this book. In addition, because working memory load plays a central role in the cognitive theory of multimedia learning, it would be useful to have more direct measures of cognitive load during learning. It would also be helpful to conduct research aimed at understanding the role of individual differences. Often multimedia presentations allow for user interaction and exploration, so additional research is needed on the role of interactivity in multimedia learning. Motivation is an important part of a complete theory of multimedia learning – as can be seen in the attraction of video games, for example – so research is needed on how motivation works in multimedia learning (Moreno & Mayer, 2007).

In summary, multimedia learning offers a potentially powerful way for people to understand things that would be very difficult to grasp from words alone. This book demonstrates the potential benefits of learning that involves the integration of words and pictures. It offers a glimpse of how we can improve upon verbal messages that have become the basis for most instruction. It offers a vision of the potential of multimedia to improve human understanding. I will consider this book a success if it helps to promote a better understanding of how to foster meaningful learning through the integration of words and pictures.

SUGGESTED READINGS

Clark, R. C., & Mayer, R. E. (2008). *e-Learning and the science of instruction* (2nd ed.). San Francisco: Pfeiffer.

Mayer, R. E. (Ed.). (2005). *The Cambridge handbook of multimedia learning.* New York: Cambridge University Press.

O'Neil, H. F. (Ed.). (2005). *What works in distance learning: Guidelines.* Greenwich, CT: Information Age Publishing.

References

Al-Seghayer, K. (2001). The effect of multimedia annotation modes on L2 vocabulary acquisition: A comparative study. *Language Learning & Technology, 5*, 202–232.

Alwitt, L. F., Anderson, D. R., Lorch, E. P., & Levin, S. R. (1980). Preschool children's visual attention to attributes of television. *Human Communication Research, 7*, 52–67.

Anderson. D. R., & Lorch, E. P. (1983). Looking at television: Action or reaction? In J. Bryant and D. R. Anderson (Eds.), *Children's understanding of television: Research on attention and comprehension* (pp. 1–33). New York: Academic Press.

Anderson, L. W., Krathwohl, D. R., Airasian, P. W., Cruikshank, K. A., Mayer, R. E., Pintrich, R. E., & Raths, J. (2001). *A taxonomy of learning for teaching: A revision of Bloom's taxonomy of educational objectives.* New York: Addison-Wesley-Longman.

Atkinson, R. K. (2002). Optimizing learning from examples using animated pedagogical agents. *Journal of Educational Psychology, 94*, 416–427.

Atkinson, R. K., Mayer, R. E., & Merrill, M. M. (2005). Fostering social agency in multimedia learning: Examining the impact of an animated agent's voice. *Contemporary Educational Psychology, 30*, 117–139.

Ayres, P. (2006). Impact of reducing intrinsic cognitive load on learning in a mathematical domain. *Applied Cognitive Psychology, 20*, 287–298.

Ayres, P., & Sweller, J. (2005). The split attention principle in multimedia learning. In R. E. Mayer (Ed.), *The Cambridge handbook of multimedia learning* (pp. 135–146). New York: Cambridge University Press.

Baddeley, A. D. (1986). *Working memory.* Oxford, England: Oxford University Press.

Baddeley, A. D. (1992). Working memory. *Science, 255*, 556–559.

Baddeley, A. D. (1999). *Human memory.* Boston: Allyn & Bacon.

Baggett, P. (1984). Role of temporal overlap of visual and auditory material in forming dual media associations. *Journal of Educational Psychology, 76*, 408–417.

Baggett, P., & Ehrenfeucht, A. (1983). Encoding and retaining information in the visuals and verbals of an educational movie. *Educational Communications and Technology Journal, 31,* 23–32.

Bobis, J., Sweller, J., & Cooper, M. (1993). Cognitive load effects in a primary school geometry task. *Learning and Instruction, 3,* 1–21.

Bodemer, D., Ploetzner, R., Feuerlein, I., & Spada, H. (2004). The active integration of information during learning with dynamic and interactive visualisations. *Learning and Instruction, 14,* 325–341.

Bransford, J. D., Brown, A. L., & Cocking, R. R. (Eds.). (1999). *How people learn.* Washington, DC: National Academy Press.

Brown, P., & Levinson, S. C. (1987). *Politeness: Some universals in language usage.* New York: Cambridge University Press.

Brunken, R., Plass, J., & Leutner, D. (2003). Direct measurement of cognitive load in multimedia learning. *Educational Psychologist, 38,* 53–62.

Brunken, R., Plass, J. L., & Leutner, D. (2004). Assessment of cognitive load in multimedia learning with dual-task methodology: Auditory load and modality effects. *Instructional Science, 32,* 115–132.

Brunken, R., Steinbacher, S., Plass, J. L., & Leutner, D. (2002). Assessment of cognitive load in multimedia learning using dual-task methodology. *Experimental Psychology, 49,* 109–119.

Calvert, S. L., & Scott, M. C. (1989). Sound effects for children's temporal integration of fast-paced television content. *Journal of Broadcasting and Electronic Media, 33,* 233–246.

Cassell, J., Sullivan, J., Prevost, S., and Churchill, E. (Eds.). (2000). *Embodied conversational agents.* Cambridge, MA: MIT Press.

Catrambone, R. (1994). Improving examples to improve transfer to novel problems. *Memory and Cognition, 22,* 606–615.

Catrambone, R. (1995). Aiding subgoal learning: Effect on transfer. *Journal of Educational Psychology, 87,* 5–17.

Catrambone, R. (1998) The subgoal learning model: Creating better examples to improve transfer to novel problems. *Journal of Experimental Psychology: General, 127,* 355–376.

Chambliss, M. J., & Calfee, R. C. (1998). *Textbooks for learning.* Oxford, England: Blackwell.

Chandler, P., & Sweller, J. (1991). Cognitive load theory and the format of instruction. *Cognition and Instruction, 8,* 293–332.

Chandler, P., & Sweller, J. (1992). The split-attention effect as a factor in the design of instruction. *British Journal of Educational Psychology, 62,* 233–246.

Chi, M. T. H., Bassok, M., Lewis, M. W., Reimann, P., & Glaser, R. (1989). Self-explanations: How students study and use examples in learning to solve problems. *Cognitive Science, 13,* 145–182.

Chun, D. M., & Plass, J. L. (1996). Effects of multimedia annotations on vocabulary acquisition. *The Modern Language Journal, 80,* 183–198.

Clark, J. M., & Paivio, A. (1991). Dual coding theory and education. *Educational Psychology Review, 3*, 149–210.

Clark, R. C., & Mayer, R. E. (2008). *e-Learning and the science of instruction* (2nd ed.). San Francisco: Pfeiffer.

Clark, R. C., Nguyen, F., & Sweller, J. (2006). *Efficiency in learning: Evidence-based guidelines to manage cognitive load.* San Francisco: Pfeiffer.

Clark, R. E. (1983). Reconsidering research on learning from media. *Review of Educational Research, 53*, 445–459.

Clark, R. E. (1994). Media will never influence learning. *Educational Technology Research and Development, 42*, 21–30.

Clark, R. E. (2001). *Learning from media.* Greenwich, CT: Information Age Publishing.

Clark, R. E., & Solomon, G. (1986). Media in teaching. In M. C. Wittrock (Ed.), *Handbook of research on teaching* (3rd ed., pp. 464–478). New York: Macmillan.

Clarke, T., Ayres, P., & Sweller, J. (2005). The impact of sequencing and prior knowledge on learning mathematics through spreadsheet applications. *Educational Technology Research and Development, 53*, 15–24.

Cognition and Technology Group at Vanderbilt (1996). Looking at technology in context: A framework for understanding technology and education. In D. C. Berliner & R. C. Calfee (Eds.), *Handbook of educational psychology* (pp. 807–840). New York: Macmillan.

Cohen, J. (1988). *Statistical power analysis for the behavioral sciences.* Mahwah, NJ: Erlbaum.

Cook, L. K., & Mayer, R. E. (1988). Teaching readers about the structure of scientific text. *Journal of Educational Psychology, 80*, 448–456.

Cooper, G., & Sweller, J. (1987). The effects of schema acquisition and rule automation on mathematical problem-solving transfer. *Journal of Educational Psychology, 79*, 347–362.

Craig, S. D., Gholson, B., & Driscoll, D. M. (2002). Animated pedagogical agent in multimedia educational environments: Effects of agent properties, picture features, and redundancy. *Journal of Educational Psychology, 94*, 428–434.

Cronbach, L. J., & Snow, R. E. (1977). *Aptitudes and instructional methods.* New York: Irvington.

Cuban, L. (1986). *Teachers and machines: The classroom use of technology since 1920.* New York: Teachers College Press.

Cuban, L. (2001). *Oversold and underused: Computers in the classroom.* Cambridge, MA: Harvard University Press.

DeLeeuw, K., & Mayer, R. E. (2008). A comparison of three measures of cognitive load: Evidence for separable measures of intrinsic, extraneous, and germane load. *Journal of Educational Psychology, 100*, 223–234.

Dewey, J. (1913). *Interest and effort in education.* Cambridge, MA: Houghton Mifflin.

Diao, Y., & Sweller, J. (2007). Redundancy in foreign language reading comprehension instruction: Concurrent written and spoken presentations. *Learning and Instruction, 17,* 78–88.

Dillon, A., & Jobst, J. (2005). Multimedia learning with hypermedia. In R. E. Mayer (Ed.), *The Cambridge handbook of multimedia learning* (pp. 569–588). New York: Cambridge University Press.

Elen, J., & Clark, R. E. (2006). Setting the scene: Complexity and learning environments. In J. Elen & R. E. Clark (Eds.), *Handling complexity in learning environments: Theory and research* (pp. 1–12). Amsterdam: Elsevier.

Fleming, M., & Levie, W. H. (Eds.). (1993). *Instructional message design: Principles from the behavioral and cognitive sciences* (2nd ed). Englewood Cliffs, NJ: Educational Technology Publications.

Fletcher, J. D., & Tobias, S. (2005). The multimedia principle. In R. E. Mayer (Ed.), *The Cambridge handbook of multimedia learning* (pp. 117–134). New York: Cambridge University Press.

Garner, R., Alexander, P., Gillingham, M., Kulikowich, J., & Brown, R. (1991). Interest and learning from text. *American Educational Research Journal, 28,* 643–659.

Garner, R., Brown, R., Sanders, S., & Menke, D. (1992). Seductive details and learning from text. In K. A. Renninger, S. Hidi, and A. Krapp (Eds.), The role of interest in learning and development (pp. 239–254). Hillsdale, NJ: Erlbaum.

Garner, R., Gillingham, M., & White, C. (1989). Effects of seductive details on macroprocessing and microprocessing in adults and children. *Cognition and Instruction, 6,* 41–57.

Gerjets, P., Scheiter, K., & Catrambone, R. (2004). Designing examples to reduce intrinsic cognitive load: Molar versus modular presentation of solution procedures. *Instructional Science, 32,* 33–58.

Gerjets, P., Scheiter, K., & Catrambone, R. (2006). Can learning from molar and modular worked examples be enhanced by providing instructional explanations and prompting self-explanations? *Learning and Instruction, 16,* 104–121.

Ginns, P. (2005). Meta-analysis of the modality effect. *Learning and Instruction, 15,* 313–332.

Ginns, P. (2006). Integrating information: A meta-analysis of spatial contiguity and temporal contiguity effects. *Learning and Instruction, 16,* 511–525.

Grice, H. P. (1975). Logic and conversation. In P. Cole and J. Morgan (Eds.), *Syntax and semantics* (vol. 3, pp. 41–58). New York: Academic Press.

Harp, S. F., & Mayer, R. E. (1997). The role of interest in learning from scientific text and illustrations: On the distinction between emotional interest and cognitive interest. *Journal of Educational Psychology, 89,* 92–102.

Harp, S. F., & Mayer, R. E. (1998). How seductive details do their damage: A theory of cognitive interest in science learning. *Journal of Educational Psychology, 90,* 414–434.

Harskamp, E., Mayer, R. E., Suhre, C., & Jansma, J. (2007). Does the modality principle for multimedia learning apply to science classrooms? *Learning and Instruction, 18*, 465–477.

Hegarty, M., & Kriz, S. (2007). Effects of knowledge and spatial ability on learning from animation. In R. Lowe & W. Schnotz (Eds.), *Learning with animation* (pp. 3–29). New York: Cambridge University Press.

Hidi, S., & Anderson, V. (1992). Situational interest and its impact on reading expository writing. In K. A. Renninger, S. Hidi, & A. Krapp (Eds.), *The role of interest in learning and development* (pp. 215–238). Hillsdale, NJ: Erlbaum.

Hidi, S., & Baird, W. (1986). Interestingness: A neglected variable in discourse processing. *Cognitive Science, 10*, 179–194.

Hidi, S., & Baird, W. (1988). Strategies for increasing text-based interest and students' recall of expository text. *Reading Research Quarterly, 23*, 465–483.

Inglese, T., Mayer, R. E., & Rigotti, F. (2007). Using audiovisual TV interviews to create visible authors that reduce the learning gap between native and non-native speakers. *Learning and Instruction, 16*, 67–77.

Jamet, E., & Bohec, O. (2007). The effect of redundant text in multimedia instruction. *Contemporary Educational Psychology, 32*, 588–598.

Jeung, H., Chandler, P., & Sweller, J. (1997). The role of visual indicators in dual sensory mode instruction. *Educational Psychology, 17*, 329–433.

Jonassen, D. H., Campbell, J. P., & Davidson, M. E. (1994). Learning with media: Restructuring the debate. *Educational Technology Research and Development, 42*, 20–38.

Jonassen, D. H., & Grabowski, B. L. (1993). *Handbook of individual differences, learning, and instruction*. Hillsdale, NJ: Erlbaum.

Jones, L. C., & Plass, J. L. (2002). Supporting listening comprehension and vocabulary acquisition in French with multimedia annotations. *The Modern Language Journal, 86*, 446–561.

Kalyuga, S. (2005). Prior knowledge principle in multimedia learning. In R. E. Mayer (Ed.), *The Cambridge handbook of multimedia learning* (pp. 325–337). New York: Cambridge University Press.

Kalyuga, S. (2005). The prior knowledge principle in multimedia learning. In R. E. Mayer (Ed.), *The Cambridge handbook of multimedia learning* (pp. 325–338). New York: Cambridge University Press.

Kalyuga, S., Chandler, P., & Sweller, J. (1998). Levels of expertise and instructional design. *Human Factors, 40*, 1–17.

Kalyuga, S., Chandler, P., & Sweller, J. (1999). Managing split-attention and redundancy in multimedia instruction. *Applied Cognitive Psychology, 13*, 351–371.

Kalyuga, S., Chandler, P., & Sweller, J. (2000). Incorporating learner experience into the design of multimedia instruction. *Journal of Educational Psychology, 92*, 126–136.

Kalyuga, S., Chandler, P., & Sweller, J. (2004). When redundant on-screen text in multimedia technical instruction can interfere with learning. *Human Factors, 46,* 567–581.

Kester, L., Kirschner, P. A., & van Merrienboer, J. J. G. (2004). Timing of information presentation in learning statistics. *Instructional Science, 32,* 233–252.

Kester, L., Kirschner, P. A., & van Merrienboer, J. J. G. (2005). The management of cognitive load during complex cognitive skill acquisition by means of computer-simulated problem solving. *British Journal of Educational Psychology, 75,* 71–85.

Kester, L., Kirschner, P. A., & van Merrienboer, J. J. G (2006). Just-in-time information presentation: Improving learning a troubleshooting skill. *Contemporary Educational Psychology, 31,* 167–185.

Kintsch, W. (1980). Learning from text, levels of comprehension, or: Why would anyone read a story anyway? *Poetics, 9,* 87–98.

Kozma, R. B. (1991). Learning with media. *Review of Educational Research, 61,* 179–211.

Kozma, R. B. (1994). Will media influence learning? Reframing the debate. *Educational Technology Research and Development, 42,* 7–19.

Lambert, N. M., & McCombs, B. L. (1998). *How students learn.* Washington, DC: American Psychological Association.

Landauer, T. K. (1995). *The trouble with computers.* Cambridge, MA: MIT Press.

Leahy, W., Chandler, P., & Sweller, J. (2003). When auditory presentations should and should not be a component of multimedia instruction. *Applied Cognitive Psychology, 17,* 401–418.

Lee, H., Plass, J. L., & Homer, B. D. (2006). Optimizing cognitive load for learning from computer-based science simulations. *Journal of Educational Psychology, 98,* 902–913.

Lehman, S., Schraw, G., McCrudden, M. T., & Hartley, K. (2007). Processing and recall of seductive details in scientific text. *Contemporary Educational Psychology, 32,* 569–587.

Lepper, M. R., Woolverton, M., Mumme, D., & Gurtner, J. (1993). Motivational techniques of expert human tutors: Lessons for the design of computer-based tutors. In S. P. Lajoie & S. J. Derry (Eds.), *Computers as cognitive tools* (pp. 75–105). Hillsdale, NJ: Erlbaum.

Levie, W. H., & Lentz, R. (1982). Effects of text illustrations: A review of research. *Educational Communication and Technology Journal, 30,* 195–232.

Levin, J. R., Anglin, G. J., & Carney, R. N. (1987). On empirically validating functions of pictures in prose. In D. M. Willows & H. A. Houghton (Eds.), *The psychology of illustration, vol. 1* (pp. 51–86). New York: Springer.

Levin, J. R., & Mayer, R. E. (1993). Understanding illustrations in text. In B. K. Britton, A. Woodward, and M. Binkley (Eds.), *Learning from textbooks* (pp. 95–113). Hillsdale, NJ: Erlbaum.

Loman, N. L., & Mayer, R. E. (1983). Signaling techniques that increase the understandability of expository prose. *Journal of Educational Psychology, 75,* 402–412.

Lorch, R. F. (1989). Text-signaling devices and their effects on reading and memory processes. *Educational Psychology Review, 1,* 209–234.

Lorch, R. F., & Lorch, E. P. (1996). Effects of organizational signals on free recall of expository text. *Journal of Educational Psychology, 87,* 537–544.

Lorch, R. F., Lorch, E. P., & Inman, W. E. (1993). Effects of signaling the topic structure of a text. *Journal of Educational Psychology, 85,* 281–290.

Low, R., & Sweller, J. (2005). The modality principle in multimedia learning. In R. E. Mayer (Ed.), *The Cambridge handbook of multimedia learning* (pp. 147–158). New York: Cambridge University Press.

Mautone, P. D., & Mayer, R. E. (2001). Signaling as a cognitive guide in multimedia learning. *Journal of Educational Psychology, 93,* 377–389.

Mautone, P. D., & Mayer, R. E. (2007). Cognitive aids for guiding graph comprehension. *Journal of Educational Psychology, 99,* 640–652.

Mayer, R. E. (1983). Can you repeat that? Qualitative effects of repetition and advance organizers on learning from science prose. *Journal of Educational Psychology, 75,* 40–49.

Mayer, R. E. (1989a). Systematic thinking fostered by illustrations in scientific text. *Journal of Educational Psychology, 81,* 240–246.

Mayer, R. E. (1989b). Models for understanding. *Review of Educational Research, 59,* 43–64.

Mayer, R. E. (1992). Cognition and instruction: Their historic meeting within educational psychology. *Journal of Educational Psychology, 84,* 405–412.

Mayer, R. E. (1993). Illustrations that instruct. In R. Glaser (Ed.), *Advances in Instructional Psychology* (vol. 4, pp. 253–284). Hillsdale, NJ: Erlbaum.

Mayer, R. E. (1997). Multimedia learning: Are we asking the right questions? *Educational Psychologist, 32,* 1–19.

Mayer, R. E. (1999a). Instructional technology. In F. T. Durso, R. S. Nickerson, R. W. Schvaneveldt, S. T. Dumais, D. S. Lindsay, & M. T. H. Chi (Eds.), *Handbook of applied cognition* (pp. 551–569). Chichester, England: Wiley.

Mayer, R. E. (1999b). Designing instruction for constructivist learning. In C. M. Reigeluth (Ed.), *Instructional design theories and models* (pp. 141–159). Mahwah, NJ: Erlbaum.

Mayer, R. E. (2000). The challenge of multimedia literacy. In A. W. Pailliotet & P. B. Mosenthal (Eds.), *Reconceptualizing literacy in the new age of media, multimedia, and hypermedia* (pp. 363–376). Norwood, NJ: JAI/Ablex.

Mayer, R. E. (2001). *Multimedia learning.* New York: Cambridge University Press.

Mayer, R. E. (2004). Should there be a three strikes rule against pure discover learning? The case for guided methods of instruction. *American Psychologist, 59*(1), 14–19.

Mayer, R. E. (2005a). Cognitive theory of multimedia learning. In R. E. Mayer (Ed.), *The Cambridge handbook of multimedia learning* (pp. 31–48). New York: Cambridge University Press.

Mayer, R. E. (2005b). Principles for managing essential processing in multimedia learning: Segmenting, pretraining, and modality principles. In R. E. Mayer (Ed.), *The Cambridge handbook of multimedia learning* (pp. 169–182). New York: Cambridge University Press.

Mayer, R. E. (2005c). Principles for reducing extraneous processing in multimedia learning: Coherence, signaling, redundancy, spatial contiguity, and temporal contiguity principles. In R. E. Mayer (Ed.), *The Cambridge handbook of multimedia learning* (pp. 183–200). New York: Cambridge University Press.

Mayer, R. E. (2005d). Principles for multimedia learning based on social cues: Personalization, voice, and image principles. In R. E. Mayer (Ed.), *The Cambridge handbook of multimedia learning* (pp. 201–212). New York: Cambridge University Press.

Mayer, R. E. (2005e). Introduction to multimedia learning. In R. E. Mayer (Ed.), *The Cambridge handbook of multimedia learning* (pp. 1–17). New York: Cambridge University Press.

Mayer, R. E. (Ed.). (2005f). *The Cambridge handbook of multimedia learning.* New York: Cambridge University Press.

Mayer, R. E. (2005g). The failure of educational research to impact educational practice: Six obstacles to educational reform. In G. D. Phye, D. H. Robinson, & J. R. Levin (Eds.), *Empirical methods for evaluating educational interventions* (pp. 67–81). San Diego, CA: Elsevier Academic Press.

Mayer, R. E. (2008a). *Learning and instruction* (2nd ed.). Upper Saddle River, NJ: Pearson Merrill Prentice Hall.

Mayer, R. E. (2008b). Research-based guidelines for multimedia instruction. In D. A. Boehm-Davis (Ed.), *Annual review of human factors in ergonomics* (vol. 3, pp. 127–147). Santa Monica, CA: Human Factors and Ergonomics Society.

Mayer, R. E. (2008c). Applying the science of learning: Evidence-based principles of multimedia instruction. *American Psychologist, 63*(8), 760–769.

Mayer, R. E., & Anderson, R. B. (1991). Animations need narrations: An experimental test of a dual-coding hypothesis. *Journal of Educational Psychology, 83*, 484–490.

Mayer, R. E., & Anderson, R. B. (1992). The instructive animation: Helping students build connections between words and pictures in multimedia learning. *Journal of Educational Psychology, 84*, 444–452.

Mayer, R. E., Bove, W., Bryman, A., Mars, R., & Tapangco, L. (1996). When less is more: Meaningful learning from visual and verbal summaries of science textbook lessons. *Journal of Educational Psychology, 88*, 64–73.

Mayer, R. E., & Chandler, P. (2001). When learning is just a click away: Does simple user interaction foster deeper understanding of multimedia messages? *Journal of Educational Psychology, 93*, 390–397.

Mayer, R. E., Dow, G. T., & Mayer, S. (2003). Multimedia learning in an interactive self-explaining environment: What works in the design of agent-based microworlds? *Journal of Educational Psychology, 95,* 806–813.

Mayer, R. E., Fennell, S., Farmer, L., & Campbell, J. (2004). A personalization effect in multimedia learning: Students learn better when words are in conversational style rather than formal style. *Journal of Educational Psychology, 96,* 389–395.

Mayer, R. E., & Gallini, J. K. (1990). When is an illustration worth ten thousand words? *Journal of Educational Psychology, 82,* 715–726.

Mayer, R. E., Hegarty, M., Mayer, S., & Campbell, J. (2005). When static media promote active learning: Annotated illustrations versus narrated animations in multimedia learning. *Journal of Experimental Psychology: Applied, 11,* 256–265.

Mayer, R. E., Heiser, H., & Lonn, S. (2001). Cognitive constraints on multimedia learning: When presenting more material results in less understanding. *Journal of Educational Psychology, 93,* 187–198.

Mayer, R. E., & Jackson, J. (2005). The case for coherence in scientific explanations: Quantitative details hurt qualitative understanding. *Journal of Experimental Psychology: Applied, 11,* 13–18.

Mayer, R. E., & Johnson, C. I. (2008). Revising the redundancy principle in multimedia learning. *Journal of Educational Psychology, 100,* 380–386.

Mayer, R. E., Johnson, W. L., Shaw, E., & Sandhu, S. (2006). Constructing computer-based tutors that are socially sensitive: Politeness in educational software. *International Journal of Human Computer Studies, 54,* 36–42.

Mayer, R. E., Mathias, A., & Wetzell, K. (2002). Fostering understanding of multimedia messages through pretraining: Evidence for a two-stage theory of mental model construction. *Journal of Experimental Psychology: Applied, 8,* 147–154.

Mayer, R. E., Mautone, P. D., & Prothero, W. (2002). Pictorial aids for learning by doing in a multimedia geology simulation game. *Journal of Educational Psychology, 94,* 171–185.

Mayer, R. E., & Moreno, R. (1998). A split-attention effect in multimedia learning: Evidence for dual processing systems in working memory. *Journal of Educational Psychology, 90,* 312–320.

Mayer, R. E., & Moreno, R. (2003). Nine ways to reduce cognitive load in multimedia learning. *Educational Psychologist, 38,* 43–52.

Mayer, R. E., Moreno, R., Boire, M., & Vagge, S. (1999). Maximizing constructivist learning from multimedia communications by minimizing cognitive load. *Journal of Educational Psychology, 91,* 638–643.

Mayer, R. E., & Sims, V. K. (1994). For whom is a picture worth a thousand words? Extensions of dual-coding theory of multimedia learning. *Journal of Educational Psychology, 84,* 389–401.

Mayer, R. E., Sims, V., & Tajika, H. (1995). A comparison of how textbooks teach mathematical problem solving in Japan and the United States. *American Educational Research Journal, 32,* 443–460.

Mayer, R. E., Sobko, K., & Mautone, P. D. (2003). Social cues in multimedia learning: Role of speaker's voice. *Journal of Educational Psychology, 95,* 419–425.

Mayer, R. E., Steinhoff, K., Bower, G., & Mars, R. (1995). A generative theory of textbook design: Using annotated illustrations to foster meaningful learning of science text. *Educational Technology Research and Development, 43,* 31–43.

Mayer, R. E., & Wittrock, M. (2006). Problem solving. In P. A. Alexander & P. H. Winne (Eds.), *Handbook of educational psychology* (pp. 287–304). Mahwah, NJ: Erlbaum.

McLaren, B. M., Lim, S-J., Gagnon, F., Yaron, D., & Koedinger, K. R. (2006). Studying the effects of personalized language and worked examples in the context of a web-based intelligent tutor. In M. Ikeda, K. D. Ashley, & T-W. Chan (Eds.), *Intelligent Tutoring Systems* (pp. 318–328). Berlin: Springer.

Meyer, B. J. F. (1975). *The organization of prose and its effects on memory.* Amsterdam: North-Holland.

Meyer, B. J. F., Brandt, D. M., & Bluth, G. J. (1980). Use of top-level structure in text: Key for reading comprehension of ninth-grade students. *Reading Research Quarterly, 16,* 72–103.

Michas, I. C., & Berry, D. (2000). Learning a procedural task: Effectiveness of multimedia presentations. *Applied Cognitive Psychology, 14,* 555–575.

Miller, G. (1956). The magic number seven, plus or minus two: Some limits on our capacity for processing information. *Psychological Review, 63,* 81–97.

Mohr, P., Glover, J., & Ronning, R. R. (1984). The effect of related and unrelated details on the recall of major ideas in prose. *Journal of Reading Behavior, 16,* 97–109.

Moreno, R. (2005). Multimedia learning with animated pedagogical agents. In R. E. Mayer (Ed.), *The Cambridge handbook of multimedia learning* (pp. 507–524). New York: Cambridge University Press.

Moreno, R. (2006). Does the modality principle hold for different media? A test of the methods-affects-learning hypothesis. *Journal of Computer Assisted Learning, 22,* 149–158.

Moreno, R., & Mayer, R. E. (1999a) Cognitive principles of multimedia learning: The role of modality and contiguity. *Journal of Educational Psychology, 91,* 358–368.

Moreno, R., & Mayer, R. E. (1999b). Multimedia-supported metaphors for meaning making in mathematics. *Cognition and Instruction, 17,* 215–248.

Moreno, R., & Mayer, R. E. (2000a). A coherence effect in multimedia learning: The case for minimizing irrelevant sounds in the design of multimedia messages. *Journal of Educational Psychology, 92,* 117–125.

Moreno, R., & Mayer, R. E. (2000b). Engaging students in active learning: The case for personalized multimedia messages. *Journal of Educational Psychology, 92*, 724–733.

Moreno, R., & Mayer, R. E. (2002a). Verbal redundancy in multimedia learning: When reading helps listening. *Journal of Educational Psychology, 94*, 156–163.

Moreno, R., & Mayer, R. E. (2002b). Learning science in virtual reality multimedia environments: Role of methods and media. *Journal of Educational Psychology, 94*, 598–610.

Moreno, R., & Mayer, R. E. (2004). Personalized messages that promote science learning in virtual environments. *Journal of Educational Psychology, 96*, 165–173.

Moreno, R., & Mayer, R. E. (2007). Interactive multimodal learning environments. *Educational Psychology Review, 19*, 309–326.

Moreno, R., Mayer, R. E., Spires, H. A., & Lester, J. C. (2001). The case for social agency in computer-based teaching: Do students learn more deeply when they interact with animated pedagogical agents? *Cognition and Instruction, 19*, 177–213.

Moreno, R., & Ortegano-Layne, L. (2008). Using cases as thinking tools in teacher education: The role of presentation format. *Educational Technology Research and Development, 56*, 449–465.

Moreno, R., & Valdez, A. (2005). Cognitive load and learning effects of having students organize pictures and words in multimedia environments: The role of student interactivity and feedback. *Educational Technology Research and Development, 53*, 35–45.

Moreno, R., & Valdez, A. (2007). Immediate and delayed effects of using a classroom case exemplar in teacher education: The role of presentation format. *Journal of Educational Psychology, 99*, 194–206.

Mousavi, S. Y., Low, R., & Sweller, J. (1995). Reducing cognitive load by mixing auditory and visual presentation modes. *Journal of Educational Psychology, 87*, 319–334.

Nass, C., & Brave, S. (2005). *Wired for speech: How voice activates and advances the human-computer relationship*. Cambridge, MA: MIT Press.

Naumann, J., Richter, T., Flender, J., Cristmann, U., & Groeben, N. (2007). Signaling in expository hypertexts compensates for deficits in reading skill. *Journal of Educational Psychology, 99*, 791–807.

Nolen, S. (1995). Effects of a visible author in statistics texts. *Journal of Educational Psychology, 87*, 47–65.

Norman, D. A. (1993). *Things that make us smart*. Reading, MA: Addison-Wesley.

O'Neil, H. F. (Ed.). (2005). *What works in distance learning: Guidelines*. Greenwich, CT: Information Age Publishing.

O'Neil, H. F. (2008). *What works in distance learning: Sample lessons based on guidelines*. Greenwich, CT: Information Age Publishing.

O'Neil, H. F., Mayer, R. E., Herl, H., Thurman, R., & Olin, K. (2000). Instructional strategies for virtual environments. In H. F. O'Neil & D. H. Andrews (Eds.), *Aircraft training: Methods, technologies, and assessment* (pp. 105–130). Mahwah, NJ: Erlbaum.

Paas, F., Renkl, A., & Sweller, J. (2003). Cognitive load theory and instructional design: Recent developments. *Educational Psychologist, 38,* 1–4.

Paas, F., Tuovinen, J. E., Tabbers, H., & van Gerven, P. W. M. (2003). Cognitive load measurement as a means to advance cognitive load theory. *Educational Psychologist, 38,* 63–72.

Paivio, A. (1986). *Mental representations: A dual-coding approach.* Oxford, England: Oxford University Press.

Paivio, A. (2006). *Mind and its evolution: A dual coding approach.* Mahwah, NJ: Erlbaum.

Paxton, R. (1997). "Someone with like a life wrote it": The effects of visible author on high school students. *Journal of Educational Psychology, 89,* 235–250.

Paxton, R. (2002). The influence of author visibility on high school students solving a historical problem. *Cognition and Instruction, 20,* 197–248.

Phye, G. D., Robinson, D. H., & Levin, J. R. (Eds.). (2005). *Empirical methods for evaluating educational interventions.* San Diego, CA: Elsevier Academic Press.

Plass, J. L., Chun, D. M., Mayer, R. E., & Leutner, D. (1998). Supporting visual and verbal learning preferences in a second language multimedia learning environment. *Journal of Educational Psychology, 90,* 25–36.

Plass, J. L., Chun, D. M., Mayer, R. E., & Leutner, D. (2003). Cognitive load in reading a foreign language text with multiple aids and the influence of verbal and spatial abilities. *Computers in Human Behavior, 19,* 221–243.

Plass, J. L., & Jones, L. C. (2005). Multimedia learning in second language acquisition. In R. E. Mayer (Ed.), *The Cambridge handbook of multimedia learning* (pp. 467–488). New York: Cambridge University Press.

Ploetzner, R., Fehse, E., Kneser, C., & Spada, H. (1999). Learning to relate qualitative and quantitative problem representations in a model-based setting for collaborative problem solving. *Journal of the Learning Sciences, 8,* 177–214.

Pollock, E., Chandler, P., & Sweller, J. (2002). Assimilating complex information. *Learning and Instruction, 12,* 61–86.

Purnell, K. N., Solman, R. T., & Sweller, J. (1991). The effects of technical illustrations on cognitive load. *Instructional Science, 20,* 443–462.

Reder, L. M, & Anderson, J. R. (1980). A comparison of texts and their summaries: Memorial consequences. *Journal of Verbal Learning & Verbal Behavior, 19,* 121–134.

Reeves, B., & Nass, C. (1996). *The media equation.* New York: Cambridge University Press.

Rieber, L. P. (2005). Multimedia learning in games, simulations, and microworlds. In R. E. Mayer (Ed.), *The Cambridge handbook of multimedia learning* (pp. 549–568). New York: Cambridge University Press.

Roy, M., & Chi, M. T. H. (2005). The self-explanation principle in multimedia learning. In R. E. Mayer (Ed), *The Cambridge handbook of multimedia learning* (pp. 271–286). New York: Cambridge University Press.

Salomon, G. (1994). *Interaction of media, cognition, and learning.* Hillsdale, NJ: Erlbaum.

Sanchez, C. A., & Wiley, J. (2006). An examination of the seductive details effect in terms of working memory capacity. *Memory & Cognition, 34,* 344–355.

Schnotz, W., & Bannert, M. (2003). Construction and interference in learning from multiple representations. *Learning and Instruction, 13,* 141–156.

Shavelson, R. J., & Towne, L. (Eds.). (2002). *Scientific research in education.* Washington, DC: National Academy Press.

Shirey, L. (1992). Importance, interest, and selective attention. In K. A. Renninger, S. Hidi, & A. Krapp (Eds.), *The role of interest in learning and development* (pp. 281–296). Hillsdale, NJ: Erlbaum.

Shirey, L., & Reynolds, R. (1988). Effect of interest on attention and learning. *Journal of Educational Psychology, 80,* 159–166.

Simon, H. A. (1974). How big is a chunk? *Science, 183,* 482–488.

Sternberg, R. J. (1980). *Metaphors of mind: Conceptions of the nature of human intelligence.* Cambridge, England: Cambridge University Press.

Stokes, D. E. (1997). *Pasteur's quadrant: Basic science and technological innovation.* Washington, DC: Brookings Institution Press.

Stull, A., & Mayer, R. E. (2007). Learning by doing versus learning by viewing: Three experimental comparisons of learner-generated versus author-provided graphic organizers. *Journal of Educational Psychology, 99,* 808–820.

Sweller, J. (1999). *Instructional design in technical areas.* Camberwell, Australia: ACER Press.

Sweller, J. (2005a). Implications of cognitive load theory for multimedia learning. In R. E. Mayer (Ed.), *The Cambridge handbook of multimedia learning* (pp. 19–30). New York: Cambridge University Press.

Sweller, J. (2005b). The redundancy principle in multimedia learning. In R. E. Mayer (Ed.), *The Cambridge handbook of multimedia learning* (pp. 159–168). New York: Cambridge University Press.

Sweller, J., & Chandler, P. (1994). Why some material is difficult to learn. *Cognition and Instruction, 12,* 185–233.

Sweller, J., Chandler, P., Tierney, P., & Cooper, M. (1990). Cognitive load and selective attention as factors in the structuring of technical material. *Journal of Experimental Psychology: General, 119,* 176–192.

Sweller, J., & Cooper, M. (1985). The use of worked examples as a substitute for problem solving in learning algebra. *Cognition and Instruction, 2,* 59–89.

Tabbers, H. K., Martens, R. L., & van Merrienboer, J. J. G. (2004). Multimedia instructions and cognitive load theory: Effects of modality and cueing. *British Journal of Educational Psychology, 74,* 71–81.

Tarmizi, R., & Sweller, J. (1988). Guidance during mathematical problem solving. *Journal of Educational Psychology, 80,* 424–436.

Thorndike, E. L. (1911). *Animal intelligence.* New York: Hafner.

Tindall-Ford, S., Chandler, P., & Sweller, J. (1997). When two sensory modes are better than one. *Journal of Experimental Psychology: Applied, 3,* 257–287.

Tufte, E. R. (1983). *Envisioning information.* Cheshire, CT: Graphics Press.

Tufte, E. R. (1990). *The visual display of quantitative information.* Cheshire, CT: Graphics Press.

van Merrienboer, J. J. G., & Kester, L. (2005). The four-component instructional design model: Multimedia principles in environments for complex learning. In R. E. Mayer (Ed.), *The Cambridge handbook of multimedia learning* (pp. 71–93). New York: Cambridge University Press.

van Merrienboer, J. J. G., Kester, L., & Paas, F. (2006). Teaching complex rather than simple tasks: Balancing intrinsic and germane load to enhance transfer of learning. *Applied Cognitive Psychology, 20,* 343–352.

van Merrienboer, J. J. G., Kirschner, P. A., & Kester, L. (2003). Taking the load off a learner's mind: Instructional design for complex learning. *Educational Psychologist, 38,* 5–13.

Wade, S. (1992). How interest affects learning from text. In K. A. Renninger, S. Hidi, and A. Krapp (Eds.), *The role of interest in learning and development* (pp. 255–277). Hillsdale, NJ: Erlbaum.

Wade, S., and Adams, R. (1990). Effects of importance and interest on recall of biographical text. *Journal of Reading Behavior, 22,* 331–353.

Wang, N., Johnson, W. L., Mayer, R. E., Rizzo, P., Shaw, E., & Collins, H. (2008). The politeness effect: Pedagogical agents and learning outcomes. *International Journal of Human Computer Studies, 66,* 96–112.

Ward, M., & Sweller, J. (1990). Structuring effective worked out examples. *Cognition and Instruction, 7,* 1–39.

Weiner, B. (1990). History of motivational research in education. *Journal of Educational Psychology, 82,* 616–622.

Weiner, B. (1992). Motivation. In M. Alkin (Ed.), *Encyclopedia of educational research* (6th ed.; pp. 860–865). New York: Macmillan.

Wetzel, C. D., Radtke, P. H., & Stern, H. W. (1994). *Instructional effectiveness of video media.* Hillsdale, NJ: Erlbaum.

Wittrock, M. C. (1989). Generative processes of comprehension. *Educational Psychologist, 24,* 345–376.

Author Index

Subject Index